Street of Ur in Abraham's time
(from Dr. Leonard Woolley's excavations 1930—31)
by courtesy of the Society of Antiquaries of London.

HISTORY OF OUR PEOPLE IN BIBLE TIMES

BY

JOSEPH HALPERN, M.A. (LOND.)

ASSOCIATE OF JEWS' COLLEGE, LONDON

WITH MAPS, PLANS, CHART, & ILLUSTRATIONS

LONDON
SHAPIRO, VALLENTINE & CO.
1935

Printed in Holland
by N. V. Ipenbuur & van Seldam, Amsterdam.

TO EVE

FOREWORD

FOREWORD

by

HERBERT M. ADLER Esq., M. B. E., M. A., LL.M.,
Director of Jewish Education

A text-book of Scripture History has long been needed
in our Jewish Schools and Classes. Teachers are constantly asking me to recommend them one, and I am
always in a difficulty. Of Bible story-books there is no
lack. We have as many as we want. But in language
and presentation they are only suited to very young
children. The time comes when the pupil is ripe for
something more mature, and when he needs to learn the
history of his people in the same atmosphere of reality
as that in which he learns the history of England in his
day-school. At this stage, he is generally offered Abraham's "Manual of Scripture History". One hesitates to
speak harshly of such a time-honoured *vade mecum*. But
it is so crammed with facts and names — many of them
of not the least consequence — that one cannot see the
wood for the trees. It has no illustrations, no index and
only one map. There are, of course, American text-
books, but I have not seen any that really meet our
requirements. They are well got-up as a rule and pro-
fusely illustrated, but they are far too expensive when
measured by our standards. Some of them, too, suffer
from a critical handling of the Bible. It is all-important
that the Bible should lose none of its sanctity, and the

children of our Classes are too young to be troubled with
the problems of Biblical criticism.

Nowadays it is generally accepted that a Scripture
history-book ought to give us the history, not just of
disconnected individuals, but of the people of Israel as
a whole.   There must be a clear thread running through
all its chapters.   We need to show the birth and development of the people, its advance upon its high purposive
mission as a nation, the adverse forces which it encount-
ered, its periodical lapses and its regeneration.   This
is practically impossible unless we give a picture of the
nomadic existence of our early ancestors and its dis-
placement after many vicissitudes by a settled agricultural
life.   We must give some idea of the effect produced
by the impact of Egyptian civilisation.   We must follow
how, almost inevitably, when entering into Canaan our
fathers came under the influence of the crude religious
rites and superstitions of the settled inhabitants, and how
they had to be laboriously weaned from them.   Babylon
and Assyria must be more than mere names or patches
on the map.   It is here, I think, that Mr. Halpern has
been particularly successful.   His descriptions, moreover,
are enlivened by the well-chosen illustrations which are
a feature of the book.   He has realised that the concrete
objects revealed by archaeologists and the scenes of
famous sites are bound to be infinitely more telling than
fanciful pictures.   The remains of Ur and the cave of
Machpelah are far more convincing than an imaginary
portrait of Abraham could be, and the real Mount Carmel
conveys a much more living message from the past than
could any fictitious presentation of the prophet Elijah.

The right kind of book must be something more than
a bare condensation of the historical chapters of the

Bible. Nevertheless the Bible must be constantly referred to. For one of our principal objects must be to
stimulate interest in the Book of books. We want our
boys and girls to feel that, with the background of
knowledge they have obtained, its pages can be full of
new meaning to them. Moreover, if the great characters
of Scripture are to become real, they must cease to be
dumb names. They must speak for themselves from
time to time in the golden utterances which the Bible
has perpetuated. Only in this way can they emerge
from the mists of time and take on bodily shape. Mr.
Halpern has shown himself well alive to this necessity,
and his frequent use of quotation gives strength and
vividness to his narrative.

I feel sure that the book will be welcomed. It seems
to me to be well adapted to the needs 'of pupils of the
age of eleven years and upwards.

June, 1935.   HERBERT M. ADLER.

PREFACE

Mr. Adler has so well expressed the purpose of this book that there is little for me to add. My intention has been to provide for the pupil who is beginning a formal study of history, and for the general reader, a guide to the Bible. It must be remembered that the Bible is not, nor does it profess to be, a history text-book. Naturally, it gives an account of the origin and development of the Children of Israel, but it also takes for granted a background of which until comparatively recently we knew very little. Words, phrases and acts which hitherto had little or no meaning for us take on a new significance when read in the light of modern archaeological discoveries in Egypt, Palestine and Mesopotamia.

It is this background which I have endeavoured to fill in, from the material provided by the work of, among others, such eminent explorers as Sir Flinders Petrie, Dr. Leonard Woolley, Professor J. Garstang, and Sir Charles Marston. At the same time I have been careful to present the Bible story as the Jew knows it, and have striven to recreate the living reality of the Biblical scenes. Such treatment calls for many notes, but I have felt it unwise to burden the text with explanations. These will be incorporated in a Teachers' Handbook, which will include also exercises for the class, selections of Biblical readings, and much other useful material. This Handbook will be issued shortly.

PREFACE

The biographical form has been chosen because it is recognised as one of the most satisfactory methods of teaching history. The four sections into which the book is divided are intended to represent the main influences which have shaped Jewish life during its first and most formative period.

The book is amply provided with maps, plans, illustrations, a Biblical index and a comprehensive subject index, and Points to remember at the end of each chapter, all intended to make it more serviceable in the schoolroom.

I take this opportunity of expressing my sincere thanks to Mr. Herbert Adler M.B.E., M.A., LL.M., for the keen interest he has shown in the progress of the work, in looking through the whole MS whilst it was being written, and for the valuable comments and suggestions he has made at every stage. My warm thanks for many helpful suggestions are also due to Dr. A. M. Silbermann, who was responsible for seeing the work through the press; Rabbi B. D. Klien B.A.; Mr. H. Klein M.A.; Mr. Barnett Samuel M.A.; Messrs. M. Clapper, and A. Baum (of Trinity College, Cambridge), who corrected the proofs and compiled the exhaustive index.

It is my hope that this small book may contribute, however slightly, to a more profound knowledge of and appreciation for the Bible.

August, 1935.   J. H.

CONTENTS

CONTENTS

PART III

PART IV

THE EXILE AND THE RETURN

LIST OF ILLUSTRATIONS

MAPS, PLANS ETC.

PART I

THE BIRTH OF A NATION

CHAPTER 1

ABRAHAM THE HEBREW

On the west bank of the river Euphrates, not far from the Persian Gulf, there lie to-day ruins and mounds where once a populous city stood. Four thousand years ago this city throbbed with the life of an old and busy civilisation. Ur of the Chaldees was then an important centre of the Babylonian Empire, ruled by the Semitic king Hammurabi. At the dawn of history, after the great Flood described in the Bible, the Semitic peoples over-ran and conquered the whole plain of Shinar, between the rivers Euphrates and Tigris. They extended their power to the north and to the west, so that when this story opens we find Hammurabi the master of a vast empire covering the whole of western Asia, from the Persian Gulf to the Mediterranean Sea. Archaeologists have explored the ruined cities of these lands, and have told us so much about the social life of the inhabitants that we can almost imagine we lived among them.

Babylonia proper was the land between the Euphrates and Tigris from the Persian Gulf in the south to an un-

Babylonia.

1

determined limit in the north. A network of canals connected the two rivers and irrigated the district. The soil being very fertile, the main occupation was naturally agriculture. At first the country was divided into a number of city-states, the most famous of which were Babylon, Kish, Erech and Ur. By the time of Hammurabi, however, the empire was organised and well administered from a central capital, Babylon. Commerce prospered and was carried on as far as India on the far east and Egypt on the west. Law, art, and science had reached an advanced stage. Hammurabi codified the laws of his empire and had them inscribed on a block of granite, which is shown on opposite page. The Babylonians used a system of wedge-shaped marks (called cuneiform) for writing, and thousands of clay tablets and cylinders so inscribed tell us of the history, superstitions, medicine, astrology and other subjects which were taught in the schools. Many of the tablets also consist of letters and dispatches of private citizens. Discoveries in the royal tombs of delicate works in gold and silver, in shell, alabaster, and lapis lazuli, testify to the skill of the craftsmen.

Religion played a great part in the life of the Sumerians, as these people have been called. Every city worshipped its own god, and built for it a temple so high that it seemed to reach to heaven. Thus, Marduk was the patron god of Babylon; at Ur, the Moon goddess was worshipped. The Sumerians were very superstitious, and consulted the gods in all matters affecting their daily life. They also believed that there was a spirit in every object in nature. Whenever they were sick or in trouble they went to the priests and brought them gifts to dispel the evil spirits.

In the midst of such a civilisation did Terah the father

Code of Hammurabi

(the king is represented in bas-relief at the top of the pillar on which the code is inscribed. He is standing before the sun-god from whom he receives the laws).

World of the Bible.

of Abraham live.   The family were descended from Eber,
a son of Shem, and are therefore called Hebrews as
well as Semites.   Terah himself worshipped
Family of Abraham. the Babylonian gods, but his son Abraham
could not do so.   Somehow he under-
stood that idols have no power and that it was foolish
to expect help in time of trouble from an image of gold
or silver.   Abraham realised that there was only One
God, who had created the world and demanded righteousness of man.   This God he worshipped.

We can imagine how hard was the life of Abraham
among all these idol-worshippers, and how glad he was
when his father decided to travel north-
They Decide to Leave Ur. wards to the district of Haran in Mesopotamia.   He followed the old caravan
route along which nomad shepherds, merchants and
armies used to go from Babylon to Egypt, that other
early home of mankind.

The map at the end of the book shows you Palestine,
which is the narrow strip of coast joining the two great
continents of Asia and Africa.   To the east
Canaan (Palestine). the desert sands of Arabia stretch in a
monotonous and dreary waste.   To the west
is the Mediterranean Sea, on which the earliest ships in
history started their journey round the world from the
Phoenician ports.   From the north flows the river Euphrates, fertilising in its passage to the Persian Gulf the lands
of Mesopotamia and Babylonia.   And to the south-west
lies Egypt.   This strip of coast, which we know to-day
as Palestine, is no more than seventy miles wide.   It
has been saved from the desert by parallel mountain
ranges split in two by a deep chasm, through which the
river Jordan flows.   The mountains and their streams,

as well as the rain-bearing winds from the coast, have
made Palestine one large oasis. For this reason the
desert tribes have flocked to it since the dawn of history.
From the earliest times, also, the empires of Egypt and
Babylon have coveted this stretch of territory and
struggled for its possession. Indeed, throughout the
centuries, the great empires of the world have striven to
be its masters.

When the caravan of Terah started their long journey
northwards, they exchanged the city-life of Ur for the
Haran. nomadic life of shepherds, pitching their
tents wherever pasture and water for their
flocks could be found. On reaching Haran, they once
more resumed their city-life, and lived in houses instead
of tents. But Abraham was not to remain in the city.
He heard the voice of God calling him to leave his father's
family, and go to another land where he would become
a great nation, and a blessing to the world.

Without question Abraham obeyed the call. With
his wife Sarah, his nephew Lot, and all who would
accompany him, he left Haran to journey
Abraham Obeys southwards. His brother Nahor and the
the Call of God. rest of the family remained in Haran, and
worshipped their old gods. Abraham went forth to teach that
only One God exists, whom everybody must acknowledge
and worship, the true and just God, full of mercy.

The family of Abraham, with their sheep and their
oxen, their slaves, their camels and their asses, travelled
on the eastern side of the Jordan, over the hills of Bashan
and Gilead, through the rich pasture-lands that still
attract even to-day the tribes of the desert. Below the
Lake of Galilee they crossed the Jordan, for we next
find them in Shechem. This city lies in the centre of

the country, in the deep valley between the hills of Ebal and Gerizim. (See illustration facing page 70). It was here that God promised to give the land to the descendants of Abraham.

Palestine is a small land, about ten thousand square miles in area, that is about one fifth the size of England and Wales. Yet this small land is so split up by mountains and valleys that already when Abraham came, he found a multitude of tribes living in it. Canaanites, Amorites, Hittites, Hivites, Rephaim, Anakim, and many other tribes jostled one another for possession of the land. The Amorites dwelt in the mountainous districts, the Canaanites in the Lowlands. The Rephaim and the Anakim were the remains of the older population of men of high stature who once inhabited the land. The Hittites were not Semitic and came from North-western Asia, making settlements in Syria and Palestine.

In spite of the fact that all these tribes and races shared this land, Abraham believed in the promise of God that it would one day belong to his descendants. His faith was perfect.

He did not stay long in Shechem, but journeyed further south, in search of pasture for his flocks. But **Egypt.** that year the rains had failed and, finding no pasture in the stony hills of Palestine, he went down to Egypt. In those days Egypt was famous for its corn, and whenever there was a famine in the surrounding countries the shepherds came pouring into Egypt to obtain food for themselves and their flocks. Egypt, the land of the Nile, was, we have seen, the home of an ancient civilisation. More than a thousand years before Abraham, Egyptian kings had built the famous Pyramids at Gizah. Abraham was well received by the Egyptian king, so that when he left that country with his caravan to return to Palestine, they found themselves very rich in flocks and herds and servants. They even possessed silver and gold. But their riches were the cause of a separation between Abraham and Lot.

So large were their flocks that the shepherds of the two kinsmen used to quarrel, for there was not enough

Lot.

unoccupied pasture-land in any one place for both their flocks. The peace-loving Abraham hated these quarrels, and suggested to Lot that they should separate, offering him the first choice of land. Lot did not consider that Abraham was the older man and should be allowed to choose first. They were at Bethel at that time, and from there Lot could see the pleasant valley of the Jordan by the shores of the Dead Sea. This place he chose. In that deep valley were the cities of Sodom and Gomorrah, where life was much easier than in the cooler hill-country. The oily waters of the Dead Sea looked brillant and alluring. The Bible says that the " Circle of the Jordan ", as it was called, was " like the garden of the Lord " in richness and fertility. The inhabitants of these cities were spoilt by the fertile soil and the warm climate. They became idle and sinful, oppressed the poor and ill-treated strangers. Yet Lot chose to live among them.

Abraham was sad when he parted from Lot, because he had no child and regarded Lot as his heir. Now, in

God's Promise to Abraham.

spite of all his wealth and large number of servants, he was a lonely old man. At this moment God appeared to him in a vision, and said:

" Lift up now thine eyes and look from the place where

The Dead Sea—"its oily waters looking brilliant and alluring"
by courtesy of the Jewish National Fund.

The Jordan (10 miles north of Jericho)
World of the Bible.

thou art, northwards, southwards, eastwards, westwards. For the whole land which thou seest, to thee will I give it, and to thy seed for ever." From Bethel Abraham had a perfect view of Palestine. Looking northwards, he could see Mount Hermon towering at a height of nine thousand feet, a hundred miles away. Below it on the east of the Jordan stretched the hills of Bashan, Gilead and Moab, broken only by the streams of the Yarmuk and the Jabbok. Twenty-five miles east of him lay the valley of Jordan, splitting the parallel ranges of mountains on either side from Mount Hermon to the Dead Sea. His eye could not see its depth. The Jordan Valley in parts is nearly thirteen hundred feet below sea level, while the Dead Sea is thirteen hundred feet deeper still! Southwards, the stony plateau of Judea stretched itself as far as the eye could reach. On the west the deep blue of the Mediterranean Sea met the horizon at a distance of thirty miles. Between the sea and the mountains were the Maritime Plain by the coast and the Shephelah or low-lying hills overlooking the Plain.

Abraham was sad no longer. He believed the promise of God. From Bethel he went by the ancient road up the centre of the Judean plateau to Hebron, and pitched his tents in the fruitful valleys near that town. Here the promise of God to Abraham was confirmed in a solemn and dramatic manner.

"Now, when the sun was going down, a deep sleep fell upon Abraham, and behold a horror of great darkness fell upon him. And (God) said to Abraham, Know of a surety that thy seed shall be a stranger in a land not theirs, and shall serve them; and they shall afflict them four hundred years. Also the nation which they serve shall I judge, and after that they shall go out with great substance."

This vision meant that the descendants of Abraham would be homeless strangers for many years, so that by their experience they might learn to be kind to strangers and treat them as equals, for to love the stranger is a rare virtue. Abraham himself practised this virtue, and entertained hospitably all who passed the door of his tent. He pressed food and drink upon them and, though he was such a great man, waited upon them himself. Tradition tells us that by his example he made the name of his God respected in the mouths of men, so that they, idol-worshippers though they were, would exclaim:

"Blessed be the God of Abraham!"

As the years passed and Sarah, Abraham's wife, was still childless, she gave her Egyptian handmaid, Hagar, **Ishmael.** to Abraham for a second wife. Hagar bore Abraham a son, whom he called Ishmael. Abraham thought that Ishmael would be his heir, but he received a divine promise that Sarah would bear him a son, through whom God's blessing would be fulfilled. As a sign that God would give the land to Abraham and his descendants, and would be their God, Abraham was commanded to circumcise himself and every male in his household. Ever afterwards every male child must be circumcised when eight days old. This is the sign of the covenant of Abraham.

Meanwhile, the wickedness of the cities of Sodom and Gomorrah, in the first of which Lot was living, was **The Destruction** so great that God decided to destroy them. **of Sodom and** Abraham, however, pleaded with God not **Gomorrah.** to destroy the righteous with the wicked, but to spare the cities even if only ten righteous people could be found in them. "Shall not the righteous Judge of all the earth do justice?" Abraham asked.

His prayer was accepted. However, only Lot and his daughters were hospitable and, warned by a heavenly messenger, they escaped the catastrophe. They fled to the mountains on the east of the Dead Sea, where the founders of the two tribes of Moab and Ammon were born.

After the destruction of Sodom and Gomorrah Abraham and his family, with all their possessions, moved

The Birth of Isaac. to the district called the Negeb, which is the hilly country south of Hebron. Here the ground is fruitful for only a few months in the year, because there is very little rain, and only a small number of wells. It is nearly a desert. The last spot before the desert really begins is a cluster of seven wells, which Abraham called Beer-sheba. In this place he pitched his tents. Very soon the promise of God was realised, and Sarah gave birth to a son, Isaac. Sarah wanted her son to be the only heir of Abraham, and asked him to send away Hagar and her son Ishmael. Abraham was sad at first because she made this request, but God promised him that Ishmael would become a great chieftain in the desert. So Abraham provided Hagar and Ishmael with food and a flask of water, and let them go. There was a road through the desert which led to Egypt, and they took that road. At first they suffered much hardship, as their water was soon gone, and they almost died of thirst. But they found a spring of water, and dwelt in the desert. Ishmael married an Egyptian woman, and became the father of the hardy tribe of Ishmaelites.

The Severest Test. After these events Abraham's faith in God was put to the hardest test. The Canaanites among whom Abraham dwelt used to sacrifice their firstborn sons to their gods, but this was an abominable custom which Abraham knew God hated. Now, suddenly, he heard this command:

" Take now thy son, thy only son, whom thou lovest, even Isaac and get thee to the land of Moriah, and offer him there for a burnt-offering upon one of the mountains of which I will tell thee."

Many years had he waited for the son born to him in his old age, a son who would continue his work in teaching by word and by example that only One God, a righteous God, exists.   Yet he obeyed without question. With his son Isaac and two servants he went to Mount Moriah.   On the mountain he built an altar on which he placed Isaac.   But as his hand clasped the knife to slay his son, a voice from heaven called to him:

" Do not anything to the lad, for I know that thou fearest God."

By this test of Abraham the whole world was shown that God values the life of every human being.   It marked the triumph of the religion of Abraham over that of his pagan neighbours.   It was a test for Isaac also.   Uncomplainingly he had gone with his father Abraham to the mountain of sacrifice, and by that action had shown that he was a worthy heir to Abraham.

Another incident is characteristic of Abraham's faith.   Sarah, his dearest companion in all his journeying from distant Ur, died in Hebron.   The **The Death of Sarah.**   Hittite owners of the territory offered Abraham a burying-place for Sarah among the best of their sepulchres. Abraham refused it, because he would not take a gift from anybody, but only from God, who had promised the land to him and his descendants.   He therefore bought from the Hittites a burying-place for Sarah his wife, and payed four hundred pieces of silver for it; the cave of Machpelah near Hebron became his possession. Visitors to Palestine can still see it to-day, for it has become one of the sacred places of the Mohammedans, who venerate Abraham.

Abraham was anxious that his son should not mix with the inhabitants of Palestine and follow their customs,

Rebecca. because Isaac had to carry on the sacred work which he had begun. So he sent his servant to Mesopotamia to find in his brother's family a wife for Isaac. Ten camels well-laden with gifts from his master accompanied the servant on his journey to the city of Haran where Nahor, Abraham's brother, dwelt. Outside the city was a well, and there, at evening, the camels rested. His master had taught him to pray, and, standing by the well, the servant prayed that God should prosper his way and bring him success. He decided upon a test. Where water is precious only a kind and generous girl would share it with a stranger, and draw water for his thirsty camels. Such a girl, was his prayer, should be of the family of Nahor. His words were scarcely ended when a girl came to the well and did exactly as he hoped. The servant was delighted when she told him that she was Rebecca, the grand-daughter of Nahor. Her parents allowed her to go with the servant, and so Rebecca became Isaac's wife.

Abraham could now die in peace. Faithfully he had throughout his life obeyed the voice of God. By word

Abraham Dies. and deed he had taught the world the truth about God, and now it remained for his son and his son's son to go on with the work, until the world was as full of the knowledge of God as the seas with water.

Old and full of days, he died and was laid to rest in the cave of Machpelah, where his wife Sarah was buried.

CHAPTER 1

POINTS TO REMEMBER

The Semites:
a) descendants of Shem, a son of Noah
b) conquered Western Asia from the Persian Gulf to the Mediterranean Sea — the Babylonian Empire.

The Babylonian Empire:
a) ruled by Hammurabi in the days of Abraham, c. 2000 B.C.E.
b) main occupation of people — agriculture
c) commerce extended to India and Egypt
d) chief cities — Babylon, Kish, Erech, Ur
e) highly civilised — cuneiform writing, history, medicine, arithmetic, astrology etc. studied
f) laws codified by Hammurabi
g) religious life — every city had high temple to its patron god; believed there was a spirit in every object of nature; very superstitious.

Palestine:
a) position — a narrow strip of coast joining the continents of Africa and Asia
b) size — 70 miles wide by 150 miles long, about 10.000 square miles in area
c) physical description — " a land split up by mountains and valleys "
d) inhabitants — large number of independent tribes — Canaanites, Amorites, Hittites, Hivites etc.

Abraham:
a) his birthplace — Ur of the Chaldees
b) his ancestry — son of Terah, descendant of Eber the Semite; therefore called a Hebrew

12

c) his call — "Get thee out of thy country, and from thy kindred, and from thy father's house, unto a land that I will show thee. And I will make of thee a great nation, and I will bless thee, and make thy name great, and thou shalt be a blessing. And I will bless them that bless thee and curse him that curseth thee, and in thee shall all the families of the earth be blessed."

d) his wanderings

    to Haran in Mesopotamia (with his father's family)

    to Shechem (with Sarah and Lot)

    to Egypt

    to Bethel (where Lot separated)

    to Hebron and the Negeb;

e) his children —

    1) by Hagar — Ishmael

    2) by Sarah — Isaac, who became his heir

    3) by Keturah — Midian and other ancestors of the desert tribes;

f) the teachings of his life —

    1) that only *One* God exists, who demands righteousness and justice of man

    2) hospitality to strangers

    3) to champion the cause of the unfortunate (Lot, prayer for Sodom and Gomorrah)

    4) love of peace

    5) unquestioning obedience to the will of God (his call; Isaac)

    6) faith in the Unseen.

Abraham and Sarah were buried in the Cave of Machpelah.

CHAPTER 2

THE PATRIARCH'S FAMILY

Isaac spent his life in the neighbourhood of Beer-sheba, in the land of the Philistines. Here he prospered exceedingly. From being a shepherd he began to settle in the land and became a farmer. In the stony soil of the district he sowed his seed and reaped a fruitful harvest. His possessions increased so much, and his household grew so large, that the Philistines would no longer allow him to live with them. They drove him further into the desert, where he had to resume his pastoral life and live in tents, moving from place to place to find pasture and water for his cattle. Still the Philistines were not content. In the Negeb, a well of water is the most precious possession a man can own. Isaac had inherited the wells dug by Abraham's servants, and these the Philistines stopped and filled with earth in their envy at Isaac's prosperity. Nor would they allow him to retain the new wells dug by his own servants. At this time God appeared to him in Beer-sheba and reassured him that he and his children would become a blessing to the world. Finally Abimelech the Philistine king came to him in Beer-sheba and made a treaty of peace with him, as an equal. The family of Isaac was now established in the land.

Isaac and the Philistines.

Isaac had two sons, Jacob and Esau. Though they were twins, Esau was the elder, and therefore he was entitled to all the privileges of the first-born.

Jacob and Esau.

Among the Semitic peoples the firstborn became the priest and the judge of the family or tribe. So, when Isaac grew old, it was Esau's duty to look after the flocks and take care of the household. He had to teach the people what was right and judge all disputes between them. But Esau preferred to hunt in the wild hilly country of the south, and was often away from home a long time. Jacob was the shepherd, dwelling in the tents of his parents, and he carried out the duties which Esau neglected. One day Esau came home tired and hungry from his hunting, and found Jacob boiling some pottage.

" Give me some pottage, for I am weary," demanded Esau. Jacob saw his opportunity.

" Sell me then your birthright," was his reply.

" As a hunter I am constantly at the point of death. Of what use is the birthright to me?" thought Esau.

This showed how little he prized the birthright. He sold it without caring what he was losing. Jacob bought it gladly, because it gave him the right to act as Isaac's heir and be the head of the family when Isaac died. A few years later Esau married two Hittite wives, to the great grief of Isaac and Rebecca, because the Hittite people did not serve God, but worshipped idols.

Yet Isaac loved Esau more than Jacob, and when he grew old he commanded his firstborn son to bring him home some venison, that he might eat of it and bless him before he died. Esau did not stop to think that he had sold the birthright to Jacob, but went out hunting to perform his father's

Jacob Obtains Isaac's Blessing.

wish. Rebecca, however, remembered, and she, favouring
Jacob, determined to get the blessing for her younger
son. Jacob did as she commanded him. He covered
his hands and the smooth parts of his neck with goat-skin
so that he should be hairy like Esau. Then, pretending
he was Esau, he went to his father and obtained the
blessing.

Rebecca and Jacob felt justified in their action, for
Esau should have told his father that he had sold the
birthright to Jacob. But that was no
Rebecca's Punishment. excuse for them, and both paid dearly
for the wrong they had done. The death
of Sarah and Rachel is mentioned in the Bible. There
is even a reference to Deborah, Rebecca's nurse. But
there is no mention of how and when Rebecca died. The
Rabbis tell us that she died at the same time as her nurse,
and neither of her children was at her side to bury her.
Of Jacob's punishment we shall learn later.

Esau hated Jacob because he had stolen his blessing,
and planned to kill him. When Rebecca heard of this,
she persuaded Isaac to send Jacob away
Jacob Goes to Laban. to her brother's family in Haran. She
told him that Jacob, his heir, ought not
to marry any of the inhabitants of Palestine, because
they were idol-worshippers. So he was sent to Haran
to get a wife from his uncle Laban's family. Isaac had
blessed him with the dew of heaven and the fatness of
the earth, yet he left his father's house poor and friendless. On his way to Haran he stopped one night at
Bethel, which means the House of God. Here he dreamt
that God appeared to him and confirmed the blessing
of Abraham that the land would belong to his descendants and that through them all the families of the

earth would be blessed. Jacob was deeply stirred by this dream, and vowed that if God would give him bread to eat and clothes to wear, he would ever afterwards give one tenth of his possessions to God.

Jacob did not mean to stay long in his uncle's house, but actually he remained there for twenty years, working as shepherd to Laban. The city of Haran **His Life with Laban.** is believed to have been situated about fourteen miles south-east of Damascus, and no doubt shared in the prosperity of that famous centre. Already in the days of Jacob it was an ancient city. It owed its importance to the river Abana which made it a veritable oasis on the edge of the vast North Arabian desert. Standing on a high plain rendered fertile by the waters of the Abana, it marked a stopping-place for the caravans coming from the Euphrates Valley. From Damascus a caravan road traversed the whole length of Eastern Palestine to the Gulf of Akaba on the Red Sea, and thus connected India with Mesopotamia. A road ran from Damascus to Gaza and so to Egypt. Thus Damascus was the market-city of three continents, while it also gave welcome shelter to the half-nomad shepherds who migrated to its outskirts. Such a family was Laban's. They lived in houses and shared the city-life of their fellow-townsmen. But they were mainly shepherds and keepers of sheep. Jacob spent his years guarding his uncle's flocks in the hills round Haran. The burning midday heat was followed by the biting cold of the desert night, but neither by day nor by night could Jacob sleep securely. He was ever on his watch against the attacks of wild beasts. The sheep and goats were entrusted to his care and he had to repay any loss.

His life was made harder still by the cunning and

craftiness of Laban. For the first seven years Jacob worked in order to marry Laban's younger daughter Rachel, whom he loved. But when the seven years passed Laban deceived Jacob and gave him as a wife his elder daughter Leah. It was only after Jacob's bitter reproach that Laban gave him Rachel also as a wife, on condition, however, that he would serve him another seven years. At the end of fourteen years he wanted to return home, but Laban persuaded him to remain, and promised to give him whatever he asked as wages. Yet ten times he deceived Jacob in his wages! In spite of all, Jacob grew rich and prosperous. His wives Rachel and Leah, and their handmaids Bilhah and Zilpah, bore him eleven sons. The flocks given him by Laban increased abundantly, and soon Laban's sons envied him, so that he decided to return to his father's house in Palestine.

What a contrast was there between the friendless exile who had come empty-handed to the house of Laban, and the wealthy father of a large family who was returning to his home! He followed the road of his grandfather Abraham and let his flocks feed in the rich pasture-lands of Eastern Palestine. As he drew near to the territory of Esau, who had settled in the district of Mount Seir, in South Palestine, he sent him a message of greeting. Esau had not yet forgiven Jacob, and set out to meet him with a company of four hundred men. So that the meeting should be in peace, Jacob sent Esau a magnificent present of hundreds of goats and sheep, camels, asses and other animals. How numerous were his cattle if he could make a gift of all these! At the same time, with deep humility he offered up a prayer to God. He re-

He Returns to Palestine.

ceived a strange answer, yet one which helped him to face his brother with courage and greet him with peace. During that night, when he was alone on the northern shore of the brook Jabbok, a man wrestled with him until day-break. Jacob fearlessly held the man and would not let him go until he had blessed him. And the man, who was really an angel of God, did bless him and called him by a new name, Israel — the prince of God.

A new chapter had begun in Jacob's life. He marked it by commanding his household to put away the idols they had brought with them from Haran. These he hid under an oak-tree in Shechem, and then proceeded south to Bethel. There God appeared to him again and renewed the promise to give the land to him and his descendants. Jacob's long exile was nearly at an end, but before he reached the city of Hebron where Isaac was living, his dearly beloved wife Rachel died while giving birth to her younger son, Benjamin.

At Hebron he rejoined his father. He settled in the land, and his sons moved about the country to tend his flocks. He hoped that his troubles were **Joseph Sold as a Slave.** over and that he would now peacefully enjoy the blessing of Isaac. He was mistaken. Trouble arose in his family because he favoured his young son Joseph and bought him a coat of many colours, a garment worn only by important people. His brothers, the sons of Leah and the two handmaids, envied Joseph for this, and they hated him still more because of his dreams which he told them, which seemed to mean that one day he would rule over them. While they were feeding their father's sheep in Dothan, Joseph came to them in his coat of many colours. Some suggested that they should kill him, but on the advice of

Reuben, the eldest brother, they cast him into a pit.
A company of Ishmaelites, carrying perfumes, spices
and medicines from the moors of Gilead to sell in Egypt,
happened to pass by. Reuben was absent at the time,
and Judah persuaded the other brothers to take Joseph
out of the pit and sell him as a slave to these Ishmaelites.
They did so, first stripping him of his coat of many
colours. This they dipped in the blood of a goat and
brought it to their father. Jacob recognised it and said:
" It is my son's coat; an evil beast hath devoured him:
Joseph is without doubt rent in pieces." He mourned
Joseph as dead for twenty-two years. Thus Jacob, who
had deceived his father Isaac with a goat, was himself
deceived by his children in the same way!

The Ishmaelites brought Joseph to Egypt and sold
him as a slave to Potiphar, the captain of Pharaoh's
guard. From Egyptian records we know
**He is Brought
to Egypt.** that by this time a horde of shepherds
from Syria had invaded and conquered
Egypt. They destroyed the temples and cities of the
Egyptians and enslaved the people. Their kings, known
as Hyksos or Shepherd Kings, reigned at Memphis, an
ancient city the ruins of which lie ten to twelve miles
south of modern Cairo. The Egyptians hated these
kings, whom they regarded as barbarians, but had to
submit to them for over four hundred years.

Joseph was brought to the notice of one of these
Shepherd Kings by his gift of interpreting dreams.
This enabled him to foretell seven years
**He Becomes a
Great Man.** of exceptional plenty, to be followed by
seven years of severe famine, when the
annual flood of the river Nile would fail. His remarkable
organising ability saved for Egypt sufficient stores of

corn to last them through the years of famine. In return for this service to the country, Pharaoh (as the kings of Egypt were called) made him Grand Vizier of Egypt. The corn was owned by Pharaoh and Joseph sold it to the people for their land, so that the whole land of Egypt became the property of Pharaoh. The famine was severe also in the countries bordering on Egypt, and their inhabitants were compelled to go down to Egypt to buy food from Joseph. One day Joseph saw bowing to him his ten brothers. He recognised them, though they did not know him, for he had been a boy of seventeen when they had sold him as a slave, and now he was a great Egyptian prince.

Joseph saw that his dreams were coming true. He accused his brothers of being spies, and put them into prison. On the third day he released **He Tests His Brothers.** them, keeping back only one of them, Simeon, and forbade them to return to Egypt unless they brought with them their youngest brother Benjamin, about whom they had told him. The brothers, speaking in Hebrew among themselves, and not knowing that Joseph understood, reproached themselves for the terrible crime they had committed twenty years earlier in selling Joseph. They felt that they were being punished for having caused so much agony to Joseph and to Jacob. Although twenty years had passed, their conscience had not allowed them to forget.

They returned home and found that the money they had paid for their corn was in their sacks. But they could not go back to Egypt to restore this money, for Jacob would not let Benjamin go, and gave up Simeon, like Joseph, as lost. But the famine was very strong,

and at last Judah persuaded Jacob to send Benjamin
with them. They returned to Egypt with double money
to buy corn. Joseph was delighted to see his brother
Benjamin, set Simeon free, and made a feast for them all.
He then decided to do a strange thing, as a result of
which he would know whether they were loyal to Benjamin, who, like himself, was Rachel's son. After the
feast he ordered his steward to put his silver goblet in
Benjamin's sack and, when the men had left, to overtake
them and charge them with the theft. It appears that
by the laws of the land the thief became the servant
of the man from whom he stole. So Benjamin was
claimed as Joseph's servant, while the brothers were
told to return home. They would not hear of it, but
all came back to Joseph. Most eloquently Judah pleaded
with Joseph:

" Now therefore I pray thee let thy servant abide
instead of the lad a bondman to my lord; and let the
lad go with his brethren. For how shall I go to my
father, and the lad be not with me? Lest peradventure
I see the evil that shall come upon my father."

Now Joseph was convinced that his brothers were
not cruel or callous, and that they would never again
Jacob and his   commit such a crime as the one against
Family Settle   him. He made himself known to them
in Egypt.   and sent for his aged father to settle with
his family in Egypt. Jacob's heart leapt with joy when
he learnt that Joseph was alive, and he eagerly set out
with the wagons provided by Pharaoh to go down with
all his family to Egypt. At Beer-sheba, God appeared
to him in a dream by night and assured him that his
family would become a great people in Egypt. But
they would not remain there, because God would bring

them up again to the land which He had promised to Abraham.

By command of Pharaoh the Israelite shepherds settled in the fertile pasture-lands of Goshen near the eastern border of Egypt. They were destined to stay there for many years, but Jacob reminded them before his death that Egypt was not their real home, and that they must keep themselves separate from the Egyptians. For the family of Jacob were the Children of Israel, a family closely bound indeed by ties of blood, but even more so by a common experience of what God required of them. Before his death, Jacob blessed his children and commanded them to carry his body to Palestine and bury him by the side of Abraham and Isaac in the cave of Machpelah, near Hebron.

The Death of Jacob.

The brothers returned to Egypt, yet a suspicion still lurked in their mind. Perhaps Joseph had not forgiven them for selling him, and had waited until his father's death before punishing them? They were mistaken. It was not in Joseph's nature to bear a grudge. " Fear not, for am I in the place of God?" he told them. " Ye thought evil against me, but God meant it unto good, to bring to pass, as it is this day, to keep alive many people." And Joseph, like his father whom he resembled so much, died with the remembrance of the divine promise upon his lips:

" God will surely visit you and bring you out of this land unto the land which He sware to Abraham, to Isaac, and to Jacob."

CHAPTER 2

POINTS TO REMEMBER

Isaac:
- a) son of Abraham and Sarah
- b) lived in South Palestine
- c) had two sons by Rebecca — Jacob and Esau.

Jacob:
- a) the younger son of Isaac
- b) character — homeloving shepherd
- c) relations with Esau:
    bought birthright from him
    deceived Isaac to obtain Esau's blessing
    sent Esau magnificent gift on returning from Laban
    parted from him in peace by the brook Jabbok;
- d) relations with Laban:
    served him as shepherd for 20 years
    was deceived ten times by Laban
    endured hard life with him;
- e) his wives:
    Rachel and Leah (daughters of Laban)
    Bilhah and Zilpah, handmaids;
- f) his children:
    by Leah: Reuben, Simon, Levi, Judah, Issachar, Zebulun, Dinah
    by Rachel — Joseph and Benjamin
    by Zilpah — Gad, Asher
    by Bilhah — Dan, Naphtali;
- g) his journeys:
    to Haran, where Laban lived
    to Hebron, where Isaac lived
    to Egypt, where Joseph ruled;
    was buried in the Cave of Machpelah.

Joseph:

    a) favoured son of Jacob

    b) relations with his brothers:

        dreamt that he would rule over them

        was hated by them

        was sold by them to Ishmaelites;

    c) in Egypt:

        was slave in house of Potiphar

        was brought to notice of Pharaoh by his ability to explain dreams

        foretold years of plenty and of famine

        made Grand Vizier

        tested his brothers who came to buy corn from him

        settled Jacob and his family in the land of Goshen, on eastern border of Egypt

    d) his children — Ephraim, Manasseh.

Jacob and **Joseph** charged the Children of Israel to remember the divine promise that God would one day give them the land of Canaan.

CHAPTER 3

MOSES

The people of Egypt, among whom the Children of Israel dwelt, had developed from the remotest past a very complex civilisation. Five social classes are distinguished in the Egyptian records — soldiers, priests, officials, royal serfs, and craftsmen. At the head of all was the King or Pharaoh, who was regarded as a god. Next to him, the most powerful man in the kingdom was the Grand Vizier, who supervised the administration of the fifty provinces into which the country was divided. His two most important functions were to control the treasury and to dispense justice.

The land was a flat sandy plain, watered for a thousand miles by the river Nile. To the east and to the west stretched the desert. Canals irrigated the whole of the Nile valley and made it fertile. To maintain this vast system of irrigation, all labouring classes had to give five days' service every year. In addition, the royal serfs, who formed the bulk of the population, were burdened with numerous taxes. These were usually paid in kind and consisted of cattle, grain, wine, oil, honey and other produce.

Naturally the collection of these taxes required the services of a vast number of officials and scribes, who formed an important part of the population. Their taxes were paid in silver, gold and linen. The writing

26

used by the scribes is called hieroglyphics, and it is not very long since scholars learnt how to understand this writing and to read the story of Egyptian life from it. In an old city of Egypt, called Rosetta, a stone was found with inscriptions in hieroglyphics and Greek, and by comparing the Egyptian with the Greek words it was possible to arrive at the meaning of the hieroglyphics. This famous stone is now one of the treasures of the British Museum.

The Egyptians were very superstitious and worshipped over two thousand gods and goddesses. Every town and district possessed its own favourite gods. Among the best known are Amon, Ra, Thoth and Hathor. Animals, such as the cat, the serpent, the lamb and the bull, were regarded as sacred. The priests, who directed the worship of the gods, were well-educated, and besides reading and writing studied mathematics and astronomy. They taught that the body and soul live on in a different world beyond the grave, and they sold magic formulas by which a person could escape the punishment of the gods after death. Many of these formulas are to be found in an ancient work called the Book of the Dead. By these means the priests became wealthy and powerful and built themselves temples which almost looked like palaces.

The wealthy Egyptians had their bodies embalmed at death. The Pharaohs built for themselves mighty pyramids and enormous rock-hewn tombs, where their embalmed bodies were preserved. In 1922 the tomb of Tutankhamen, an Egyptian king of the Eigteenth Dynasty, was discovered in the Valley of the Kings, near Thebes. The outer chamber of the tomb contained life-size statues of the king, chariots, beds, magnificent alabaster vases, and furniture of every kind. The tomb-chamber was filled with beautiful jewels, images of gods and goddesses, and the royal throne itself.

Until the rise of the Eigteenth Dynasty, Egypt was under the domination of the Hyksos or Shepherd Kings.
The Children of Israel. It is probable that they ruled the kingdom for over four hundred years. The Hyksos, as you remember, were Semites who came from Syria, and naturally they treated with favour the Israelite shepherds who dwelt in the land of Goshen. The Children of Israel were organised into tribes according to the names of the twelve sons of Jacob, and were governed by the elders of these tribes. They did not worship the gods of Egypt, but remembered the God of their ancestor Abraham and kept the covenant of circumcision. The small family of seventy persons which Jacob had brought down with him to Egypt multiplied in the land, and became a strong and numerous people. Most of them were shepherds, but some of them learnt the arts and crafts of the Egyptians, and became skilful in gold and copperwork, while others became farmers.

A change came, however, when the native princes of Thebes felt sufficiently strong to rebel against the Hyksos.
A New Pharaoh. The Shepherd Kings were driven out of Egypt and every trace of their hated rule was wiped out by the victorious Pharaoh, who was the founder of the Eighteenth Dynasty, one of the most famous in the history of ancient Egypt. The Pharaohs of this dynasty pursued the Hyksos into Palestine and Syria and brought these lands under their power. Wealth poured into Egypt as a result of these foreign wars, while the influence of the army and the priesthood grew infinitely stronger.

Hebron, general view, including Cave of Machpelah

by courtesy of the Jewish National Fund.

Entrance of the Valley of the Kings.

The lot of the Israelites, who were of the same race as the Hyksos, was now far from happy. The Pharaohs were afraid that they, living on the eastern frontier of Egypt, might join with the desert tribes to overthrow the new dynasty. So the Israelites were enslaved and set the task of building fortresses and store-cities to protect the borders. They were forced to labour in the fields and in the cities, while taskmasters were appointed over them to see that they were not slack in their work. Gangs of men dragged the heavy stones along the rough roads, and were allowed no rest in the heat of the Egyptian day. Others had the task of making bricks, and were beaten if they were slack in their work. We know the names of two cities which the Israelites built for Pharaoh — Pithom and Raamses. The ruins of Pithom were discovered by an explorer about fifty years ago. Store-houses have also been found built of bricks with the name Raamses stamped upon them.

The life of the Israelites was bitter indeed. Yet in spite of all oppression they increased in number. Their spirit was not crushed, and they main- **The Cruel Decree.** tained their faith in God. But a Pharaoh was on the throne who was determined to destroy them and to wipe them out utterly from the earth. The records of Egyptian history suggest that this monarch was Thothmes III, who reigned jointly with the Princess Hatshepsut at the beginning of the fifteenth century B. C. E. He ordered the male children of the Israelites to be killed at birth, but his command could not be obeyed. Then he issued a decree that every newborn boy should be cast into the river Nile and drowned. Little did he dream that through this very decree he would help to rear in his own palace the child who was one day to lead the Israelites out of Egypt.

It happened in this way. Jochabed, the wife of Amram the Levite, who already had two children, gave birth to a boy after the barbaric law of Pharaoh was issued. For three months the child was kept hidden in the house. Then Jochabed placed him in a box of bulrushes, which she concealed among the reeds on the banks of the river Nile, while his sister stood at a distance to guard it. A daughter of Pharaoh, probably the Princess Hatshepsut, coming to bathe in the waters of the Nile, found the little box of bulrushes. She had pity on the child and adopted him as her own. Through Miriam she took as a Hebrew nurse for the child his own mother, though the princess did not know this. Thus the child learnt from his own mother the story of his people and their undying hope. Pharaoh's daughter gave him the name of Moses, because she had drawn him out of the water, and this is the meaning of that name.

The Birth of Moses.

In the palace of Pharaoh Moses was taught the wisdom of Egypt by the priests and magicians. He learnt to read and write, and became acquainted with many of the secrets of the priesthood. Yet he could not forget that he was a Hebrew, although he was dressed and spoke like an Egyptian. When he was old enough he went out among the people in the land of Goshen, and it hurt him to see the Hebrews working as slaves and being beaten by the Egyptians. One day he was so enraged at seeing a Hebrew being flogged by an Egyptian taskmaster, that he immediately struck the Egyptian dead and buried his body in the sand.

In Pharaoh's Palace

When Pharaoh heard of this action he realised that

Moses, though brought up as an Egyptian, was really a Hebrew, a member of the race he was trying to crush. Also at this time, the year 1487 B. C. E., scholars tell us, the Princess Hatshepsut, Moses' protector, died, and Thothmes III tried to destroy everything she had done, because he hated her memory. Moses knew that he could expect no mercy from Pharaoh, so he fled to the land of Midian in the Arabian desert. At an oasis in this desert he saw some shepherds stealing the water which the daughters of Jethro, the priest of the Midianites, had drawn for their own flocks. Again Moses showed that he was always on the side of the oppressed. He helped the daughters of Jethro against the shepherds, and watered their flock. Jethro invited Moses to his tent, and eventually he married one of his daughters, Zipporah, and became his shepherd.

His Flight to Midian.

It meant a great change for Moses. Instead of the noise and bustle of a capital city he enjoyed the silence of the desert, broken only by the bleating of sheep. In the place of houses and temples and other stone buildings, his eyes saw the unending plateau covered with patchy grass, and the unclouded sky meeting the earth in the distance. The whole district is a mass of hills, from four to five thousand feet above sea-level, wild and uncivilised, as different from the cultivated land of Egypt as day from night. Among these hills Moses tended the flocks of Jethro, and thought about his people in Egypt.

His Life There.

Forty years passed and Pharaoh died, but his death made no difference to the Hebrew slaves, for his successor, Pharaoh Amenhetep II, went on oppressing them. So harsh was their slavery that some of the men of the tribe of Ephraim, not waiting for God to redeem them, decided to leave the country, and break their way into Palestine. They were unsuccessful, and **The Persecution Grows Harsher.** were killed by the men of Gath, a strong city on the coastland of Palestine. As for the remainder who were in Egypt, they groaned in their misery, but clung to the hope that one day God would fulfil His promise made to their ancestors and take them into a better land.

It was at this time that, while Moses was tending the flock of Jethro at Horeb in the Peninsula of Sinai, he saw a strange sight. A thorn bush was burning **The Call of Moses.** in the desert, yet the fire did not seem to harm it. It was an unearthly fire.

" I must go near," said Moses, " and see this strange sight, why the bush is not burnt."

But as he stepped forward, he heard a voice calling him:

" Moses, Moses, draw not nigh hither.... for the place whereon thou standest is holy ground. I am the God of thy fathers, the God of Abraham, Isaac and Jacob," the voice went on. " I have seen the affliction of My people, who are in Egypt.... Come now, therefore, and I will send thee unto Pharaoh, that thou mayest bring forth My people, the Children of Israel, out of Egypt."

When he heard the voice, Moses hid his face between his hands. He was a very modest man, and he answered:

" Who am I that I should go to Pharaoh and that I should bring forth the Children of Israel out of Egypt?"

The Children of Israel, he declared, would not believe him if he came to them and claimed to be their leader. Pharaoh would laugh at him. Moreover he was not an eloquent man, but rather slow of speech.

But the Voice was insistent. The Children of Israel would listen to him because God would give him signs to show that he was His messenger. Pharaoh would not easily let the people go, yet in the end would himself drive them from his land. And, if he felt that he could not speak well, let his elder brother Aaron speak for him to the people and to Pharaoh.

Moses obeyed the call of God. Leaving his family with his father-in-law Jethro, he returned to Egypt with Aaron,

Moses Returns to Egypt. who had come to meet him in the desert. They assembled the elders of the Children of Israel, and Aaron told them God's message. The elders believed his words, and their hearts were glad.

Not so Pharaoh. He would not listen to the two brothers.

" Who is the Lord, that I should obey His voice? I know not the Lord, neither will I let Israel go.... Rather let more work be laid upon the men, that they may labour therein, and let them not regard vain words."

This was his answer. Through the coming of Moses the burdens of the Children of Israel were increased.

Pharaoh is Obstinate. They were no longer given straw with which to make bricks, but had to find it themselves. Yet they had to complete the same number of bricks each day, as when they were given the straw. Naturally this was impossible, and they were beaten. The Children of Israel protested to Pharaoh, but he would not listen to them. He told them they were lazy, and must work harder.

The elders of the people now turned against Moses and Aaron, and loaded them with reproaches. Moses was dumbfounded. He had meant to do good, and evil had resulted. In a voice full of anguish he cried to God:

"Why hast Thou sent me? Since I have come to Pharaoh to speak in Thy name, he has done evil to this people; neither hast Thou at all delivered Thy people."

The voice of God answered him:

"Now shalt thou see what I will do to Pharaoh, for with a strong hand shall he let them go, and with a strong hand shall he drive them out of his land."

This meant that not only would Pharaoh give the Children of Israel permission to leave the land, but he would himself implore them to go. And Moses believed the word of God and prepared himself to obey His commands. He and Aaron were not afraid to go to the mighty Pharaoh and tell him the message of God. Unless he allowed the Hebrews to go out of Egypt, with their young and with their old, with their sons and with their daughters, with their flocks and with their herds, in fact with all their possessions, disaster would befall him and his land. But the proud king laughed at the brothers, and mocked at the signs they gave. Then one plague after another came to the country. First the waters of the Nile became infected and were changed to blood. Frogs and all sorts of noisome insects swarmed over the land, bringing disease to man and beast. Added to all these horrors, tempests of hail and rain wrought havoc with the crops. An unnatural darkness also descended upon the land of Egypt for three days, during which no man could move from his place. Yet Pharaoh remained obstinate, in spite of the advice of his counsellors, who saw in the plagues the hand of the God of the Hebrews, and urged Pharaoh to let them go.

Before the Children of Israel were redeemed, however,

The Plagues.

they were tested. They were commanded to take on the tenth day of the first month every man a lamb, slaugh-

The Paschal Lamb. ter it on the fourteenth day, and sprinkle its blood on the door-posts of their houses for all to see. The lamb was a sacred animal of the Egyptians, and you can imagine what courage was required of every Israelite to keep it in his house for four days and then to slaughter it. The Egyptians, when they saw the blood of the lamb upon the door-posts of the Hebrews, might rush in to kill them for this crime. Yet the Children of Israel did as the Lord commanded Moses and Aaron. By this act they showed their firm belief in the God of their fathers, and proved themselves worthy of being redeemed.

Meanwhile, Moses had threatened Pharaoh that unless he allowed the Children of Israel to leave Egypt, every firstborn child of the Egyptians would die.

The Last Plague. At midnight on the fourteenth day of the first month, one great cry was heard throughout the whole of the land of Egypt. In every house, as Moses had foretold, the firstborn child was dead. Pharaoh and his counsellors rose up in the night and begged the Children of Israel to go out from Egypt:

" Take your flocks and your herds, as ye have said, and be gone; and bless me also."

Thus, on the fifteenth day of the first month, four hundred and thirty years after they had first come to

The Exodus. Egypt, the Children of Israel left that country for ever. Six hundred thousand men, besides women and children, assembled at Raamses, a frontier town of Egypt, and were joined by a large multitude of Egyptians. The promise of God to Abraham was fulfilled; his descendants took with them great riches from the country in which they had been oppressed and treated as strangers for many years. It marked the end of their slavery and the beginning of a new period in their history. They were no longer one family, nor merely a collection of tribes. They were a people united by a common thought of service to God. And they obeyed one leader — Moses. The day and the month in which they were redeemed from Egypt took precedence over all others in the Jewish year. Nisan, the month of spring, became the first month of the year. The evening of the fourteenth day of the month was observed from then onwards as the Feast of Passover. The festival was to be kept for seven days each year, during which only unleavened bread must be eaten, as a memorial of the fact that the Children of Israel had no time to bake their bread properly when they went out of Egypt. A new era began, and every date was reckoned "after the Exodus from Egypt."

In spite of the haste in which they left the country, Moses remembered Joseph's dying request, and carried his bones with him out of Egypt, so that **Moses Takes Joseph's Bones.** Joseph, like his ancestors, might be buried in the land of Israel.

From Egypt the nearest road to Palestine followed the coast to Gaza and the Maritime Plain. Here the Philistines were at that time trying to gain a **The Road to Palestine.** foothold. They were a non-Semitic people who overflowed from Crete, an island in the Mediterranean Sea, and established themselves on the coast. The country was named after them, because in early times it was called Canaan, and only later was it known as Palestine, the land of the Philistines.

God did not wish Moses to lead the Children of Israel

by this short road, lest they should come in contact with war. He rather led them through the desert to the east of Egypt.

When Pharaoh heard that the Children of Israel were wandering in the desert between Egypt and the Red Sea, he thought that they were trapped in the wilderness. He regretted now that he had let them go. With a host of six hundred chosen chariots of iron, each occupied by two soldiers, an archer and a charioteer, he rushed to overtake them. The northern part of the Red Sea is split into two gulfs by the Peninsula of Sinai. The western gulf, known as the Gulf of Suez, is to-day about 130 miles long, and has an average width of 18 miles. In ancient times this gulf extended much further northwards. The Israelites were encamping at the nothernmost point of the gulf when Pharaoh's host overtook them. Thus they were at bay between the sea and their dreaded enemy. In their despair they uttered bitter words against their leader Moses.

Pursuit by Pharaoh.

" Fear ye not," he answered, " stand still and see the salvation of the Lord.... The Lord shall fight for you, and ye shall hold your peace."

That night the two camps faced each other, separated only by the " Pillar of Fire " which accompanied the Children of Israel. That same night God commanded Moses to lift up his rod over the waters of the Red Sea and bid the people cross over. An east wind blew and divided the waters for the Israelites to pass over on dry land. The people courageously marched across the sea, with the waters piled up like a wall on either side of them. The Egyptians pursued them and also went into the channel

The Red Sea Crossed.

made by the wind. But towards morning the wind changed, and the waters came pouring over the chariots of Egypt and their soldiers, and overwhelmed them all. Not one was left alive.

When the Children of Israel saw the great miracle of their escape, a song of praise to God burst from their lips.

" I will sing unto the Lord," they began, " for He hath triumphed gloriously; the horse and his rider hath He thrown into the sea. The Lord is my strength and song, and He is become my salvation."

The crossing of the Red Sea finally made them a free people. With the bonds of slavery thrown off for ever, they now went forward to the mountain of God to offer Him their service.

The journey to Mount Sinai took six weeks. Unaccustomed to travel in the desert, the people found much **The Manna.** cause to complain. Often they went for days before they came upon an oasis with wells of water and palm trees. The stores of food they had taken with them from Egypt were soon eaten up, and then the Israelites in their hunger remembered with longing the abundance of food they had enjoyed in Egypt. By the grace of God they did find water in the desert, and food was provided for them, resembling coriander seed, but white, and tasting like honey-cake, which the people called Manna. They gathered it every day, each man according to the needs of his household. On the sixth day they found a double portion, which was to serve for the seventh day as well. For that day was singled out by God to be for ever the Sabbath, the day of rest. In the desert they also met enemies. The Amalekites, a wild tribe of nomads, attacked them, but were defeated in battle by the Children of Israel.

At length, the whole congregation of the Children of Israel reached the wilderness of Sinai on the first day of

Mount Sinai. the third month, counting from the Exodus from Egypt. The people pitched their tents in the broad plain opposite Mount Sinai, while Moses ascended the Mountain. He brought down a message from God:

" If you will indeed obey My voice and keep My covenant, then you shall be unto Me a peculiar treasure above all peoples, for the whole earth is Mine. And you shall be unto Me a kingdom of priests and a holy nation."

The people in their joy answered with one voice:

" All that the Lord hath spoken shall we do."

For the next three days the Israelites purified themselves, while Moses set bounds around the Mountain of God to prevent them from drawing too near.

" On the third day when it was morning, there were thunders and lightnings, and a thick cloud upon the Mountain, and the sound of the trumpet, exceedingly loud. And all the people that were in the camp trembled."

The most tremendous event in the history of the world was about to happen. God, the Creator of the world,

who had chosen Abraham and his descend-
The Ten Com- ants to make His ways known in the
mandments. world, was about to give His law to these descendants, the Children of Israel. So that no one among them afterwards could ever deny the Law, God uttered it from Mount Sinai in the presence of the whole people. They saw no image or form, only a cloud enveloping the mountain-top, and they heard a voice. The words which that voice spoke were the Ten Commandments. These commandments are the basis not only of Jewish Law, but of the laws of every civilised country

in the world. They were addressed to every person standing at the foot of the Mountain, and to their descendants for ever:

1. I am the Lord thy God who brought thee out of the land of Egypt. Thou shalt have no other gods beside me.
2. Thou shalt not make unto thyself any graven image.
3. Thou shalt not take the name of the Lord thy God in vain.
4. Remember the Sabbath day to keep it holy.
5. Honour thy father and thy mother.
6. Thou shalt not kill.
7. Thou shalt not commit adultery.
8. Thou shalt not steal.
9. Thou shalt not bear false witness against thy neighbour.
10. Thou shalt not covet.

The people were truly awed by the majesty of the spectacle, and they stood afar off. Moses then ascended the Mountain again to receive God's commands. Forty days he stayed there, accompanied only by his servant Joshua, who waited at the foot of the mount.

Aaron and the elders were left in charge of the people. For some days all went well, but soon the people grew restive at Moses' long absence. They were **The Golden Calf.** not yet used to the idea of an invisible God, because in Egypt they had always seen the images which the Egyptians worshipped. Now they clamoured that Aaron should make such an image of God for them. They thought that only if the image was there God was among them, and did not realise that they would be breaking the second of the Ten Commandments.

For the sake of peace Aaron agreed. The people eagerly tore off from themselves and from their wives all the jewels and ornaments which they wore, earrings and nose-rings, and bracelets, and gave them to Aaron, and he fashioned for them an image — a golden calf. Aaron proclaimed a feast to God for the next morning, and the people first offered sacrifices and then began to dance round the golden calf, singing as they danced and played:

" These are thy gods, O Israel, which brought thee out of the land of Egypt."

On that day Moses and Joshua were coming down from the Mountain, and they heard the shouting of the people.

Moses Shatters the Tablets of Stone. " There is sound of battle in the camp," said Joshua.

" No," answered Moses, " it is not the voice of them that shout for mastery, neither is it the voice of them that cry for being overcome, but the voice of them that sing do I hear."

The sight that met his eyes struck horror into his heart. As soon as he came near the camp he saw the calf and the dancing of the people. In his hands were the two tablets of stone on which the Ten Commandments were inscribed. The Children of Israel had already broken some of these Commandments. In an outburst of fury he cast the tablets out of his hands and broke them into fragments beneath the Mountain. In that moment it seemed to him that his whole life-work was shattered and that he had laboured in vain.

CHAPTER 3

POINTS TO REMEMBER

The Egyptians:
- a) their land — valley of Nile — a flat sandy plain bordered by the desert to the east and to the west
- b) organisation — divided into fifty provinces administered by governors
- c) social classes — soldiers, priests, officials, royal serfs, craftsmen
- d) culture — very ancient — hieroglyphic writing
- e) religion — worshipped over two thousand gods and goddesses embalmed bodies of the dead
- f) history — ruled by Hyksos for many centuries

  Hyksos expelled by Pharaohs of XVIII Dynasty, who then carried war into Palestine and Syria
- g) Pharaohs of the Oppression and the Exodus

  Thothmes III 1501—1447 B. C. E.

  Amenhetep II 1447—1423 B. C. E.

Israelites (or Hebrews):
- a) under the Hyksos — dwelt happily in Goshen

  were organised in Tribes and kept the covenant of Abraham (circumcision)

  were mainly shepherds, but some became craftsmen and farmers
- b) under the Pharaohs of the XVIII Dynasty

  were oppressed and enslaved

  built fortresses and store-cities on the frontier for Pharaoh yet maintained their faith in God.

Moses:
- a) son of Jochabed and Amram
- b) was hidden near the Nile to be protected from the barbaric decree of Pharaoh

c) was saved by daughter of Pharaoh and brought up in the palace
d) championed cause of Israelite and killed his taskmaster
e) fled to Midian to escape Pharaoh's wrath
f) life in Midian — defended daughters of Jethro
    married Zipporah, a daughter of Jethro
    became Jethro's shepherd
    his " call "
g) his return to Egypt:
    accompanied by brother Aaron
    Israelites believed his message
    Pharaoh scornful
    the Ten Plagues
    the Paschal Lamb
h) the Exodus:
    600,000 men, besides women and children and a mixed multitude, assembled at Raamses
    left Egypt by way of desert
    pursuit by Pharaoh
    the crossing of the Red Sea
    the journey through the wilderness
    the Ten Commandments
    the Golden Calf
    Moses shattered the tablets of stone.

CHAPTER 4

AARON

Moses seized hold of the golden calf and burnt it.   Then he turned to Aaron and demanded:

The Tribe of Levi Faithful. " What harm have this people done to thee, that thou hast brought upon them such great sin?"

Aaron defended himself:

" Thou knowest the people, that they are bent on evil. They said to me, Make us a god which shall go before us, for we know not what has happened to this man Moses.... and so with their gold I made this calf."

Soon Aaron showed strikingly that he had never forsaken God.   Moses stood in the gate of the camp and cried:

" Who is for the Lord, let him come to me."

The whole tribe of Levi answered his call.   Of that tribe Aaron was the eldest member and, next to Moses, the most respected.   When it came to the test, and he and every Israelite had to choose between God and the golden calf, there was no question — he and his tribe were for the Lord.

The next day was one of shamefaced repentance.   The people knew that they had sinned grievously, and were sorry.   Would God forgive them?   Long **God Pardons the People.** and earnestly did Moses pray on their behalf, and God, remembering His covenant with their ancestors Abraham, Isaac, and Jacob, pardoned them. He also gave Moses new tablets of stone inscribed with the Ten Commandments in place of those which Moses had broken.

The incident of the golden calf had shown how far the Israelites still were from a true knowledge of God. It

Heathen Customs.

was essential for them to feel the presence of God in their midst and that they should do Him personal service. Therefore Moses was commanded to build a Sanctuary to God from the free-will offerings of the people.

The Egyptians and the Canaanites had ornate temples and thousands of altars, on every one of which they offered sacrifices every day. In Palestine especially every hill and every fertile piece of ground had its own god, where the most abominable customs were practised. Children were even killed and passed through the fire to the gods. Enchantment and divination, witchcraft and magic, and every kind of horrible superstition were used in their worship.

These customs the Children of Israel were forbidden to imitate. Instead, they were commanded to make a

Sacrifices.

Tabernacle, to furnish it very simply, and at its entrance to build only one altar where sacrifices could be offered. The sacrifices were few in number: a burnt-offering, a meal-offering, a peace-offering, a sin-offering, and a trespass-offering. The burnt-offering, so called because the whole animal was burnt upon the altar, was to be sacrificed twice a day, one lamb in the morning and another in the evening. The other offerings were brought mainly on account of sin, and their object was to teach man not to sin. Nobody would lightly do wrong if he knew that because of it he would have to bring a sacrifice to the courtyard of the Tabernacle, lay his hands upon the animal and publicly confess the wrong he had done.

The Children of Israel eargerly obeyed the command to bring a free-will gift for the building of the Tabernacle.

The Gifts of the People. In their crowds men and women came to Moses' tent, and freely gave their bracelets and their earrings, and all their jewels of gold. Whoever had blue and purple, and scarlet wool and fine linen, and goat's hair, and skins of rams dyed red, and badger's skins, brought them. The princes of the tribes gave rich stones, spices, and olive oil for the lamps. Gold and silver and brass poured in abundantly, more than enough. The women spun the linen with their own hands and brought it to Moses.

Great was the activity in the camp of Israel opposite Mount Sinai. Bezalel, a man of Judah, and Aholiab of the tribe of Dan, were in charge of the **The Golden Ark.** skilled craftsmen who did the work. First they made the Ark which was to contain the new tablets of stone which Moses had brought down from Mount Sinai. The Ark consisted of three caskets, one inside the other. The middle one was made of acacia wood, a tree which is very common in many parts of the Peninsula of Sinai. The other two caskets were made of pure gold. On the Ark were two Cherubim. The Ark was to be placed in the holiest part of the Tabernacle and separated from the rest of it by a curtain.

The Tabernacle itself was a tent built of upright boards of acacia wood covered with layers of hangings, one **The Building of the Tabernacle.** layer being of goat-skin, which was the usual material with which tents were covered. In the Tabernacle were placed a golden candlestick with seven lamps, a golden table, and a small golden altar on which spices and sweet incense were offered. Near the entrance to the Tabernacle stood an altar of acacia wood, overlaid with brass.

All day long for day after day, the Israelites worked hard to build this Tabernacle for the glory of God. But on one day every week no sound of work was heard in the camp. On the Sabbath day all the people rested, even from the holy work of building the Tabernacle, because to keep the Sabbath day holy was part of the covenant between God and Israel.

When the Tabernacle was completed, men had to be appointed to serve in it, and to guard it. While the **The Priesthood.** Israelites were in Egypt they had continued the tradition of their ancestors that the firstborn in each family should be the priest of God. But they had proved unworthy of this privilege, because they had shared in the worship of the golden calf. Only the tribe of Levi had taken no part in this sin. So this tribe was chosen to guard the Tabernacle and to carry it in its journeys with the Israelites through the wilderness. For the service in the Tabernacle, Aaron and his sons were appointed, and they and their descendants for ever became the priests of God. Aaron, quiet and peaceloving by nature, was the ideal man to act as priest and to make atonement for the Children of Israel.

Great was the rejoicing in the camp of Israel when the Tabernacle and all its vessels, and the holy garments for **The Consecration.** Aaron and his sons, were completed. On the first day of the first month, a year after the Israelites had left Egypt, Moses set up the Tabernacle in the Plain of Sinai in the presence of all the people. Aaron, clothed in the gorgeous garments of the High Priest, with his four

sons Nadab and Abihu, Eleazar and Ithamar, stood
at the entrance of the Tabernacle and were solemnly
consecrated as the priests of God. It was an impressive
spectacle. Only the sound of the golden bells at the hem
of Aaron's robe was heard as he went about performing
the consecration ceremony. On the breastplate which
he bore near his heart gleamed the bright colours of the
twelve precious stones, each inscribed with the name of
one of the Twelve Tribes. The sacrifices were offered,
and Moses and Aaron stood up and blessed the people.
" Then fire came out from before the Lord and consumed
the offering on the altar. And when the people saw
it they shouted for joy and fell upon their faces." From
that moment onwards a cloud rested over the Tabernacle,
a sign of God's presence among the people.

But two of Aaron's sons, Nadab and Abihu, took fire
of their own and brought it near the altar. They had
done wrong, and their punishment came terribly and
swiftly. They died at once, and the joy of that day
was turned to mourning. Yet Aaron accepted the
tragedy with that quiet trust in all God's actions which
showed the greatness of his character. He kept silent.

The duties of the priests were much more than only
to offer sacrifices. It was their task to heal diseases in
the body and the mind. They were the
The Law of Moses. doctors and the teachers of Israel. The
laws which they had to teach are to be
found in many parts of the Torah, as the Five Books of
Moses are called. The object of the laws was to make
the Children of Israel a holy nation and a kingdom of
priests to the rest of the world. First and foremost they
were forbidden to imitate any of the evil customs of the
countries from which they came and to which they were

going. They were commanded to worship God only, to be pure in their family life, to deal justly with their fellow-men, and to love the stranger. Here are some of the laws from chapter 19 of the Book of Leviticus, the Third Book of the Torah:

" Ye shall fear every man his father and his mother, and keep My Sabbaths."

" Turn ye not unto idols, nor make to yourself molten gods."

" And when ye reap the harvest of your land, thou shalt not wholly reap the corners of thy field.... neither shalt thou gather every grape of thy vineyard.... thou shalt leave them for the poor and the stranger."

" Ye shall not steal, neither deal falsely, nor lie to one another."

" And ye shall not swear by My name falsely, neither shalt thou profane the name of thy God."

" Thou shalt not defraud thy neighbour, neither rob him."

" Thou shalt not curse the deaf, nor put a stumbling-block before the blind."

" Ye shall do no unrighteousness in judgment; thou shalt not respect the person of the poor, nor honour the person of the mighty, but in righteousness shalt thou judge thy neighbour."

" Thou shalt not go up and down as a talebearer among thy people."

" Thou shalt not hate thy brother in thine heart."

" Thou shalt not avenge, nor bear any grudge against the children of thy people, but thou shalt love thy neighbour as thyself."

" Ye shall not eat anything with the blood; neither shall ye use enchantments."

" Thou shalt rise up before the hoary head, and honour the face of the old man, and fear thy God."

" And if a stranger sojourn with thee in thy land, ye shall not vex him. The stranger that dwelleth with you shall be unto you as one born among you, and thou shalt love him as thyself; for ye were strangers in the land of Egypt."

" Ye shall do no unrighteousness in judgment, in meteyard, in weight, or in measure."

" Just balance and just weights shall ye have."

" I am the Lord thy God who brought thee out of the land of Egypt. Therefore shall ye observe all My statutes, and all My judgments, and do them: I am the Lord."

Besides the Sabbath day, special holydays were appointed: Passover, the Feast of Weeks, the New Year, the Day of Atonement, and the Feast of Tabernacles. On these occasions the people, free from their work, could assemble and hear the word of God explained to them by the priests. The Festivals also marked special events in the life of the Israelites and in the seasons of the year, and through them they were taught the goodness of God. They were even commanded to be holy in the very food they ate. And so we find in the Torah not only laws about caring for the stranger, the poor and the fatherless, and about justice and kindness in all one's actions, but also laws forbidding the eating of certain animals and foods, laws about the Sabbaths and Festivals, and laws about the priesthood and sacrifice. The object of all the laws was to draw the Israelite away from the bad customs and practices of his neighbours and to enable him to live a good life. Jews all over the world still observe these laws to-day, over three thousand years since they were given to our ancestors from Mount Sinai.

CHAPTER 4

POINTS TO REMEMBER

The Golden Calf:
>Tribe of Levi rallied round Moses
>the people pardoned
>new tablets of stone given to Moses.

The Tabernacle:
>1) built from the gifts offered by the people
>2) consisted of tent divided into 2 unequal parts: the smaller, the Holy of Holies, contained the Ark;

in the larger, the Holy Place, were
>the golden candlestick
>the golden table
>a small golden table for incense;

near the entrance stood the brazen altar of sacrifice.
>3) was guarded by the Tribe of Levi.

The Priesthood:
>1) Aaron and his sons chosen to serve in the Tabernacle
>2) their duties: a) the service of the Tabernacle
>   b) to teach the people the ways of God.

The Law of Moses:
>deals with every aspect of human life.

CHAPTER 5

THE WILDERNESS

On the twentieth day of the second month, in the second year after the Exodus, the Children of Israel began their journey northwards to Palestine. **The Israelite Camp.** Moses blew the two silver trumpets which he had made. At once the three tribes encamped on the east side of the Tabernacle prepared themselves to march forward. Then came the Levites, who took down the Tabernacle and its vessels, which they placed in covered wagons provided by the princes of the tribes for the holy service. The Golden Ark, however, the Kohathites, a special section of the Levites, bore reverently on their shoulders until the Tabernacle was set up wherever the camp was pitched. The other tribes followed in companies of three, each with its own banner. The Israelite hosts made an imposing sight as they set forward with joyful heart from the mountain near which they had encamped for almost a year.

The country which they traversed was the eastern end of the Peninsula of Sinai. The peninsula is a barren tract of limestone hills to the south of **Trials on the Way.** Palestine, rich in copper. Triangular in shape, it is enclosed by the Gulf of Suez on the west, and the Gulf of Akaba on the east. These inlets join the Red Sea at the southern apex of the triangle. The only outlet by land is to the north, where lay the territory of Edom and the Negeb. Beyond this stretched

THE ISRAELITE CAMP

In the centre was the Tent of Assembly (the Tabernacle); surrounding it were the families of the Levites; the outermost ring was formed by the Twelve Tribes.

the Promised Land, towards which their steps were now directed. But the journey was beset with untold hardships. The blazing heat of the summer days and the dull monotony of the limitless desert as far as the eye could reach, reacted upon the Israelites. They started to find complaints against their leader. At one time they grew tired of the Manna, which was their food in the wilderness, and they longed for meat. The sound of their murmuring weighed heavily upon Moses' heart. His one desire was to weld the people together and lead them forward on their high purpose as a united nation, but he felt that it was impossible for himself alone to guide such a great multitude. So, by divine command, he chose seventy elders to assist him in ruling the people. Earlier, at Sinai, on Jethro's advice, he had appointed judges to deal with the minor causes which required attention. With these elders Moses now had the nucleus of a government.

At last the Israelites reached Kadesh-Barnea, an oasis in the wilderness of Paran and a well-known stopping-place on the route between Palestine and Egypt. They were within sight of the Promised Land! Urged on by the people, Moses picked out twelve men, one from each tribe, and sent them to spy out the land. They followed the road over the steep mountain ridges of the Negeb and proceeded as far north as Hebron. From one of the fruitful valleys near this city they cut a big branch with a cluster of grapes, so heavy that two men had to carry it on a pole. They also brought back with them other fruits of the land, such as pomegranates and figs.

The Twelve Spies.

After forty days the spies returned to the camp of Israel in Kadesh-Barnea and gave their report to the whole assembly. "The land," they said, "is very fruit-ful, but the people are strong that dwell in it, and the cities are well fortified. The Amalekites dwell in the Negeb, the Hittites, the Jebusites and the Amorites dwell in the mountains, and the Canaanites dwell by the sea and by the side of Jordan. We cannot go up against these people, for they are stronger than we."

Their Report.

A startled cry went up from the Israelites as they heard these words.

"Would to God," they exclaimed, "that we had died in Egypt or in this wilderness."

The report of the spies terrified them, and they had no faith in the promise of God that He would lead them into the land. In their despair they turned against Moses and spoke of appointing another leader to take them back to Egypt.

Two of the spies, however, Joshua and Caleb, did have faith in God, and they turned to the rebellious people and said:

Joshua and Caleb.

"The land which we spied out is ex-ceedingly good. If the Lord delight in us He will bring us into this land and give it to us.... Only rebel ye not against the Lord, neither fear ye the people of the land." But the Israelites would not listen and threatened to stone them.

You can imagine the feelings of Moses when he saw the whole congregation of Israel turn against him in their terror. He had given up everything for them. He could have been a prince in Egypt. Instead, he led this people out of Egypt where they had been slaves, and brought down to them the Law of God. It was his object to lead them

The Greatness of Moses.

further into a land of their own where they could become a free and noble nation, an example to mankind. They, however, had no courage. At the first thought of danger they were prepared to desert him and to abandon their whole future. They still had the mentality of slaves.

At this moment the divine voice proclaimed to Moses that the Children of Israel would be destroyed and that he would become the father of a great people instead. Moses again revealed the nobility of his character. His thought was all for the people, weak and disloyal though they had shown themselves. He prayed to God to pardon them, and not to destroy them for their faithlessness. And God, because He is long-suffering and merciful, did pardon them. Yet they had shown that they were not worthy to enter Palestine. For forty years, therefore, He decreed, they must wander in the Wilderness, until the whole generation which had left Egypt had died. Then, their children would enter the Promised Land. Only Joshua and Caleb, who had proclaimed their courage and faith in God, would be allowed to enter Palestine.

When the Israelites heard this dread decree, they grew desperate and decided to make an immediate attack on Palestine. Moses tried to prevent them, but they would not obey him. They attacked the mountainous district of the Negeb, while Moses and the Ark remained in the camp. Naturally, the undisciplined army of Israelites was severely defeated by the Amorites and the Canaanites who dwelt in the hill-country.

The Attack on the Negeb.

The Israelites now sullenly accepted their fate and put themselves again under the leadership of Moses. There were, however, several men who felt they could still stir

up the people to revolt. Korah, a Levite, and a cousin
of Moses and Aaron, was envious of Aaron because he
was High Priest, and gathered round him
The Revolt of members of the tribe of Reuben to challenge
Korah. the authority of Moses. The people flocked
round Korah, and Dathan and Abiram, the leaders of
the revolt. Moses realised Korah's ambitions and denounced him and his followers:

" Hear now, ye sons of Levi; seemeth it a small thing
unto you that God hath separated you from the congregation of Israel to do the service of the Tabernacle....
and seek ye the priesthood also?"

Dathan and Abiram were even more defiant than
Korah. They would not obey the command of Moses to
come up to him, and insolently added:

" Is it a small thing that thou hast brought us up out
of a land flowing with milk and honey to kill us in the
wilderness, that thou must also make thyself a prince
over us?"

The rebellion was now formidable, and only a miracle
from God could show the people that Moses was indeed
the messenger of God in all that he had
The Rebels done. This miracle happened. In sight
Punished. of the whole people, who were assembled
round the tents of Korah and his company, the earth
trembled and Korah and the other rebels, with all their
possessions, were destroyed in an earthquake. The rest
of the people fled, terrified, in all directions. Their complaints however, did not cease until it was made plain
to them all that God had also chosen Aaron to be High
Priest. The prince of every tribe was commanded to
place in the Tabernacle his rod with his name inscribed
on it. The next morning Moses brought out the rods to

the princes, and it was found that Aaron's rod had budded and brought forth almond blossoms, which was the sign that God had chosen him to be High Priest. After that nobody dared to challenge the authority of Moses and Aaron.

For thirty-eight years the Children of Israel now wandered in the wilderness in the neighbourhood of Kadesh-Barnea. It was a significant period, **The Forty Years' Wandering.** though the Bible is silent about it. Pastoral life in the desert is always the same, and the habits of desert tribes to-day recall the movements of the Israelites over three thousand three hundred years ago. Oases are the only stations in the wilderness. When a watering-place is reached, the camp settles down and tents are pitched. The flocks are allowed to graze on the scanty vegetation, and when this has been consumed the camp moves on to the next oasis. The same round of the few watering-places is made year by year, and grazing rights are acquired. Yet there is always the danger of attack from hostile and more powerful tribes. And when drought comes, the nomads are faced with the alternatives of death by starvation or a long trek to the more fertile lands to the north.

To the Israelites fresh from the comparative luxuries of Egypt this life was trebly hard, for they had no hope of any better time. They lived and waited at the gates of Palestine in order that their children might possess the qualities which would enable them to enter the Promised Land as the Chosen People. It was the iron will of their inspired leader which inculcated in them the ideas of cohesion and discipline, pure worship, honest dealing, and sacrifice for the common good. The leaders had to set an example of unfaltering faith in God. The slightest lapse could not go unpardoned. One such instance is recorded, at the end of the forty years of wandering. The new generation of Israelites had returned to Kadesh-Barnea, where Miriam, the sister of Moses and Aaron, died. The people murmured against Moses and Aaron because they could find no water to drink. God showed Moses a rock from which water would flow when he spoke to it in the presence of the people. Moses assembled the people before the rock, but impatiently reproached them as rebels and then struck the rock twice, when water flowed from it abundantly. At once the divine decree went forth to the two brothers:

" Because ye believed Me not, to sanctify Me in the eyes of the Children of Israel, therefore ye shall not bring this congregation into the land which I have given them." The name of this place was called The Waters of Meribah, which means The Waters of Strife.

Moses and Aaron accepted the decree of God uncomplainingly.

Meanwhile, the Children of Israel were ready to march forward to Palestine. The king of the Edomites would **Aaron Dies.** not allow them to cross his territory, so they went out of their way to the south of Edom and then proceeded northwards to the river Arnon, which was the boundary of the land of Moab, on the east side of the Jordan. Shortly after they began this long and arduous journey, Aaron the High Priest, at the command of God, went up Mount Hor which is at the edge of the land of Edom, not far from Kadesh-Barnea. His brother Moses and his son Eleazar accompanied him to the top of the mount, and there Eleazar was sanctified as High Priest. Aaron died on the summit of the mountain, and was deeply mourned by the whole congregation of Israel.

The journey through the wilderness by the boundary of Edom was a terrible trial for the people. For hundreds of miles they were moving southwards, away from Palestine. The land through which they went was mountainous and dry, with very little pasture and full of serpents and wild beasts. It is no wonder that sometimes the spirit of the Israelites failed them and they murmured against God and against Moses. At length, however, they came to the brook Zered, which, as the map shows you, seperated the broken hilly country of Edom from the high plateau of Moab. The territory of Moab formerly stretched from the brook Zered in the south, to beyond the river Arnon in the north. But before the coming of the Israelites, Sihon, an Amorite king of Western Palestine, had crossed the Jordan and driven the Moabites south to the river Arnon. The Israelites proceeded from the brook Zered, keeping east of Moab until they reached the upper valleys of the river Arnon. To cross the Jordan they had to pass through the territory of Sihon, the king of the Amorites. Moses sent messengers to Sihon, craving permission to pass through his land. Sihon refused and marched to his frontier-town of Yahas to do battle with the Israelites. He was defeated, and the Israelites took possession of his land, from the river Arnon to the river Jabbok.

The First Victory.

This victory meant much to the Israelites. After many years of homeless wandering they now possessed territory of their own, where they could build houses and settle. Further north lay the fertile pasture lands of Gilead and Bashan, with their forests and cornfields, their delightful valleys yielding pomegranates, apricots, olives, and vines, and

Og Defeated.

their plains and moors full of fragrant herbs. The Israelites advanced to these districts, and when Og, king of Bashan, came out to do battle with them at Edrei, they defeated him and his army and conquered his land.

The whole of the territory east of the Jordan, from Mount Hermon in the north to the river Arnon in the south, was now in the hands of the Israelites. As Balak, the king of Moab, looked out upon the tents of the Israelites stretching away into the distance, he grew afraid and sought for means to destroy them. Suddenly he thought of Balaam, the famous heathen prophet who lived in Syria. He believed, as did all the heathen peoples of that time, that the blessing or the curse of a soothsayer would be effective. So he sent messengers to Balaam bidding him come to curse Israel.

Balak is Afraid and Sends for Balaam.

At first Balaam refused to go because he was told in a divine vision that he must not curse the people, for they were blessed. But Balak pressed him to come, offering him honour and wealth, and at last he agreed, although divinely warned to say only the words which God would put into his mouth.

Balak went out to meet Balaam at the border of Moab, and received him with honour. The next morning they went to one of the hills of Moab, from which they could see a part of the Israelite camp. Balak built an altar and offered sacrifice, and then Balaam, turning to Balak and the princes of Moab, began:

Balaam Blesses Israel.

" From Aram hath Balak brought me,
The king of Moab from the mountains of the East,
Come, curse me Jacob,
And come, defy Israel.

How shall I curse whom God hath not cursed?
And how shall I defy whom the Lord hath not defied?"

Then, to the amazement of Balak and his princes, he went on to glorify Israel. Balak, strange as it may seem, thought that if he saw Israel from another hill Balaam might change his mind and feel prompted after all to curse them. But it was not so. Three times Balaam saw the tents of Israel, from three different hills, and three times he blessed them, inspired by God. Balak, in great rage, smote his hands together and exlcaimed:

" I called thee to curse mine enemies, and behold thou hast altogether blessed them these three times. Therefore now flee to thy place; I thought to promote thee unto great honour, but the Lord hath kept thee back from honour."

Before Balaam went, however, in a prophetic vision he showed Balak the great future of the people of Israel. Balak felt that he could not contend with this divinely-protected people.

Yet there was one way in which the Israelites could forfeit the protection of God, and that was by disobeying **Israel's Lapse.** His laws. And while the Israelites were encamped opposite the plains of Moab, many of them accepted the invitation of the Moabites and Midianites to a sacrificial festival to the gods of Moab. They took part in their barbarous heathen idol-worship, even in the sight of Moses and the elders of Israel. But Phineas, the grandson of Aaron, championed the cause of God, and slew Zimri, a prince of the Simeonite tribe, who had sinned in the presence of the whole people. The evil-doers were punished, and vengeance was taken on the Midianites; yet the incident showed how easily the people could be led away from the true service of God.

This weakness, the desire to imitate their neighbours, was to prove a stumbling-block more than once in the history of Israel.

It was for this reason that Moses, before his death, prayed to God that He might appoint "a man over the congregation, who may go out before them and come in before them; who may lead them out and who may bring them in; that the congregation of the Lord be not as sheep which have no shepherd."

Joshua Chosen as Successor to Moses.

God answered his prayer and told him to appoint his servant Joshua in the presence of the whole congregation. This Moses did, and laid his hands upon Joshua, as a sign that he would be his successor as leader of the people.

The nation of Israel was now ready to cross the Jordan and conquer Palestine. Two and-a-half Tribes, however, Reuben, Gad, and half the tribe of Manasseh, approached Moses and asked to be allowed to settle on the east of the Jordan and not to cross over to Palestine proper. Their reason was that the land was very suitable for cattle-grazing and they had large herds of cattle.

The Two and-a-half Tribes.

At first Moses was shocked at their request. He thought that they were behaving like their fathers, who had been afraid to enter Palestine, and that the other tribes might follow their example. But when they promised to send their armed men with the other tribes across the Jordan, while the women and children remained on the east of the Jordan, Moses agreed that they should possess these lands. To Reuben and Gad was assigned the land between the rivers Arnon and Jabbok, while half the tribe of Manasseh occupied the territory of Gilead and Bashan, further north.

At the same time the ideal boundaries of Palestine, west of Jordan, were laid down. This territory of Israel was to stretch from the southern end of the Dead Sea to the river of Egypt in the south, the whole length of the Mediterranean coast on the west, and as far as the Phoenician city of Sidon on the north, and the whole length of the Jordan on the east.

The Boundaries of Palestine.

The work of Moses in the Wilderness was nearly over. On the first day of the eleventh month, in the fortieth year after the Exodus from Egypt, he assembled the people by the border of Moab and charged them to remain faithful to God. He went over the course of their history and showed them how from one man, Abraham, they had grown to become a great and numerous nation. He reminded them of the laws they had received in the Wilderness and exhorted them to observe those laws faithfully. He also reminded them of their shortcomings and of their faithlessness to God time and again. Lest they be ensnared by the nations they would meet in Palestine, he enjoined them to stamp out ruthlessly all signs of idol-worship and not to worship God in that manner. They must have only one altar in the whole country on which to offer sacrifices to God. If they observed the laws, he declared, they would live long upon the land which God had promised to give to their ancestors and to them. He ended by blessing each one of the tribes.

The Last Words of Moses.

With a last look at the people for whom he had done so much, Moses at the command of God ascended Mount Nebo, opposite Jericho. From this high hill he had a magnificent view of the land which he himself was not allowed to

The Death of Moses.

enter. The whole Jordan valley from Engedi in the
south to the source of the river Jordan in Mount Hermon
on the north was visible to his eye. The hills of Gilead
and of Ephraim seemed to meet and form one range.
Jericho, the city of palm-trees, stood opposite him across
the Jordan. To the south-east he saw the hills of Judea
and the arid soil of the Negeb, as well as the valley of
the Dead Sea. He heard the voice of God saying:

" This is the land which I swore to Abraham, to Isaac,
and to Jacob, saying, to thy seed will I give it. I have
caused thee to see it with thine eyes, but thou shalt not
go over thither."

So Moses, the faithful servant of God, died on that
mountain, though no man knows his burying-place. The
whole people of Israel mourned his death, for now they
realised how truly great he was and that no prophet like
him had ever arisen in Israel, nor ever would.

Inspired by his work, and treasuring the law of God
which he had given them, the people held themselves
in readiness under the leadership of Joshua, to take
possession of the land where they could live as a free
people, a united nation.

CHAPTER 5

POINTS TO REMEMBER

The Israelite Camp. — See plan, facing page 52

Forward to Palestine:
    March to Kadesh
    difficulties by the way
    the twelve spies
    the false report of the ten
    courage of Joshua and Caleb
    cowardice of the people
    nobility of Moses.

Forty Years' Wandering:
    the rebellion of Korah
    the vindication of Aaron
    the period of waiting and preparation
    death of Miriam at Kadesh
    the lapse of Moses and Aaron
    death of Aaron on Mount Hor.

Conquest of Eastern Palestine:
    the journey round Edom
    the victory over Sihon and Og.

By the Plains of Moab:
    Balak and Balaam
    the Midianites — zeal of Phineas
    Joshua chosen to succeed Moses
    Reuben, Gad, and half Manasseh settled in Eastern Palestine
    Moses' last words
    his death.

PART II

JUDGES, PRIESTS AND KINGS

CHAPTER 6

JOSHUA

The land which Joshua and the Children of Israel were about to enter had undergone a great change since the days of Jacob. In the lifetime of the **The Masters of Palestine.** Patriarchs, Palestine was dominated by the same race that ruled Egypt, the Hyksos. They over-ran Palestine and invaded Egypt, where they ruled for two dynasties, the fifteenth and sixteenth. They brought with them the culture and the language of Babylonia. They also introduced the horse into Palestine and Egypt. In Palestine, moreover, they built or rebuilt a large number of hill-cities which they fortified in a peculiar manner, with sloping ramparts, unlike other races, who preferred upright walls. After many centuries, as we have already seen, the Pharaohs of the Eighteenth Dynasty drove out the hated Hyksos from Egypt. The Pharaohs went even further and invaded Palestine and Syria. Thothmes III, the Pharaoh of the Oppression, invaded Palestine twelve times and subjugated the whole country. His successors Amenhetep II and Thothmes IV continued his policy of conquest and set up Egyptian governors all over the land.

It was thus a Palestine weakened by Egyptian conquest which Joshua set out to attack.   Yet his task was by no

Joshua's Task. means easy. The country was full of strongly-fortified cities, all situated on hills, which their inhabitants, Canaanites, Hittites, Hivites and others, would doubtless defend to the last.   There was always the fear that the Israelites would try by peaceful means to settle among these peoples and learn to imitate their idolatrous and immoral customs.   Therefore Joshua was commanded utterly to exterminate the heathen inhabitants of Palestine and to destroy all signs of their pagan worship.   In its place he was to implant the true service of God.

His first step was to send two men secretly to spy out Jericho, the city on the west side of the Jordan immediat-

Rahab. ely facing the Israelite camp.   The cities of Palestine were small, but enclosed by high and broad walls. Normally a large number of the inhabitants lived outside the walls and kept within the city-gates only in time of danger.   The two spies found no difficulty in entering Jericho, and lodged with an innkeeper named Rahab, whose house was built on the wall, near the citadel.   From her they learnt how terrified the inhabitants of Palestine were at the approach of the Israelites.   They had heard of the wonders which God had wrought for the people in taking them out of Egypt, and defeating the Amorite kings Sihon and Og on the other side of the Jordan.   Meanwhile word reached the king of Jericho of the presence of the spies, and he sent messengers to Rahab to capture them.   She hid them on the flat roof of her house among stalks of flax, thus saving their lives.   For this action they promised that her family would be spared when the city was captured by the Israelites. Jericho had only one gate, and this was heavily barred, so Rahab let the spies down outside the wall by a rope from her window. The two men hid in the neighbouring hills for three days until the search for them was over. They returned to the Israelite camp with the glad news that the inhabitants of the city were terror-stricken by fear of the Israelites.

That night the Israelites spent on the east bank of the river Jordan, possibly wondering how the great host of warriors (there were 600,000 men of war) and women and children would cross the river. It was the tenth day of Nisan in the year 1407 B. C. E., and harvest-time in the Plain of Jericho. The river Jordan, swollen by reason of the melting snows from Mount Hermon, was overflowing both its banks. The valley of the Jordan from the Lake of Galilee to the Dead Sea is 65 miles in length and about two miles broad, except at two places, near Beth-shan and Jericho, where it widens into a plain of 14 miles. The river itself is a rapid stream about 100 feet broad flowing through an old sea-bed of volcanic nature.

The Crossing of the Jordan.

Joshua commanded the priests to bear the Ark and to march about a mile in front of the army. The hosts of Israel followed them in eager expectation. No sooner did the feet of the priests touch the waters of the river, than the earth trembled and the clay mud-banks collapsed and caused the rushing waters to turn back. The lower waters discharged themselves swiftly into the Dead Sea, so that the Israelites were able to march across the river Jordan on dry land. The priests stood in the midst of the river-bed until all the people had passed over. To perpetuate the miracle, Joshua set up a memorial of twelve large stones at the spot where the priests had stood, and another memorial in the Plain of Jericho at Gilgal where the camp was pitched that day. Inspired by this event with invincible courage, the Israelites willingly followed the leadership of Joshua. At Gilgal they circumcised themselves (because the generation that was born in the wilderness had not been circumcised) and then observed their first Passover in the Promised Land.

Meanwhile the high walls of Jericho barred their progress through the country. At the command of God, Joshua ordered all the Israelite warriors **The Fall of Jericho.** to march round the walls of Jericho once a day for six days, while seven priests went at their head blowing on seven trumpets. The citizens of Jericho must have been greatly surprised at this silent and mysterious siege. They soon knew the reason. On the seventh day the Israelite host marched round the city seven times, and at the seventh time they uttered a piercing shout. At the noise the earth trembled, and the two walls of Jericho collapsed and fell outwards. The Israelites rushed into the surprised city and destroyed it utterly by fire, saving only the family of Rahab. They were forbidden to take any of the spoil for themselves. Achan of the tribe of Judah, however, stole one goodly Babylonian garment, two hundred shekels of silver, and a wedge of gold weighing fifty shekels, which he hid in the floor of his tent. For this crime he was punished by death. Moreoever, Joshua put the city of Jericho under a ban, saying:

" Cursed be the man before the Lord that riseth up and buildeth this city, even Jericho."

The next city to fall before the Israelites was Ai, situated on a hill north of Jericho and having 12,000 inhabitants. Joshua burnt Ai too, and killed its king.

Shechem, between Mount Gerizim and Mount Ebal

World of the Bible.

Having thus obtained a foothold in the country, he now made a dash to Shechem.

Joshua at Shechem. There, between the two hills of Ebal and Gerizim, he performed the ceremony of the Blessing and the Curse, as commanded in the Book of Deuteronomy. Six of the tribes stood upon Mount Ebal and six upon Mount Gerizim. The priests, with the Ark, stood in the valley. They turned to the people assembled on Mount Gerizim and began:

" Blessed be the man who will not make an idol."

Altogether they pronounced twelve blessings. Then they turned to Mount Ebal and pronounced a curse on all who would not perform the Law of God. At the same time Joshua wrote there upon unhewn stone pillars the whole of the Torah. One day those pillars may be found, just as so many ancient tablets and other articles have already been discovered in Palestine and other countries of the East.

The people returned to their camp at Gilgal knowing that they inspired terror in all the inhabitants of Palestine.

The Gibeonites. The Hivites dwelt in four cities west of Jericho, and their capital city was Gibeon. They were afraid that they would meet the fate of Jericho and Ai. So they deceived Joshua and made a covenant of peace with him, by sending him messengers who pretended to come from a very distant country. Discovering their deceit, the Israelites could not break their oath, but made the Gibeonites their bondmen: hewers of wood and drawers of waters for the congregation and for the altar.

Now Gibeon was an important city in Palestine, and when the Amorites heard that it had made peace with Israel they immediately determined to attack it. Adoni-zedek, king of the hill-city of Jerusalem, made a league with the kings of Hebron, Yarmuth, Lachish, and Eglon, all strongly-fortified hill-cities in the south of Palestine, and together the five kings went up with a large army to besiege Gibeon. The Gibeonites at once sent an urgent appeal to Joshua:

" Come up quickly to save us, and help us; for all the kings of the Amorites that dwell in the hill-country are gathered together against us."

Joshua acted without delay. The Israelite army left the camp at Gilgal by night and made a surprise-attack upon the Amorites. The enemy was defeated and driven from Gibeon. They fled down the valley of Ajalon along the road to Beth-horon, and were caught in a terrific hailstorm which killed a great number of them. The five kings hid themselves in a cave at Makkedah, where they were discovered and slain by command of Joshua. The Israelites then besieged and captured the cities of these kings, and in this way made themselves masters of the whole of the centre and south of Palestine. But Jerusalem still held out, and many years passed before it fell. We shall hear of this later.

Meanwhile, the kings of northern Palestine gathered themselves at the Waters of Merom to make a stand against the Israelite invaders. These Ca-

The Battle of the North. naanites, Amorites, Hittites and Hivites of the north were led by Jabin, king of Hazor, an important city about ten miles north of the Lake of Galilee. With them they had many horses and chariots, which could be used in the open plains of northern Palestine.

Once again Joshua struck suddenly. He led his army speedily from the camp at Gilgal and caught the hosts of

the enemy by surprise at the Waters of Merom. They fled before him and were pursued in two directions, to Sidon on the north-east and also eastwards. After the battle he returned, captured the city of Hazor, and burnt it to the ground. The cities of the other kings also fell before his victorious army, so that Joshua was master of the whole country from Baal-gad in the valley of Lebanon to the mountains of Edom in the south. In all he conquered thirty-one kings and their cities.

But what was Egypt doing at this time, that it allowed these Israelite invaders to conquer the country? The answer to this question is given by the Tel-el-Amarna Tablets. In the year 1887, in the ruins of the city of Tel-el-Amarna in Egypt, there were discovered 320 clay tablets written in the Babylonian cuneiform language. These tablets, one of which can be seen facing page 80, have been deciphered by scholars and found to be letters written by the governors of Palestine and Syria to Pharaohs Amenhetep III and Akhenaton. The governors of Palestine appeal to the Egyptian kings for help against the invasion of a people whom they call Habiru. This people is identified by scholars with the Hebrews. In other words, these letters give us the story of the Israelite invasion from the point of view of the Egyptian governors of Palestine. These rulers were untrusworthy men who often deceived the Pharaohs and made a league with the invaders. The letters appealed to Egypt for help, but we know that Akhenaton was too concerned with changing the religion of Egypt to care much about retaining the provinces of Syria and Palestine in his empire. One of the letters mentions the fate of Hazor which, we have seen, Joshua burnt. These are its words:

" Let my Lord the king recall what Hazor and its king have already had to endure."

Akhenaton reigned from 1377 to 1361 B. C. E., so that the conquest of Palestine by Joshua must have taken many years after the capture of Jericho in 1407 B. C. E. Yet even after the battle with the kings of the north, many parts of the country were still unconquered. But Joshua had already grown old, and he decided to divide the land among the tribes of Israel before his death.

The tribe of Judah was the first to enter into its inheritance. Its territory stretched from the southern to the northern end of the Dead Sea and included **The Division of the Land.** all the land to the west of it right up to the Mediterranean Sea, an area about 55 miles long and 25 to 30 miles wide. It contains three of the four divisions which distinguish the whole of Palestine, namely the Coastal Plain, the Shephelah, and the Central Range of mountains. In place of the fourth division, that is the Jordan valley, it has the Wilderness of Judea, a desolate and fearful stony desert running down from the Central Range to the Dead Sea. But the Coastal Plain and the Shephelah were still in the hands of the Canaanites and Philistines, so that the tribe of Judah possessed only the stony hills. Yet these stony hills were clad in those days with fertile vineyards, while many of the cities sacred to the Patriarchs were situated on their hilltops. In Judah were Hebron, Beer-sheba and Jerusalem, although this last-named city was still occupied by the Jebusites.

The tribes of Manasseh and Ephraim were the next to take possession of their land. Part of Manasseh had chosen its inheritance east of Jordan. The remaining part shared with the tribe of Ephraim the centre of

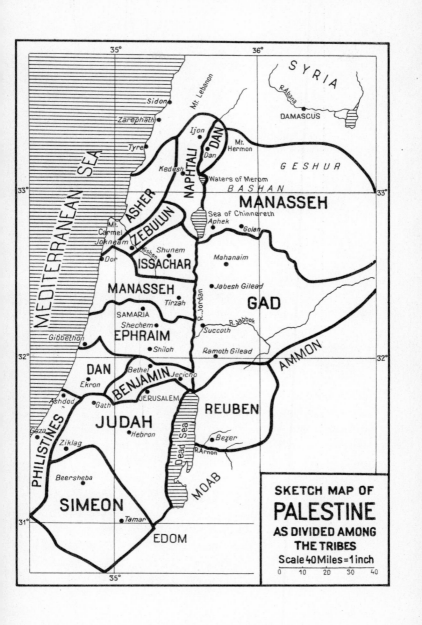

SKETCH MAP OF
PALESTINE
AS DIVIDED AMONG
THE TRIBES
Scale 40 Miles = 1 inch

0   10   20   30   40

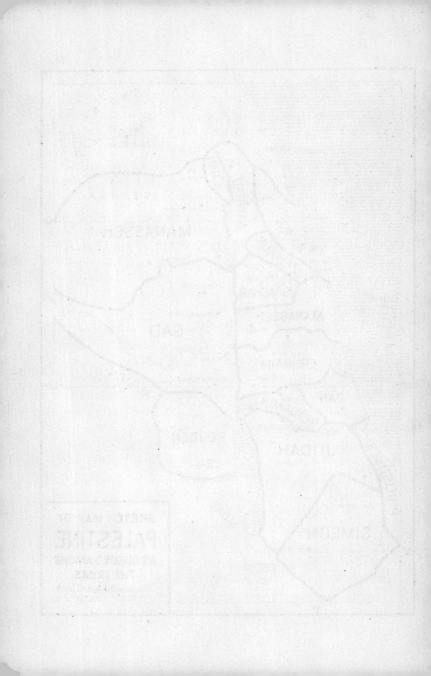

Palestine, Ephraim going to the south, Manasseh to the north. Their territory, later known as Samaria, is nearly square, being about forty miles in length and in breadth. Mount Ephraim dominates it, with the ancient city of Shechem in the valley between the hills. The slope to the Jordan is not so rugged as in Judea, and the Jordan valley with its cornfields, date-palms and balsam-trees must have appealed strongly to these Israelites from the barren desert. Even the hill-country is intersected by pleasant valleys and fruitful plains, while the summits of high mountains slope by gentle ridges to the Plain of Sharon. This is an open plain by the sea-coast over which the armies and traders of the ancient world crossed from Egypt to Syria and from Syria to Egypt.

At Shiloh, in the territory of Ephraim, Joshua set up the Tabernacle, and there all Israel now assembled to divide by lot the rest of the land to the remaining seven tribes. The portion of Benjamin was between Judah and Ephraim, and to the west of Benjamin lay the land of Dan. The tribe of Simeon was given its inheritance in the land of Judah. To Issachar and Zebulun was allocated the broad Plain of Esdraelon, which marked the northern boundary of Manasseh. This plain commands the pass over the slopes of Mount Carmel to the Plain of Sharon, and so became in later times the great battlefield of Palestine. Asher and Naphtali were to share the hills of Galilee, Naphtali possessing the Lake of Galilee, while Asher held the coastland to the north of Zebulun. Thus nine and-a-half tribes received their land in Palestine, while the two tribes of Reuben and Gad, and half the tribe of Manasseh possessed the land given to them by Moses on the east of Jordan. Only the tribe of Levi received no portion of the land. When all the land had been divided among the tribes in this manner, the Children of Israel granted to their leader Joshua the city of Timnath-Serah in Mount Ephraim as a perpetual possession.

Then Joshua chose from among the cities of the tribes forty-eight cities wherein the priests and Levites should dwell. Six of these cities, three on the west of Jordan, and three on the east, were marked Cities of Refuge, to which any person guilty of manslaughter could flee, if he were able to prove that the act was not a crime but an accident.

The work of conquest and of the division of the land was over, so Joshua permitted the warriors of Reuben, **The Two and-a-Half Tribes Return.** Gad and Manasseh, who had faithfully observed their promise and fought side by side with the other tribes, to return to their homes on the east of Jordan.

" Ye have kept all that Moses the servant of the Lord commanded you," he said to them, " and now the Lord your God hath given rest unto your brethren, as He promised them; therefore return ye and get ye unto your tents and unto the land of your possession on the other side of Jordan. But take diligent heed to do the commandment and the Law which Moses charged you, to love the Lord your God and to serve Him with all your heart and with all your soul."

The two and-a-half tribes returned to their homes. But, at the banks of the Jordan, before they crossed the river, they built an altar, after the pattern of the altar which was in the Tabernacle at Shiloh. Their object was not to worship at this altar, but to remind their children that they were a part of the people of Israel, and that the Jordan was no barrier between the tribes.

Joshua, now an old man, gathered the elders of Israel together and addressed them at Shechem.   He recounted to them the history of their fathers and the wondrous deeds which God had wrought for them.

The Assembly at Shechem.

" And now," he went on, " fear the Lord and serve Him in sincerity and in truth....   And if it seem evil unto you to serve the Lord, choose ye this day whom ye will serve, ...but as for me and my house, we will serve the Lord."

And the people answered and said:

" God forbid that we should forsake the Lord to serve other gods."

When Joshua heard the answer of the people his heart was glad, for he felt that his work had not been in vain. Shortly afterwards he died, leaving a united nation with a common ideal, living upon its own land, the land in which the Patriarchs had lived and which now belonged to the Children of Israel.

CHAPTER 6

POINTS TO REMEMBER

Condition of Palestine — full of strongly-fortified hill-cities.

Joshua's steps to conquer the country:
   a) Spies sent to Jericho
   b) Jordan crossed and Jericho besieged
   c) Jericho captured and burnt
   d) Ai taken and burnt
   e) ceremony of Blessing and Curse at Shechem.

Defensive steps of inhabitants:
   a) Hivites of Gibeon and neighbouring district made peace with Joshua
   b) Amorite kings of Centre and South formed league against Joshua — defeated in Battle of Beth-horon
   c) Canaanites, Amorites, Hittites and Hivites of North, led by Jabin of Hazor, combined against Joshua — defeated at Waters of Merom.

Joshua conquered 31 kings and their cities.

Account of Invasion from Canaanite standpoint in Tel-el-Amarna Letters.

Division of the Land among the Tribes — shown in sketch-map facing page 74.

Tabernacle set up in Shiloh, in territory of Ephraim.

Two and-a-half Tribes returned to their homes on east of Jordan.

Final assembly at Shechem.

CHAPTER 7

FOUR JUDGES

Joshua left no successor, and after his death each of the tribes fought separately for the possession of its territory. The fortress-cities of the Canaanites overlooking the great Plains of Palestine (Beth-shan, Taanach, Megiddo), were too strong for the Israelites, so that none of the tribes was altogether successful in driving out the Canaanites from its land. But the Israelites were masters of the hill-country in Judea and Samaria, and after a time they were content to share the land with the Canaanites. They occupied houses which they had not built, and fields and vineyards which they had not planted. They gave up the pastoral life of the desert and began to till the soil of Palestine. Gradually they became an agricultural people, living at peace with their neighbours and engaging in war only when they were forced to do so.

Israel in Palestine.

But it was not long before the Israelites learnt to imitate the Canaanites in their religious life. That which Moses and Joshua had feared came to pass. Many of the Israelites took daughters of the Canaanites for wives, and daughters of Israel were married to these pagan peoples. They joined them in their feasts and soon began to worship their gods as well. Every city in Palestine had its own Baal and Ashtoreth, or Lord and Mistress of the place. To these gods a temple was dedicated, usually on a hill, in which were a stone altar for sacrifice, stone pillars pointed at the top, a sacred tree called Asherah, and images of the gods. The Israelites did not forget God, they rather worshipped Him in this idolatrous way and so broke the laws which He had commanded them. A story of this time shows how far the Israelites had fallen from the true service of God.

The tribe of Dan had been given its inheritance on the seacoast, between Judah and Ephraim, and to the west of Benjamin. The coast-land, however, was then inhabited by the Philistines, and only with difficulty could the Danites settle there. So they sent five spies to search Palestine for a more suitable territory in which to dwell. These spies chanced to come to the house of a man named Micah who lived in Mount Ephraim. Now the mother of Micah, who thought herself a pious woman, had made a Canaanite temple in her house, complete with all the objects of heathen worship. She even had a young Levite to act as the priest in that temple. When the Danite spies saw this temple and the Levite priest, they asked him whether God would prosper their way. The young man replied that He would, and the spies continued their journey rejoicing. In the far north of Palestine, near Mount Hermon, they came upon a city named Laish which was so spacious and well situated that they planned to capture it.

The Idols of Micah.

They returned to their countrymen, and six hundred warriors from the tribe of Dan journeyed northward to Laish. On their way they stopped at the house of Micah in Mount Ephraim and persuaded the Levite to steal the images from Micah, go with them, and be their priest. The Levite agreed, in spite of the protests of Micah, who was thus robbed of his costly idols and of his priest.

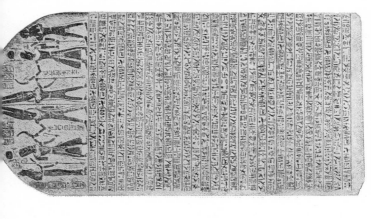

"The Stone of Israel"—memorial tablet of
Pharaoh Mernepthah, referred to on p. 81
World of the Bible.

Letter in cuneiform script from Abd-Khiba,
ruler of Jerusalem, to Pharaoh. He complains
about the inroads of the Habîru (Hebrews) who
are conquering the land
World of the Bible.

The Danites captured Laish and burnt it to the ground. On its site they built a city which they called Dan, and there the Levite set up a new temple for his idols. For many generations he and his descendants remained the priests of the tribe of Dan.

It is not surprising to find that when the Israelites began to worship idols, they also became corrupt in their moral life. The men of Gibeah, a city belonging to Benjamin, were particularly debased, and one action of theirs stirred the whole of Israel to anger. They ill-treated a certain Levite and his wife who were passing through the city, and the woman died as the result of their cruelty. The Levite reported the crime to all the tribes of Israel, who demanded that the tribe of Benjamin should give up the criminals for punishment. The Benjamites refused, so the heads of the tribes assembled at Mizpeh and decided to make war on the Benjamites. For three days a fearful battle was fought at Gibeah between the tribes of Israel and the tribe of Benjamin. Many thousands of warriors were slain on both sides, the city of Gibeah was burnt with fire, and of the whole tribe of Benjamin only six hundred men were left alive. For a time the tribe was in danger of total extinction, through the unwillignes of the other tribes to intermarry with it.

The Civil War with Benjamin.

Such lawless barbarities were the consequences of forsaking the Law of God and imitating the idolatrous worship of the Canaanites. That Israel was not disturbed much during this period by the surrounding nations was due to the tight hold which Egypt exercised over Palestine. Facing page 80 is a photograph of the Stele of Pharaoh Mernepthah, the successor of the great Rameses II.

Mernepthah's Stele.

Both these kings fought important battles in Palestine and Syria, and Mernepthah records his victories in these words:

" The Hittite land is at peace; plundered is Canaan with every evil; Askelon is carried off; Gezer is seized; Yenoam is made as though non-existent; Israel is desolated; her seed is not; Kharu (south Palestine) hath become a widow; all lands are united and pacified; everyone that is turbulent is bound by king Mernepthah."

The words are boastful and exaggerated, but they do show that Egypt maintained firm rule over the nations of Palestine during the reigns of the powerful Pharaohs Rameses II and Mernepthah. In the year 1210 B. C. E., however, Mernepthah died, and Egypt for a time fell into a state of anarchy.

The Canaanites dwelling in the Plain of Esdraelon at once seized their opportunity, and for twenty years Jabin, king of Hazor, oppressed the Children of **The Canaanite Oppression.** Israel. The plain divides the hills of Galilee from the mountains of Ephraim, so that the tribes of the north, Issachar, Zebulun, Asher and Naphtali, were cut off by the Canaanites from the more powerful tribes of Manasseh and Ephraim in the centre. Yet it was from Ephraim that the revolt against Jabin began.

In Mount Ephraim, between the cities of Ramah and Bethel, there dwelt a Prophetess named Deborah, who acted as Judge to the tribes of Israel. **The Judges.** The name Judge is the same as that which the Phoenicians and later the Carthaginians gave to their chief magistrates and rulers. Among the Israelites the title was given to the man who, inspired by God, saved the people in time of great trouble, delivered them from their oppression, ruled them, settled their disputes, and made plain to them the meaning of the Law. Really these were the special duties of the priests and the Levites, but after the death of Phineas, the grandson of Aaron, no outstanding priest fit to rule the people arose for many generations. The Tabernacle was situated in Shiloh, and to this place the Israelites flocked for worship year by year. The priests and the Levites performed the ceremonies there, and many of them no doubt did their best to keep alive a knowledge of the Law of God. But they did not *lead* the people.

Thus it was that at this time the Israelites came to the Prophetess Deborah in Mount Ephraim to guide them in

Deborah. their perplexity. She saw and felt the great danger to the whole people which the oppression of the Canaanites meant, and was determined to end it. Divinely inspired, she sent a message to Barak the son of Abinoam, of the harassed tribe of Naphtali, to arise and lead the men of Israel against Sisera, the commander of Jabin's army. Barak would not go without Deborah. She was asking him to undertake an almost superhuman task. It must be remembered that the Israelites had neither spears nor shields with which to fight against the iron chariots of the enemy. Barak required her presence to inspire him with moral courage and heroism. Deborah left her house in Mount Ephraim and went to the city of Kedesh in Naphtali. Barak gathered ten thousand men from the tribes of Naphtali and Zebulun, and, accompanied by Deborah, led them to the foot of Mount Tabor. This mountain in the hills of Galilee was a strong fortress overlooking the Plain of Esdraelon. When Sisera heard of the Israelite preparations, he assembled his forces at Harosheth Hagoyim, and, with nine hundred iron chariots, proceeded across the plain. The river Kishon, which flows through the plain, was in full flood, so that the ground was swampy and difficult for the chariots. Barak and his men made a sudden wild onslaught upon the slowly-moving chariots, and completely put to flight the host of Sisera.

At the same time a fierce storm arose and added to the discomfiture of the enemy. Sisera himself dismounted from his chariot and fled on foot. He escaped to the tent of Jael the Kenite, near the town of Kedesh, but she killed him when he was asleep in her tent, and delivered his body to Barak. Deborah uttered a song of thanksgiving, a beautiful poem which paints a truly wonderful picture of the conditions of the country and the life of the people, besides giving a graphic account of the battle.

As a result of this great victory the power of the Canaanites was broken for ever, and they never again threatened the peace of Israel. Mean-

Egyptian Influence Withdrawn. while, in Egypt, another great Pharaoh had arisen, Rameses III, who maintained the Egyptian power in Palestine and in Syria. During this period of rest the Israelites continued to mingle with the other inhabitants of Palestine, and to forget more and more the Law of Moses. Yet in times of trouble they remembered the marvellous help which God had extended to their ancestors, and they would turn to Him again for help. After the death of Rameses III, in 1167 B. C. E., the power of Egypt declined and for two hundred years had no influence in Palestine. It was then that the smaller nations around Palestine attempted to become its masters, and in so doing fought against the Children of Israel. The struggle against these enemies brought to the front several outstanding champions in Israel, and helped to unite the people as no event had done since the days of Deborah.

The first enemy to swoop down upon Palestine was the Midianites. This nomadic tribe had moved up from the Peninsula of Sinai and, crossing the Jordan with other marauders from the desert, invaded the land of Israel for plunder. They ravaged the fields, seized the corn and barley which the Israelites had sown, and took as booty all the cattle they could seize. From the Jordan they roamed throughout the country right up to Gaza on the Mediterranean coast. The Israelites, terrified at the onrush of these fierce tribesmen, hid in caves, ravines, and mountain fastnesses to escape from them. Some, however, put up a heroic defence. Among these heroes was a man named Gideon of the tribe of Manasseh, whose brothers were killed while defending their home against the raiders. He was determined to avenge their death. One day, while he was threshing wheat by a winepress in Ophrah to hide it from the Midianites, he heard the voice of God commanding him:

The Midianites: Gideon.

" Go and save Israel from the hand of Midian... and I shall be with thee."

Gideon's father Joash had a temple to Baal. One night after this event Gideon took ten men, and with their help overthrew the heathen altar and cut down the sacred tree or Asherah near it. In its place he built to God an altar on which he sacrificed a sacred bull of Baal. The next morning the inhabitants of the town saw what Gideon had done, and wanted to put him to death. But Joash saved his son.

" Will you plead for Baal?" he asked them. " If he is a god he will punish him himself for having pulled down his altar." For this reason the townspeople called Gideon Jerubbaal, which means " Let Baal plead."

Gideon was now full of confidence that God was with him, and he called together the tribes of Manasseh, Asher, Zebulun, and Naphtali to march with him against the Midianites, who had pitched their tents in the broad valley of Jezreel. A large army flocked to Gideon, but all who were afraid he sent home. Ten thousand men were left, but even these were too many for his purpose. Two miles south of the Midianites, at Ain Harod near Mount Gilboa, he tested his men by the way they drank water. Three hundred men lapped the water with one hand, the others bowed down on their knees and drank. Gideon chose the three hundred and sent the others home. At dead of night Gideon led his three hundred men to the Midianite camp. Each man carried a lamp in an earthen pitcher, with a horn slung on it. Arrived at the enemy's camp, they blew their horns, broke their pitchers and, taking the lamps in their left hands and the trumpets in their right, they shouted:

" The sword of the Lord and of Gideon!"

The Midianites and their allies were panic-stricken and fell one upon another. They fled by way of Beth-shan over the Jordan, pursued by the victorious Israelites. The men of Ephraim now joined in the pursuit and held the fords of the Jordan. Gideon crossed the Jordan and utterly routed the Midianites, slaying their chieftains.

The Israelites Want to Make Him King. When Gideon returned in triumph from the battle, the grateful Israelites wanted to make him their king. This was the first time that the Israelites entertained the idea of setting up a king, like the nations round about them. They thought that a hereditary king would be better able to defend them from their enemies, and to lead them in peace as well as in war.

But Gideon nobly refused, saying:

" I shall not rule over you, neither shall my son rule over you. The Lord shall rule over you."

He was nevertheless held in high honour by the people and during his lifetime the Midianites dared not attack

Abimelech. Israel. Wealth and prosperity returned to the tribes dwelling in northern Palestine. With part of the rich spoil taken from the enemy Gideon made an Ephod which he set up in his native city of Ophrah as an expression of gratitude to God. Unfortunately the Israelites worshipped this Ephod idolatrously as a symbol of God. When Gideon died, one of his sons re-opened the question of kingship. This son, Abimelech, was the offspring of Gideon's marriage with a Canaanitess from Shechem. The Canaanite population of this city helped Abimelech to kill the sons of his father, and then made him their king. One son, however, named Jotham, had escaped the massacre. Ascending to the summit of Mount Gerizim which overlooked Shechem, he told the Israelite party the famous parable of the trees.

" The trees," he said, " wanted to elect a king over them. The olive, the fig, and the vine all refused the honour. Only the lowly bramble accepted. But, said the bramble, if in truth ye anoint me king over you, come and trust in my shadow. And if not, let fire go forth from the bramble and consume the cedars of Lebanon."

" So," explained Jotham, " if ye have dealt truly in making Abimelech king and slaying the sons of Gideon who did good to you, then rejoice in Abimelech. If not, let a fire go forth from Abimelech and consume the men of Shechem."

For three years Abimelech reigned as king over Israel in Shechem. This city, being in the centre of the country, was very suitable for a capital. Abimelech, however, was unpopular with the mixed citizens, Israelites and Canaanites, and a conspiracy was formed against him. He destroyed Shechem, but was himself killed while besieging the city of Thebez. Thus ended the first attempt at setting up a monarchy in Israel.

On the other side of the Jordan the Ammonites now attacked the tribes of Israel living in Gilead. The Ammonites lived on the edge of the desert **The Ammon-ites: Jephthah.** and claimed that the fertile lands of Gilead belonged to them. For eighteen years they oppressed Israel, and once they even crossed the Jordan and raided the territory of Judah, Benjamin and Ephraim. The Israelites in their great distress turned to Jephthah, a dauntless warrior of Gilead who had been driven away from his home by his half-brothers. He refused to assist them unless they made him their chieftain. When they agreed, he prepared to attack the Ammonites. But first he made a peculiar vow to God. "If," he said, "Thou wilt give the Ammonites into my hand, then that which goes out from the doors of my house to meet me when I return in peace from the Ammonites, it shall be the Lord's, and I will offer it for a burnt-offering."

His attack was completely successful. The Ammonites were subdued by the Children of Israel. Jephthah returned in triumph to his house in Mizpah. **His Vow.** To his horror his only daughter was the first to meet him with joyful music. At sight of her Jephthah remembered his vow, and rent his clothes in sorrow. So barbarous were his ideas, and so utterly removed from the teaching of the Law of Moses, that he deemed it his duty to sacrifice his own daughter rather than get his rash vow annulled.

His next action was no better. The men of Ephraim were angry because they had not been called to fight against the Ammonites. Instead of calming them he opened war against them, and his army killed many thousands at the fords of Jordan.

While the Ammonites were attacking Israel from the east, the Philistines were advancing from the west. **The Philistines.** After the death of Jephthah the menace of the Philistines threatened the very existence of Israel as a people. We have already seen how the Philistines came up the coast-land from Egypt about the same time as the Israelites crossed the Red Sea. They were a war-like nation who originally came from Crete. In Palestine they took over the religion and the culture of the Canaanites. Living by the coast, they were on the main trade route of the East. Through their five cities of Gath, Ekron, Ashdod, Ashkelon and Gaza passed the caravans of Syria, of Egypt, and of India, bearing the trade of the ancient world. The Maritime Plain was very fertile, and the Philistines therefore engaged also in agriculture. In Gath lived the survivors of the race of tall men who once inhabited the whole of Palestine. These giants, as they were called, became the champions of the Philistines. As the centuries passed, they pressed further into the country and came in conflict with Israel. It became a struggle for life and death.

Samson. At first the Philistines were successful. We remember how they forced many of the Danites to seek a new home in the north of Palestine.

From the tribe of Dan, however, there now came a man who, single-handed, troubled the Philistines for twenty years. His name was Samson. He was born in the town of Zorah, in the low hills of the Shephelah which overlook the Philistine Plain. From his birth he was made a Nazarite. That is, he was not allowed to drink wine or cut his hair. While quite a young man he showed his great strength by rending a lion with his hands. He was fond of mixing with the Philistines, and married one of their daughters. Her father, however, gave her to another man, and Samson took a savage revenge by setting fire to some of their crops.

Samson took refuge in the hills of the Shephelah. The Philistines marched into Judea and threatened to ravage it unless Samson were delivered into their hands. The men of Judah bound Samson and brought him to the Philistines. No sooner did he come into their midst, however, than he burst his bonds asunder, seized a dry jaw-bone of an ass which lay upon the ground, and hacked his way free from his captors. You must all have read of Samson's wonderful exploits. The Philistines sought in many ways to capture this dangerous foe. At length he was lured into their hands by a woman. She called in the Philistines, and this time they captured him without difficulty. Like the barbarians they were, they cut out his two eyes, bound him in fetters, and set him to grind corn in the city of Gaza.

Then the Philistines arranged a great feast to their god Dagon to celebrate their victory. The temple was full of exultant men and women. " Call Samson and let him disport before us," they ordered. So the blind Samson was led from the prisonhouse to the temple, and he played before them. They

His Death.

left him for a moment beside the pillars. " Let me touch the pillars," he said to the lad who held his hand. When Samson's hands touched them he uttered a prayer. " O Lord God," he said, " remember me now and strengthen me this once, that I may be avenged on the Philistines."

He took hold of the pillars, and shouting, " Let my soul die with the Philistines," he brought down the temple on the concourse of people, thus killing more in his death than during his life.

On Samson's death the Philistines renewed their war on Israel. The scene of battle was one of the numerous valleys leading from the Philistine cities to the highlands of Judea. The Israelites were defeated in the first encounter. The elders of Israel reformed the camp at Eben-ezer and sent to Shiloh for the Ark of God, superstitiously thinking that its mere presence would give them a miraculous victory. At Shiloh dwelt the High Priest Eli, now an old man of ninety-eight. With a trembling heart he sent the Ark to the battlefield in charge of his two sons, Hophni and Phineas, and the Israelites shouted with joy when it reached the camp.

The Battle of Eben-ezer.

Hearing the jubilation in the Israelite camp, the Philistines redoubled their efforts and fought so valiantly that they defeated Israel, captured the Ark, and took it in triumph to their cities. An Israelite soldier escaped from the battlefield and brought the news to Shiloh. " I have escaped from the battlefield," he told Eli; " Israel has fled before the Philistines; a great destruction has befallen the people; thy two sons Hophni and Phineas are dead; and the Ark of God has been captured."

The Ark is Captured.

The dread news was too much for the aged Eli. He

collapsed and died. His daughter-in-law, the wife of Phineas, was giving birth to a child when the news came to her. And she called the name of the child I-chabod, for she said, " The glory is departed from Israel."

The Philistines followed up their victory by destroying the Tabernacle at Shiloh and conquering the whole of the land up to Mount Carmel. It was a tragic day for Israel.

CHAPTER 7

POINTS TO REMEMBER

Penetration of Palestine:
> Israelites masters of the hill-country in Judea and Samaria
> fortress-cities in the hands of Canaanites.

Life of Israel in Palestine:
> became agricultural people
> imitated religious worship of Canaanites and intermarried with
>   them
> stories of the Danites and the civil war with Benjamin.

The Judges:
> Land at rest until the collapse of Egyptian power c. 1210 B.C.E.
> a) oppression by **Canaanites** under Jabin king of Hazor, 20 years;
>   deliverance through **Deborah** and **Barak;**
> b) invasion of **Midianites** 7 years; defeated by **Gideon**
>   Gideon offered kingship by grateful Israelites
>   his son Abimelech made king of Shechem
>   Jotham's parable
>   Abimelech's death;
> c) **Ammonite** oppression, 18 years
>   **Jephthah's** success
>   his rash vow;
> d) struggle with **Philistines:**
>   exploits of **Samson**
>   the battle of Eben-ezer
>   the Ark captured
>   Shiloh laid waste.

CHAPTER 8

SAMUEL AND SAUL

The capture of the Ark and the destruction of Shiloh awakened the people of Israel to their moral and religious

Shiloh. obligations. After the death of Joshua, for over three hundred years they had mixed with the inhabitants of Palestine, worshipped their gods, and imitated their rites and customs. They had disobeyed the Law of Moses and built temples all over the land. As a result, the Tabernacle at Shiloh was ignored. Some Israelites still made pilgrimages to it year by year and brought their sacrifices to the priests. But even the priests were corrupt and abused their sacred office. They snatched away the best part of the sacrifices for themselves, and degraded the whole priesthood. In the last days of Shiloh, the High Priest was Eli, a descendant of Aaron's younger son. His two sons, Hophni and Phineas, were among the worst of the priests, yet their father only rebuked them with fruitless words.

Among the Levites serving the Tabernacle at Shiloh was a young man named Samuel. His mother, Hannah, had been childless, and when he was born she dedicated him entirely to the service of God. While he was yet a boy, the word of God came to him.

" Behold," it said, " I am about to do a thing in Israel at which the ears of everyone that heareth it shall tingle. I shall judge the house of Eli because his sons made themselves vile and he restrained them not."

That thing was the overthrow of Shiloh and the death of Eli's sons. Samuel told Eli this fatal message. When it was fulfilled, he became famous throughout all Israel as a Prophet.

When Shiloh was destroyed, the priests and the Levites there were scattered. Ahitub, a grandson of Eli, saved

The Ark Returned. some of the holy vessels and carried them to Nob, a city in Benjamin, north of Jerusalem. As for the Ark, it did not remain long in the hands of the Philistines. The jubilant Philistines brought it first to their city of Ashdod. But a plague that broke out here and afterwards at Gath — to which place they removed it — persuaded them that they were better without this dangerous trophy than with it. So they restored it to the Israelites, and eventually the Ark found a home in Kirjath-jearim, until David many years later brought it to Jerusalem.

The Israelites were without a national centre, and they were oppressed by the Philistines. Their enemies forbade

Samuel's Great Work. them to make either sword or spear, and when they needed to sharpen their plough-shares and axes they had to go to the Philistine smiths. Yet a new spirit was breathed into the people by their leader Samuel. He taught the Israelites that their troubles had come upon them because they had not served God with all their heart, nor obeyed His Law. He gathered round him a body of young men who faithfully observed the Law of Moses and earnestly desired to be inspired by God. Bands of these young men went up and down the country with harps and psalteries, stirring in the hearts of the people a new love of God and His Law. They became a guild of Prophets. Even the city of Dan in the extreme north of Palestine was affected by Samuel's teaching and pulled down the idolatrous temple of Micah.

Samuel himself did not stay in one place and wait for the people to come to him for advice. He went from town to town, from Bethel to Gilgal, and from Gilgal to Mizpeh to act as judge and teacher to Israel, while he appointed his two sons as judges in Beer-sheba. His own home was in Ramah in Benjamin. He was upright and incorruptible as a judge, and never took a bribe from any man. Neither did he use the cattle or goods of anyone for his own service. By his example he showed the Israelites how to live a noble life such as the Torah prescribed.

By these means he gradually brought the Children of Israel to realise their duty to observe the Torah, to keep themselves apart from their heathen neighbours and to worship God truly. At length he called a solemn assembly at Mizpeh in Benjamin, proclaimed a fast, and urged the people to give up their evil ways.

" If ye return to God with all your heart," he said, " remove the strange gods and Ashtaroth from your midst.... and serve God alone."

The Israelites confessed their fault and determined never again to go astray.

The Philistines, hearing that the Israelites were assembled at Mizpeh, feared that they were preparing for attack. So, in order to crush them, they **The Victory at Eben-ezer.** marched up the hills to Mizpeh. The Israelites, however, were victorious, and pursued their defeated enemies to Eben-ezer. From that day they were not troubled by the Philistines for some years.

In time, however, Samuel grew old. His two sons,

Joel and Abijah, were not upright, for they misgoverned the people and took bribes. The elders of Israel were

The People Demand a King. afraid that when Samuel died they would have no leader, and would consequently sink back into the anarchy from which Samuel had rescued them. So they came to Ramah and begged him to appoint a king over them. Already in the days of the Judges, you remember, some of the Israelites had asked for a king. Gideon had refused, but his son, Abimelech, who was half-Canaanite, had made himself king by force. Samuel did not want the people to have a king. He was afraid that the king would behave as Abimelech had done, or as the kings of the surrounding nations. These kings were despots and obeyed no law but their own. An Israelite king would have to obey the Law of Moses.

" This will be the manner of the king who will rule over you," said Samuel to the elders. " He will take your sons and make them his charioteers and horsemen, and they shall run before his chariot.... Your goodly fields, vineyards, and olive-groves he will take and give to his courtiers.... Your best slaves, maid-servants, and young men, and your asses he will take and use for his work. He will take a tenth of your cattle, and ye shall be his slaves."

Nevertheless, the elders would not listen to Samuel and repeated their demand for a king. Samuel, divinely in-

Saul Chosen. spired, chose a man from Benjamin, one of the smallest tribes in Israel — Saul the son of Kish. His family was wealthy and respected, and he himself was distinguished in character and physique. But he was also modest and did not seek the honour. When Samuel assembled the people at Mizpeh a second time to elect the king, they could not find Saul at first, because he had hidden himself. They searched and found him, and he stood in the midst of the people, a head and shoulders taller than any of them.

Then said Samuel:

" See ye the man whom the Lord hath chosen, for there is none like him among all the people." And all the people shouted, " Long live the King!"

An occasion soon arose for Saul to show his prowess. The Ammonites, encouraged by the success of the Philis-

He Saves Jabesh-Gilead. tines, resumed their attack upon Israel. Nahash, king of the Ammonites, besieged Jabesh-Gilead on the east of Jordan. The citizens of Jabesh-Gilead sent to Gibeah in Benjamin for help. Saul, though king, was still a farmer, and was returning to the city with his oxen when he saw the messengers. Instantly he took a yoke of oxen, cut them in pieces, and sent them throughout the land of Israel with these words:

" Whoever cometh not forth after Saul and after Samuel, so shall it be done to his oxen."

The tribes of Israel rallied to his standard at Bezek, on the road from Shechem to the Jordan. That night Saul crossed the Jordan and made a surprise-attack on the Ammonites, and routed them. Saul had justified his choice as king.

Samuel once again assembled the Children of Israel, this time at Gilgal, near Jericho, to consecrate Saul as

Samuel Adresses the People. king, and to resign his own office as Judge. He reminded the people of their wonderful history and charged both them and their king to be faithful to the Law of Moses. "As for me," he concluded, " I shall not cease to pray for you, and to teach you the good and right way."

Saul now established himself as king. He chose a body-guard of two thousand men who remained with him at Michmash, while his son Jonathan commanded a thous-and men at Gibeah. It was Jonathan who struck the first blow for freedom against the Philistines. The Philistines had established a strong garrison at Geba in Benjamin. You have probably noticed that all the battles between the Philistines and Israelites took place in Benjamin. The reason for this was that the hills of Judea extended northwards into Benjamin, where the valleys into the Maritime Plain began. The Philistines were always trying to be masters of those valleys and so have control over the whole country.

Jonathan with his men attacked the Philistine garrison at Geba. It became a signal for a general rising. The Philistines grew alarmed and sent a **Saul Rebuked by Samuel.** strong force to subdue Israel. A small body was left at Michmash, while the rest divided into three companies and raided the land of Israel. The Israelites were terrified, and many crossed the Jordan to take refuge in the hills of Gilead. Others hid in the caves which abound in the hills of Judea. Saul had been commanded to wait seven days at Gilgal for Samuel, before engaging in battle with the Philistines. During those days Saul's army dwindled to about six hundred men. On the seventh day, Saul, though not a priest, impatiently offered sacrifices to God, a sacred office which only the priests were allowed to fulfil. No sooner had he done so than Samuel appeared.

" What hast thou done?" asked Samuel in dismay.

" I saw the people deserting me; thou hadst not come.... and I thought now the Philistines will come down against me to Gilgal and I have not yet besought the Lord.   So I sacrificed the burnt-offering," Saul answered.

" Thou hast acted foolishly.   Thou hast not kept the commandment of the Lord thy God," said Samuel.

The king had acted as though he were above the Law, and the Prophet rebuked him.   You see the difference between the kings of Israel and the kings of other nations. It was this difference which kept the people of Israel from being swallowed up by the mighty empires which arose later, for all the other small nations were absorbed and exist no longer.

It was Jonathan who again started the attack against the Philistines.   This brave prince, accompanied only **Jonathan's Courage.** by his armourbearer, daringly climbed the steep rock towards the Philistine garrison.   When the enemy saw them, they said mockingly:

" Look, the Hebrews are coming out of the holes in which they have hidden themselves.   Come up to us."

Jonathan and his armour-bearer came, but not as the Philistines had expected.   Alone, they courageously attacked the Philistines, slaying about twenty of them. The rest, imagining that the Israelites were behind them, fled for their lives.   An earthquake at the same time added to their terror.   Saul, at Gibeah, saw the commotion and hastily pursued the enemy.   Israelites joined him almost at every step and the Philistines retreated to their own territory.   Saul now took the offensive. He drove the enemy out of Judah and Benjamin.   He also crushed the Moabites and Ammonites on the east and the Edomites on the south.   For the first time Israel was free of enemies on all its borders.

The king faithfully observed the commands of the

Torah.   At one time he had joined a band of the Prophets and this gave rise to the saying " Is Saul also among the Prophets?"   The land being at rest,

The Land at Peace. he sought to put away all the evil practices which the Torah forbade.   He punished with death every witch and magician.   All idols were swept away.   In his own house at Gibeah he set an example of the true worship of God.   He observed every festival and every New Moon's day, and on those occasions made a feast for his family, his generals, and his courtiers. His nephew Abner was the commander of his army, and his eldest son Jonathan was heir to the throne.

The happiness of Saul's reign was disturbed by himself. The Amalekites, the savage tribe, you remember, which attacked the Children of Israel when they

Saul's Disobedience. left Egypt, were still troublesome in the South.   Samuel commanded Saul to exterminate them and to destroy all their property.   Saul marched at the head of a large army to the Negeb and crushed the Amalekites.   But he brought back their king alive to Gilgal, and also took as spoil the best of their sheep and oxen and the fattest of their rams, thinking to sacrifice some to God.   Samuel went to meet the king at Gilgal, and denounced him in the presence of his courtiers.

" Hath the Lord delight in burnt-offerings and sacrifices?" he asked angrily, " as in obeying the voice of the Lord?   Behold, to obey is better than sacrifice, and to hearken than the fat of rams.... Because thou hast rejected the word of the Lord, He hath rejected thee from being king."   Then Samuel had Agag the king of the Amalekites brought before him.   " As thy sword hath made women childless, so shall thy mother be childless among women," he said, and executed him.

The Prophet and the king separated, Samuel going to his home in Ramah, and Saul returning to Gibeah. They never met again. Samuel, by command of God, secretly anointed another man to be king of Israel — David, the youngest son of Jesse, a descendant of Ruth the Moabitess. He was a shepherd lad in Bethlehem, with kindly eyes, and a charming manner. Alone with his father's sheep in the hills of Judea, he learnt to be courageous and self-reliant. In those days lions and other wild beasts were quite common in Palestine. Often a lion or bear would raid the flock and snatch away a lamb. David fearlessly went after it, rescued the lamb out of its mouth, and killed the wild animal in the struggle. He also had days of quietness and peace when he sat upon a hillside and played upon his harp tunes so sweet that they made him famous. At such times he saw the beauty and the glory of nature and spoke about them in the Psalms which you know so well. You remember the Psalm which begins:

David.

" The Lord is my shepherd, I shall not want."

Himself a shepherd, he thought of God as a gentle Shepherd leading His flock in pleasant places and protecting them even in the darkest valleys.

His fame as a musician reached the ears of the king. After his quarrel with Samuel, Saul became moody and depressed, and only music could soothe him. So David was brought to Saul's palace, where he played before Saul whenever the sad spirit came upon him.

The Philistines now felt strong enough to attack Israel again. They marched up the winding valley of Elah and encamped at Sochoh, where a deep trench made by three streams cut off the road to the Judean hills. Saul's army took up its position

Goliath.

on a hill overlooking Sochoh. Both armies were thus strongly placed, and for forty days neither side dared to begin the attack. The Philistines, however, had in their camp one of those enormously tall men who still lived in Gath. His name was Goliath, and every day he came out of the Philistine camp and challenged the Israelites to single combat.

" I defy the armies of Israel," he shouted across the valley. " Give me a man and we shall fight together. If he wins, then we shall be your slaves; and if I win, then you will be our slaves." As he came forth, over nine feet tall and clothed in sparkling bronze armour from head to foot, the Israelites kept in terror to their tents. In Saul's army were the three eldest sons of Jesse. Bethlehem was only twelve miles away from the camp, and one day Jesse sent his youngest son David to the battlefield to get news of his brothers. David came and heard Goliath challenging the Israelites. He heard also that Saul had promised to give his elder daughter as wife to the man who would accept the challenge. David was stirred and, with Saul's permission, went out to meet the Philistine. Saul's armour was too heavy for him, so he went unarmed, except for his shepherd's stick, a sling, and five pebbles which he picked up from the river bed.

When Goliath saw who was approaching, he shouted: " Am I a dog that thou comest against me with a stick?" David's answer was: " Thou comest against me with sword and spear and shield; but I come against thee in the name of the Lord of Hosts, the God of the armies of Israel which thou hast defied." As Goliath approached, David quickly slung a stone at his forehead. It stunned him, so that he fell. At once David ran forward, snatched the sword from Goliath, and cut off his head. When the

Philistines saw that their champion was killed, they fled. The Israelites pursued them all the way to their city of Ekron.

David returned to the Israelite camp a hero. Jonathan admired him and they soon became fast friends. Saul

Saul Hates David. would not allow David to return to his father's house in Bethlehem, but made him one of his commanders. The Philistines feared him, and he often made successful attacks against them. When the Israelite army returned from the war, the women of Israel came out to greet the victorious king with music and dancing.

> "Saul hath slain his thousands,
>
> And David his ten thousands,"

they sang. When Saul heard this he was extremely angry. From then onwards he was jealous of David and sought to do him harm. Yet his younger daughter, Michal, loved David, and Saul allowed her to marry him. But several times, when his mad moods came upon him, he tried to kill David. Once he even sent to his home to capture him, and David escaped only by the help of his wife Michal. On another occasion he fled to Samuel at Ramah and took refuge with the guild of the Prophets there.

Jonathan was grieved by his father's attitude to David, but was sure that he meant him no harm. David, however, was certain. "There is only a step

Jonathan Helps David. between me and death," he told Jonathan. The two friends decided to test Saul. On the next festival of the New Moon David absented himself from Saul's table. "Why cometh not the son of Jesse to the banquet?" Saul asked his son. He hated David so much that he would not even mention him by name. Jonathan answered that he had given David permission to attend a family festival in Bethlehem. Saul could not restrain his anger.

"So long as the son of Jesse is alive," he shouted, "thou and thy kingdom will not be established. Send and bring him to me, for he shall die." In his frenzy he threw a javelin at Jonathan, fortunately missing him. Like the true friend he was, Jonathan told David and sent him away in peace.

David fled for safety. He stopped first at the priestly city of Nob, where the sword of Goliath was kept. Ahi-

David an Outlaw.

melech, the High Priest, the great grandson of Eli, unaware that anything was wrong, supplied him with food and gave him the sword. David then took refuge in the low hills of the Shephelah, and established himself in the stronghold of Adullam. Here his family joined him, and about four hundred adventurers whom he formed into a band. Saul slew Ahimelech and the priests of Nob because they had helped David. Only one son of Ahimelech escaped the slaughter, Abiathar by name, and he took refuge with David.

Saul pursued David relentlessly and forced him and his men to live as outlaws. No one place was safe for them and they stayed first in the hills of the Shephelah, then in the wilderness to the east of Judea, and later in the Negeb, south of Hebron. They helped the shepherds in these districts and begged food as a reward from the rich farmers whose flocks they protected. Twice Saul fell into David's hands, yet David would not harm the king, nor did he allow his men to touch him. At those times, Saul regretted that he had made David an outlaw, and showed his old generous spirit. But these moods did not last long. Saul felt himself deserted, and his mad mood took stronger hold upon him. During these troubled days Samuel the Prophet died, and Saul missed the presence of this guide and counsellor of his happier days.

After Samuel's death, David considered it unsafe for him to remain in the land of Judah. He therefore went to the Philistine city of Gath, with his band of men, now six hundred in number. Achish, king of Gath, knew that he was an outlaw and received him well. He gave him the city of Ziklag, where David and his men remained for a year and four months. From there they made raids upon the wild tribes to the south of Judah, and brought back much spoil. Achish, thinking the raids were against Judah itself, was glad.

The Philistines had taken advantage of the trouble between Saul and David and had advanced very far into Palestine. They conquered the whole **The Philistine Invasion.** of the Maritime Plain and penetrated to the Plain of Esdraelon. It was their intention to control the trade route to Damascus and the East, and they set out to capture Beth-shan. This city was situated in a commanding position in the Jordan Valley and was strongly fortified. For a long time it was held by Egypt. Later the Canaanites defended it successfully for many generations against the tribe of Manasseh. It was well supplied with water by three streams, and the broad valley around it abounded in palm-groves and other fertile products.

The Philistine army assembled at Aphek. David and his men went with Achish, but the lords of the Philistines sent them back to Ziklag. They were afraid that during the battle David might go over to the side of Saul. When David returned to Ziklag he found it plundered and burnt. In his absence the Amalekites had attacked the city and taken its inhabitants captive. David pursued them with four hundred men. They were fortunate in finding a wounded Egyptian lad whom the Amalekites had left to die by the wayside. He directed them to the Amalekite camp. David fell upon the enemy and recaptured the spoil and the prisoners. On his return he sent gifts to the elders of Judah.

Meanwhile the Philistines advanced to Shunem, at the head of the Valley of Jezreel. Saul followed them with his army and took up his position on the slopes of Mount Gilboa. facing the enemy.

The Witch of Endor.

Saul was lonely and desparate. He had no encouraging word from Prophet or priest on the eve of battle. The priests he had slain, and Abiathar the High Priest was in exile with David. Samuel was dead. Saul, you remember, had put to death every witch and magician. But he now wanted someone to make the spirit of Samuel speak to him. His courtiers told him of a witch who lived in Endor. This town lay among the hills of Galilee, beyond the Philistine lines. At dead of night Saul, disguised, and accompanied by only two servants, crossed the enemy camp and reached the house of the witch. With difficulty he persuaded her to exercise her craft, and presently he heard the voice of Samuel uttering dark forebodings of defeat.

" The Lord will give thee and Israel into the hands of the Philistines, and to-morrow thou and thy sons shall be with me," said the voice. Saul, weakened by fasting and this dread message, fainted. His servants and the witch revived him, and they returned to the Israelite camp that night.

The next morning the Philistines marched to Jezreel

and attacked Mount Gilboa from the easy slopes to the
west.   The courageous king and his army put up a desperate resistance and defended every step
The Battle of Gilboa. against the enemy.   Saul's three sons, including Jonathan, were slain.   Saul himself
was mortally wounded by an archer's arrow.   He turned
to his armour-bearer.   " Draw thy sword and thrust me
through," he said.   The armour-bearer was afraid.   Saul
took his sword and fell upon it.   When the armour-
bearer saw that Saul was dead he killed himself too.
Israel suffered its most crushing defeat in battle.

   After the battle the enemy came to strip the dead.
They found the bodies of Saul and his sons, and joyfully
announced the tidings throughout all the Philistine
cities.   His armour they placed in the temple of Ashtoreth in Beth-shan.   His head they fixed in the temple
of Dagon.   A few years ago both these temples were
discovered in the ruins of Beth-shan.   They were Canaanite temples built in the reign of Pharaoh Rameses II,
one to the god Resheph, the other for the goddess Antit.
The Philistines hung the bodies of Saul and his sons on
the wall of Beth-shan, a reproach to the Children of Israel.

   The inhabitants of Jabesh-Gilead, on the east of the
Jordan, remembered the kindness of Saul to them in
earlier days.   They crossed the Jordan that night and
took down the bodies, which they buried in Jabesh-
Gilead.   They fasted and mourned for Saul for seven days.

   Two days later the news of the disastrous battle reached
David.   He was grief-stricken at the tragedy of Saul and
of Israel, and the loss of his noble friend
David's Lament. Jonathan moved him to tears.

   " Saul and Jonathan," he lamented, " were lovely and
pleasant in their lives,

Mount Gilboa—scene of the death of Saul and Jonathan

by courtesy of the Jewish National Fund.

And in their death they were not separated....
How are the mighty fallen in the midst of battle!
I am distressed for thee, my brother Jonathan;
Very pleasant hast thou been unto me.
Thy love to me was wonderful,
Passing the love of women.
How are the mighty fallen,
And the weapons of war perished!"

CHAPTER 8

POINTS TO REMEMBER

Samuel:
At Shiloh
    son of Elkanah and Hannah
    a Levite dedicated to the service of God from birth
    ministered in the Tabernacle.

Prophet and Judge
    became famous as Prophet
    acted as Judge on overthrow of Shiloh
    breathed new spirit into people
    founded Guild of Prophets
    judged Israel in yearly circuits
    upright and incorruptible
    brought people back to true worship of God
    led Israel successfully in war against Philistines
    lived in Ramah.

Relations with Saul
    chose Saul as king
    rebuked Saul for usurping the priest's office and offering
      sacrifice at Gilgal
    commanded Saul to exterminate the Amalekites
    denounced Saul for failing to obey his command
    secretly anointed David as king in place of Saul.

Saul:
Early Life
    son of Kish, a Benjamite
    family wealthy and respected
    himself distinguished in character and physique
    elected king by national assembly at Mizpeh
    delivered Jabesh-Gilead from Ammonite attack.

War with Philistines
>   exploits of Jonathan
>   Philistine garrison at Geba attacked
>   Saul's impatience and rash sacrifice at Gilgal
>   Philistines driven out of Judah and Benjamin.

War with border Tribes
>   Moabites and Ammonites on east ⎫
>   Edomites on south   ⎬ crushed.
>   ⎭

Administration
>   a) put to death every witch and magician
>   b) swept away all idols
>   c) set example of true worship — held feast on every Festival
>   and New Moon's day
>   d) nephew Abner commanded army; Jonathan heir to throne.

Disobedience in War with Amalekites
>   did not exterminate them as Samuel had commanded
>   spared life of king Agag and brought back best of the spoil.

Relations with David
>   appointed him court musician
>   made him a commander after he had killed Goliath
>   envied him his popularity and sought to do him harm
>   feared him as successor to the throne and aimed at his death
>   pursued him relentlessly.

His Death
>   renewed war with Philistines
>   faced enemy on slopes of Mount Gilboa
>   inquired of Witch of Endor result of the battle
>   courageously resisted Philistines and met his death in battle.

David:
>   youngest son of Jesse the Bethlehemite
>   shepherd lad, fearless and self-reliant
>   was famous for his harp-playing and became Saul's musician
>   secretly anointed king of Israel by Samuel

defied and slew Goliath
became close friend of Jonathan
was feared by Philistines for his prowess
married Michal, daughter of Saul
helped by Michal and by Jonathan to escape from Saul
lived as outlaw among the hills of the Shephelah
formed band
spared Saul's life twice
took shelter with Philistines after death of Samuel
dwelt in city of Ziklag
went with Philistine army to Aphek
sent back to Ziklag by Philistine lords
avenged sack of Ziklag by Amalekites
lamented death of Saul and Jonathan

CHAPTER 9

KING DAVID

At the death of Saul the Israelites were subject to the Philistines. The hundred years' struggle between the two peoples seemed to have ended in victory for the enemies of Israel. Yet the struggle had not been in vain, for it brought together and united the Tribes of Israel. They stopped imitating the customs of the Canaanites and turned more to the Law of Moses. Once again, as in the days of Joshua, they felt themselves to be a people chosen by God, and though defeated by the Philistines, were strong in spirit. In their midst were the " Sons of the Prophets," those disciples of Samuel who went among the people, teaching and explaining the Law of Moses. In David, moreover, they had a leader who could fight their battles and make them again a free and independent nation.

David Becomes King.

David, you remember, had been secretly anointed king by Samuel in the lifetime of Saul. After the battle of Gilboa he left the Philistine country and settled with his band in Hebron. The elders of Judah came to him there and made him king. But Saul's commander-in-chief, Abner, retreated to the east of Jordan and, in the city of Mahanaim, in Gilead, set up Ish-bosheth, Saul's youngest son, as king. There were thus two rival kings in Israel. The tribes of Israel, except for Judah, were faithful to the House of Saul. But Ish-bosheth was not a great leader and depended entirely on his commander-in-chief, Abner. David's power grew stronger day by day, while the House of Saul became weaker. Abner quarrelled with Ish-bosheth and decided to offer the whole kingdom to David. While the negotiations were taking place, Joab, David's general, treacherously killed Abner, without David's knowledge. A few days later Ish-bosheth was murdered by two of his own servants. The rivalry between the two kings had lasted seven years, and the whole nation was glad when it was over. The elders of the people came to David in Hebron and solemnly made him king of all Israel.

The Philistines, who were not at all pleased that David was now king over all Israel, immediately invaded Judea, establishing a garrison at Bethlehem.

The Philistines Subdued. David retired to his former stronghold of Adullam with his trusted band of warriors. They fought the Philistines and defeated them many times in battle, driving them back to their coast-land and even capturing their strong border-city of Gath. After this the Philistines never again troubled Israel.

It was during the wars with the Philistines that David thought of changing his capital. The city of Hebron was important both by position and through

Jerusalem Made the Capital. its history. It was situated on the main road which ran through the centre of the Judean plateau. South of it lay Beer-sheba. Northwards it led to Bethlehem, Jerusalem and Bethel. Abraham and Isaac, two of the Patriarchs, had lived there. In the cave of Machpelah nearly all the Patriarchs were buried. But it was too far south to be the capital of the whole country. There was one city in Palestine, Jerusalem, which the Israelites had never conquered and

General View of Jerusalem

by courtesy of the Jewish National Fund.

which was much more suitable for a capital than Hebron. It was a very ancient and famous fortress inhabited by the Jebusites, and really formed part of the northern mountain range. On every other side it was separated from the hills of Judea by deep ravines. That on the east, the Valley of Kidron, was nearly straight from north to south. The western gorge, the Valley of Hinnom, made a sudden bend eastwards and met the Valley of Kidron, at the south-east corner of the city. Thus, on three sides, south, east and west, Jerusalem was surrounded by high natural walls of rock and a trench like the ditch of a fortress. By position it was an ideal pivot for a leader anxious to maintain a hold on the Northern Tribes and on Judah. The city itself was also split into two hills by a central valley running north to south. The western hill was higher than the eastern, and was known as Zion, or the Upper City. The Lower City was not so strong and was soon captured by David's men. But the Upper City seemed so safe that the Jebusites boasted that they need defend it only with blind and lame men. David was stung by the insult.

" Whoever first smites the Jebusites shall be my chief captain," he declared to his army.

Now there was one entrance to the city, by a tunnel cut in the rock from the spring Gihon on the south. Through this tunnel Joab and his daring men crawled, surprised the Jebusites, and captured the city.

The news of the capture of Jerusalem spread David's fame throughout the land. When Hiram, King of the Phoenician seaport of Tyre, heard of it, he sent messengers to David bearing gifts of cedar-wood from Lebanon, and craftsmen, who built a palace for David in the Upper City. For the Phoenicians, who inhabited the coast-land

of Syria, were great builders and skilled craftsmen, as
well as the most famous traders of the ancient world.
From their cities of Tyre and Sidon ships sailed to every
part of the world, bringing back treasures of gold, silver,
tin and precious cargoes. Old tin mines which they
worked have been found even in Cornwall.

It was an ancient custon for the conqueror of an
important city to call it by his own name, so the Upper

The Ark Brought to Jerusalem. City was called the City of David. The
old name, Jerusalem, meant the City of
Peace, and it was David's dream to make
it indeed a city of peace. For he was an inspired poet
as well as a prudent and wise king, and he yearned to
make his city the centre of the true worship of God. The
Ark, you remember, was in the house of Abinadab in
Kirjath-jearim. With great pomp and ceremony David
now transferred it from there to Jerusalem.

He set it in a tent near his palace; but the contrast
between his gorgeous palace and the plain tent troubled
him, so he determined to build a beautiful

David Desires to Build a Temple. temple to God.
"See now," he said to his counsellor and
friend, the prophet Nathan, "I dwell in a house of
cedar-wood while the Ark of God abideth within curtains."

That night, however, the word of God came to the
Prophet:

"Go and say to my servant David, thus saith the
Lord, Thou shalt not build a house for My name. I shall
be with thee and cut off all thine enemies from before
thee. Moreover, I shall appoint a place for My people
Israel and shall plant them firmly that they may dwell
in a place of their own and move no more. And when
thy days be fulfilled then will I set up thy son after thee

and establish his kingdom. He shall build a house for My name, and thy house and thy kingdom shall he established for ever before Me."

When David heard these words, his heart was filled with joy, and he offered a moving prayer of thanksgiving to God. Although he himself could not build the Temple, he stored away for it gold and silver and copper in abundance from the spoil of the many wars which he was now forced to undertake. He also brought the priests and Levites to Jerusalem and arranged the service of the Tabernacle. Abiathar was High Priest, while Asaph and his brother Levites chanted Psalms every day before the Ark. The altar of sacrifice, however, was in Gibeon, under the charge of Zadok the priest, a descendant of Aaron's elder son. There also Levites accompanied the service with songs of praise and thanksgiving.

Around him in Jerusalem David had a faithful group of friends and advisers. Foremost among them were the two Prophets Nathan and Gad, who may have received their training in the prophetic guild of Samuel. They guided the king in his conduct, and were never afraid to reproach or rebuke him when he did wrong. The king in ancient times was the chief judge of the people, and to David in Jerusalem came all who had disputes to settle. David's army was formed round the trusted band of heroes who had lived with him as outlaws in the days of Saul, with Joab and Abishai, the two sons of David's sister Zeruiah, at their head. Upon them fell the direction of the wars which now began.

The Wars of David. The Ammonites, whose territory touched that of the Israelite tribes on the east of Jordan, were the first to provoke David, by their treatment of his ambassadors. Fearing reprisals, they assembled a mighty army, re-inforced by the chariots and horsemen of their Syrian allies. Joab, David's chief general, crossed the Jordan with his army, and met the enemy in battle outside their capital Rabbah, which was situated in the valley of the river Jabbok. The battle was fiercely fought on both sides, but in the end David's army put to flight the Syrian hosts. Joab's war-cry is interesting:

" Be of good courage and let us act as men," he called to his troops, " for our people, and for the cities of our God; and let the Lord do that which seemeth Him good."

The war was not yet over, for the Syrians gathered in greater strength the next year, under Shobach, the chief general of Hadarezer, king of Zobah, who was overlord of the Syrian kings. David himself took the field with an enormous army and completely defeated the Syrians. The Syrian kings became vassals of David, and even the renowned city of Damascus paid him tribute. The Ammonites still held out until the following year when Joab, after a long siege, conquered their strongly-fortified capital, Rabbah. So loyal was he to David that he sent for him to enter the city in person so that it might be called by David's name, and not by his own.

The Moabites suffered the same fate as their neighbours the Ammonites, both being very severely treated by David. Further south, Joab crushed the Edomites in a decisive battle and made his name feared through Edom. In all these conquered provinces David placed governors who sent him a yearly tribute. The spoil from these wars, and the gifts he received from neighbouring kings who wished to be at peace with him, was immense, and much of it David dedicated for the Temple to be built by his son.

For these wars David required a much larger force

than the voluntary band which joined him at first, and in order to raise this large army he ordered Joab to take a census of the people. Joab, realising that its purpose was contrary to Israelite tradition, was against the census, but obeyed the king's command. With the captains of the army he went throughout the country from Dan to Beer-sheba, and at the end of nine months reported the number of all the men over twenty years of age as 1,300,000. This was more than twice the number which had entered Palestine under Joshua. David was now conscience-stricken that he had counted the people, and saw in a plague which ravaged them for three days the punishment of God. In the threshing-floor of Araunah the Jebusite, where the plague ceased, he built an altar and offered sacrifice to God. The place of that altar, which he bought from Araunah, he reserved as the site of the future Temple.

As a result of these wars the territory of Israel was increased, and stretched from the Red Sea in the south **David's Empire.** to the River Euphrates in the north, and from the Mediterranean Sea on the west to the desert on the east. The promise of God to the Patriarchs was fulfilled and the Children of Israel dwelt securely in their own land. When David was at rest from all his enemies he uttered a stirring song of thanksgiving to God, because he realised that not his own strength had made him victorious, but the help and protection of God:

" Thou art my lamp, O Lord.
The Lord will lighten my darkness....
Thou teachest my hands to war,
So that a bow of steel is broken by mine arms.
Thou givest me the shield of Thy salvation,
And Thy gentleness hath made me great."

David showed himself merciful and magnanimous to the House of Saul. He sought out the son of Jonathan his friend, a lame man named Mephibosheth, restored to him his father's property in Gibeah, and made him welcome at his table in Jerusalem.

Yet David had many faults, and one crime he committed left a lasting impression on his life. During the war with the Ammonites he took into his harem **David and Bath-Sheba.** Bath-Sheba the wife of one of his officers, Uriah the Hittite, and commanded Joab to put Uriah in the forefront of the battle, so that he might be killed. Then Nathan the Prophet came to the king and told him a parable.

" Two men," he said, " lived in a city, one rich, the other poor. The rich man had very many flocks and herds, while the poor man had nothing, save one little ewe lamb, which he had bought and nourished up; and it grew up together with him, and with his children; it did eat of his own meat and drank of his own cup, and was unto him as a daughter. And there came a traveller unto the rich man, and he spared to take of his own flock and of his own herd to prepare for the wayfaring man; but took the poor man's lamb and prepared it for the man who had come to him."

David thought it was a cause which he had to judge. He was very angry and said:

" As the Lord liveth, the man that hath done this thing shall surely die, and the lamb he shall restore four-fold, because he did this thing and had no pity."

Then said Nathan fearlessly to David:

" Thou art the man. Thus saith the Lord, I anointed thee to be king over Israel.... why then hast thou despised the commandment of the Lord, and hast done evil in

His sight? Uriah the Hittite thou hast caused to be slain with the sword, and his wife hast thou taken to be thy wife.... Now, therefore, the sword shall never depart from thy house, because thou hast despised Me."

It was courageous of Nathan to speak so fearlessly to David. For in those days the kings of other nations committed even worse crimes and none dared to rebuke them. But the Prophets of Israel had to impress upon the people what God required of them, and even the king was bound, like every Israelite, to observe the Law of Moses.

David was humbled. "I have sinned against the Lord," he said. A Psalm he composed at this time expresses his deep feeling of contrition:

"Be gracious unto me, O God, according to Thy loving-
kindness;
According to the multitude of Thy tender mercies blot
out my transgressions....
For I acknowledge my transgressions,
And my sin is ever before me....
Create in me a clean heart, O God,
And renew a right spirit within me.
Cast me not away from Thy presence,
And take not Thy holy spirit from me."

In David's later years many troubles arose in his own family, and in them he saw the punishment for his sin.

Absalom's Rebellion. His eldest son Amnon, the heir to the throne, ill-treated Tamar, the sister of his half-brother Absalom. Two years Absalom waited to avenge the wrong done to his sister. Then, at a feast to celebrate his sheepshearing, he killed Amnon in the presence of all the king's sons. Absalom fled to Geshur, east of Jordan, where he remained for three years.

Although in disgrace, he was now heir to the throne, and when David recalled him he began to plot a rebellion against his own father. He was a handsome man, and popular with the people. He made it his habit to sit in state at the gate of Jerusalem, where all matters for judgment were decided, and used to say to everyone who had a lawsuit:

" See, thy cause is just, but there is no one deputed by the king to hear thee. Would that I were judge in the land, that every man who hath any suit or cause might come to me, and I would do him justice."

In this manner Absalom stole the hearts of the people away from David. When the conspiracy was ripe, Absalom deceitfully asked leave of David to go to Hebron, and in this city of Judah he proclaimed himself king. With Absalom in the rebellion were all who had a grudge against David, among them Ahitophel, David's wisest counsellor, who was the grand-father of Bath-Sheba.

David was dumb-founded when he heard of the rebellion, but he would not allow war to enter his holy city. Hastily he assembled his faithful followers and left Jerusalem. The priests Zadok and Abiathar prepared to follow their master, with the Ark of God, but David would not hear of it.

" Take back the Ark of God to the city," he command- ed. " If I find grace in the sight of God, then He will bring me back and I shall see it again. But if He say, I desire thee not, behold, let Him do to me what is good in His sight." So the Ark was returned to the city, while David and his followers walked weeping barefoot, and with head covered as a sign of mourning, up the Mount of Olives east of Jerusalem on their way to the Jordan.

Absalom entered Jerusalem and immediately called

a council of war. Ahitophel was for striking against David at once, an excellent plan which might have succeeded. But in the council was Hushai, David's friend, who craftily suggested that it would be better for Absalom to assemble an army from all Israel and then march in overwhelming force against David. Hushai's advice was taken, so that David and his men had time to cross the Jordan and arrange their forces at Mahanaim. On this side of Jordan David found many friends, even among his former enemies the Ammonites, who supplied welcome food and shelter to the weary fugitives.

Absalom's army, under the command of Amasa, a cousin of Joab, crossed the Jordan and prepared to attack David. Joab would not allow the king to go out with the army to battle, so David sat in the gate of the city, waiting anxiously for the result of this unnatural civil war. Yet he still loved his son Absalom and commanded his captains to deal gently with him. The engagement was fought in the Wood of Ephraim, and the men of Israel were heavily defeated by David's warriors. Even the wood was against the Israelites and, in the words of the Bible, devoured more people than the sword. Absalom met his fate in the wood. He was riding through it on his mule when his long hair was caught in the thick bough of a great oak. The mule went on, so that Absalom was left hanging by his hair. One of David's soldiers saw him thus, and reported it to Joab. Instantly Joab rushed to the spot and shot three arrows into Absalom's heart, in spite of David's command. With Absalom dead, the men of Israel fled, and the battle was over.

When the news reached David, he went up to a room over the gate and wept bitterly for his son.

" O my son Absalom, my son, my son Absalom! Would that I had died instead of thee, O Absalom, my son, my son." It was only after Joab had spoken sternly to the king that he returned to his seat at the gate and welcomed his victorious army.

But fresh trouble awaited him at the fords of Jordan on his way back to Jerusalem. The Israelites quarrelled with the men of Judah as to who should **Sheba the Son of Bichri.** have the honour of first receiving the king. Fierce words were spoken on both sides when suddenly a Benjamite, Sheba the son of Bichri by name, raised a new standard of revolt, crying:

" We have no portion in David, neither have we inheritance in the son of Jesse; every man to his tents, O Israel." The Israelites followed him and the rebellion looked like becoming grave. But Joab pursued the rebels and besieged Sheba in the city of Abel-Beth-Maachah, where a wise woman saved the situation by prevailing upon the inhabitants to surrender the head of the rebel Sheba.

The ease with which the Northern Tribes were stirred up against Judah and its kings shows that there was no real unity between them. This point ex- **Preparations for the Temple.** plains a great deal of subsequent history. For the time, however, David succeeded in reigning over a united nation. Once more at peace, he again gave thought to the building of the Temple. He prepared plans, provided materials of cedar-wood, hewn stone and marble, dedicated offerings of precious stones, gold, silver, iron and copper, and gathered skilled workmen. To Solomon, his youngest son, he said:

" It was in my mind to build a house unto the name of the Lord my God. But the word of the Lord came to me saying, Thou shalt not build a house unto My name because thou hast shed much blood upon the earth in my sight. Now, my son, the Lord be with thee; and prosper thou, and build the house of the Lord thy God. Only the Lord give thee wisdom and understanding, and give thee charge concerning Israel, that thou mayest keep the Law of the Lord thy God."

It was David's intention to make his son Solomon king, but Adonijah, his surviving eldest son (for Amnon and Absalom were dead), conspired with **Adonijah's** Joab and Abiathar to make himself king. **Conspiracy.** This rebellion was easily crushed and, to prevent further dispute, Solomon was forthwith anointed king by Zadok the priest in the presence of Nathan the Prophet. Before his death David exhorted Solomon,

" to keep the charge of the Lord thy God, to walk in His ways, and to observe His commandments as it is written in the Law of Moses."

He also warned him of the character of some of his counsellors and charged him to reward the kindness of his friends.

After reigning for forty years, seven years in Hebron and thirty-three in Jerusalem, the second king of Israel **The Psalms of** died, leaving to his son Solomon a rich **David.** legacy — a large empire and a contented people. To the world he has left a more enduring legacy than a kingdom — the book of Psalms. Not all the Psalms are by David, but in the sense that he composed many of them himself and set the example to others he may be said to be the inspirer of them all. And when we weigh up his adventurous life we think less of the cruel treatment he meted out to his foes, less of the faults in his character, and remember the man who poured out his soul to God in prayer, meditation and thanksgiving.

From his youth the experiences of his life marked him out as a leader of men. The calm, medidative hours of the music-loving shepherd were replaced by days and years of battle and outlawry. In both periods the future king displayed that courage and chivalry which endeared him to his followers and later to his subjects. His was indeed a magnetic personality, and when we add to it his unwavering trust in God and his profound remorse for his own shortcomings, we possess the secret of his success. His psalms became a part of the daily life of the Jewish people and of the world, and have remained so for nearly three thousand years.

CHAPTER 9

POINTS TO REMEMBER

King David:
His struggle for power:
- a) after Battle of Gilboa left Philistine country and settled in Hebron
- b) made king of Judah in Hebron
- c) warred with Ish-bosheth, youngest son of Saul, who had been made king of Israel by Abner
- d) made king of all Israel on death of Abner and Ish-bosheth
- c) Jerusalem captured and made the capital.

His wars:
- a) against Philistines for mastery of Palestine
- b) against Ammonites and their Syrian allies
- c) against Moabites
- d) against Edomites.

His Dominions:
> From the Red Sea in the South to the River Euphrates in the North
>
> From the Mediterranean Sea in the West to the desert beyond Jordan on the East.

His administration:
- a) brought Ark to Jerusalem and put it in charge of Abiathar
- b) altar of sacrifice was at Gibeon in charge of Zadok
- c) Nathan and Gad were Prophets at court
- d) David was chief judge
- e) Joab and Abishai commanded the army
- f) Mephibosheth, a grandson of Saul, was well treated at court
- g) planned to make Jerusalem a City of Peace
- h) told by Nathan that his son would build Temple

    i) promised by Nathan that his dynasty would last

    j) preparations for building of Temple.

Court Intrigues:

    a) David's sin with Bath-sheba

    b) Absalom's rebellion

    c) revolt of Sheba son of Bichri

    d) Adonijah's rebellion.

His Character:

    religious; chivalrous, passionate, courageous; poet; wrote the Psalms.

Made Solomon king before his death, and charged him to keep the Torah.

CHAPTER 10

KING SOLOMON

Solomon was eighteen years of age when he became king, and he ruled over Israel for forty years. His kingdom extended from the River Euphrates to the boundary of Egypt, and all the nations whom David had conquered — Syrians, Ammonites, Moabites, Edomites — were subject to him and paid him yearly tribute. Egypt, after a long period of strife, was once more rising to importance, and Solomon, deeming it wise to be friendly with the Egyptian Pharaoh, married his daughter. With Hiram, king of Tyre, he renewed the league of friendship which David had made. Thus, Solomon's long reign was one of enduring peace.

Solomon Establishes Himself.

At the beginning, however, trouble arose within the court circle itself. Adonijah made another attempt to seize the throne, but Solomon, by immediately crushing the rebels, prevented an outbreak of civil war. He ordered Adonijah and Joab to be slain, while he banished Abiathar to the priestly city of Anathoth in Benjamin. In his place he appointed Zadok as High Priest, so that this office now passed back from the House of Eli to the older branch of Aaron's family.

His Dream at Gibeon.

The kingdom now firmly established under him, Solomon visited Gibeon, where the Tabernacle was still situated, and there, in the presence of his people, offered numerous sacrifices to God. In a dream that night, he heard the voice of God saying:

" Ask what I shall give thee."

" Thou hast made Thy servant king in succession to my father David over a great people which cannot be numbered for multitude," he answered. " Yet I am a little child. Give therefore to Thy servant an understanding heart to judge Thy people, that I may discern between good and bad."

His answer pleased God, and he was promised a wise and understanding heart, and unparalleled wealth and honour.

The first task to which Solomon set his hand was the building of the Temple. He began it in the fourth year of his reign, four hundred and eighty **He Builds the Temple.** years after the Exodus from Egypt, that is in the year 967 B. C. E., and it took seven and-a-half years to build. The king spared no expense and effort over it. Hiram helped him in the work by providing skilled Phoenician craftsmen and stonemasons, as well as cedar and fir-trees felled from Lebanon. Solomon raised a levy of Israelites who hewed the wood in Lebanon, and a larger number Canaanites who worked in the quarries near Bethlehem and under the Temple rock in Jerusalem. All the stones were cut and polished in the quarries and then carried by other Canaanites to the Temple area, so that, in the words of the Bible, " neither hammer, nor axe, nor any tool of iron was heard in the Temple while it was in building."

The Temple itself was made after the pattern of the Tabernacle which Moses erected in the Wilderness, except that it was built of hewn stone and was twice the size of the Tabernacle. The building was sixty cubits in

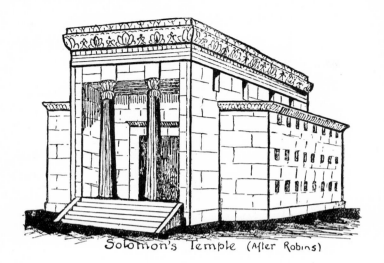

Solomon's Temple (After Robins)

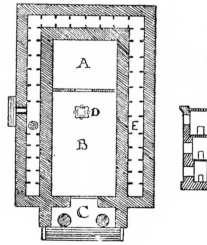

Plan.

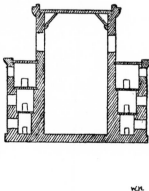

Section.

SOLOMON'S TEMPLE

(A) Holy of Holies, (B) Holy Place, (C) Porch with Pillars, (D) Altar,
(E) Chambers for Storage, etc.

length, twenty cubits wide, and thirty cubits high.   The
walls were of hewn stone covered with cedar-wood, overlaid with gold, and all were decorated with precious
stones to strike the eye with beauty.   The most western
part was lower than the rest, and formed a perfect cube,
being twenty cubits in height, length and breadth.
This was the Holy of Holies in which only the Ark was
placed, surrounded by two Cherubim of olive-wood overlaid with gold, which stretched from one wall to the
other.   In the Ark were the two tablets of stone en-
graved with the Ten Commandments.   Separating the
Holy of Holies from the Holy Place, as the rest of the
Temple building was called, there hung a curtain of blue,
and purple, and crimson, and fine linen, embroidered
with Cherubim, in front of two small doors of olive-wood,
beatifully carved and overlaid with gold.

In the Holy Place stood a golden altar of incense, a
golden table on which twelve loaves of shewbread were
placed every Sabbath, and ten golden candlesticks.   The
Temple opened out on the east to a porch 10 cubits long,
20 cubits wide, and 120 cubits in height, overlaid with
gold, and supported on either side by two pillars of
brass.   Surrounding the Temple were two courts, the
outer planted with trees and made for the people, the
inner somewhat higher and reserved for the priests.   In
the Inner Court stood the great brazen altar of sacrifice
and the accessories of the Temple such as the Molten Sea,
in which the priests purified themselves, and the lavers
where the parts of the sacrifices were washed.   Round
the Temple were three galleries divided into chambers
for the use of the priests, where the Temple untensils of
gold and brass were kept.

At the end of the seven and-a-half years the Temple

was completed, and to consecrate it to the service of God, Solomon made a great feast in the seventh month. To

The Consecration. the western hill of Jerusalem on which it was situated flocked the Children of Israel from every city in Palestine. They were all eager to be present at the consecration of the Temple and to observe for the first time in the City of God the pilgrim festival of Succoth. The Levites bore the Ark to the entrance of the inner court, where the priests received it reverently and carried it to its place in the Holy of Holies, under the outstretched wings of the Cherubim. Solomon turned to the assemblied multitude in the outer court and, in a voice full of gratitude, said:

" Blessed be the Lord, the God of Israel who spoke with His mouth unto David my father, and hath with His hand fulfilled it saying, " Thy son shall build the Temple unto My name. For I have arisen in the place of David my father and have built the Temple to the Lord God of Israel."

Then, spreading his hands towards the sky, Solomon uttered a moving prayer to God, begging him ever to be attentive to the prayers of His people directed towards that Temple, no matter how scattered and far away the Children of Israel might be.

" Also concerning a stranger, who is not of Thy people Israel," he went on, " but cometh out of a far country for Thy name's sake, when he shall come and pray towards this Temple, do Thou hear in heaven, and do according to all that the stranger calleth Thee for; that all the people of the earth may know Thy name, to fear Thee, as do Thy people Israel."

Then Solomon impressed upon the people the need to

serve God with a perfect heart, and both he and the
people observed the festival of Succoth with joy and
gladness. The Children of Israel returned to their homes
at the end of the festival joyful and glad of heart for all
the goodness which God had shown to the House of
David and to His people Israel.

The Children of Israel were happy. Their land
from Dan to Beer-sheba was secure from enemies, and
**The Life of
the People.** they could plough their ground and reap
its harvest of wheat and barley without
fear. In the valleys and the plains and
on the mountain-slopes they planted orchards wherein
grew the vine, the fig-tree and the olive. On the hills
of Judea and the moors of Gilead shepherds tended
their flocks of sheep and goats. Every Sabbath day
and New Moon the people rested from their work, and
every seventh year the ground lay fallow and was not
tilled. On the Festival of Passover, the Feast of Weeks,
and the Feast of Succoth, the Israelites went with their
families to Jerusalem, taking with them the produce
of their land, barley on Passover, wheat on the Feast of
Weeks, and fruits of all kinds (grapes, figs, pomegranates,
olives and dates) at the Feast of Ingathering held on
Succoth. These were also religious Festivals, and on
these days the outer court of the Temple was thronged
with crowds, bringing their sacrifices to be offered by
the priests upon the brazen altar in the inner court of
the Temple. Levites accompanied the service with
harps and psalteries, cymbals, flutes and trumpets, and
sang Psalms of praise and thanksgiving to God.

The people lived mainly in villages, and life there
was very simple. The men built their own houses of
timber or sun-baked bricks, covered by flat roofs, and

constructed the plain wooden furniture for the rooms—chairs, tables, beds. The women of the house baked their own bread, and prepared homely meals of fruits and herbs for the family. Meat was eaten only on special occasions. The women also wove and spun, made the family clothes of wool and linen, helped their husbands in the fields at harvest time, and often tended the flocks and herds. Children were strictly controlled by their parents, and taught at an early age to read and write.

In the towns lived the craftsmen and the wealthier people. The number of town-dwellers increased enormously during the reign of Solomon.

In the Towns. Through Palestine the caravans bearing the trade of the ancient world had to pass, and the king exacted a toll from the traders. He himself engaged in the export of horses with the Egyptians, the Hittites, and the Syrians. Solomon also joined Hiram in fitting out a merchant fleet of ships from the port of Ezion-Geber (now called Akaba) on the Red Sea, in the land of Edom. This navy sailed to Spain and Africa, and possibly to India, taking three years for the voyage, and brought back gold and silver, ivory, apes and peacocks. The world was opened out to the Israelites, and they readily learned from it. The towns soon filled with Israelite craftsmen who imitated the work of the foreign silver-smiths and goldsmiths, metal-workers, potters and weavers.

Moreover, Solomon was a great builder. Besides the Temple, he built in Jerusalem a palace for himself, a house for his Egyptian wife, a Court of Justice and a magnificent public building known as the House of the Forest of Lebanon because of the forty-five cedar columns in the lower hall. All this building-activity brought to Jerusalem foreign craftsmen, architects and stonemasons, from whom the Israelites also learnt these trades and professions. With the increase in trade came a more luxurious civilisation. The princes and the nobles had beautiful houses built for themselves, fitted up with the choicest furniture and comforts.

Solomon also extended the fortifications of Jerusalem and built or strengthened other important cities, such as Hazor, Megiddo, and Gezer. Through-
Solomon's Court. out the country he established store-cities and armouries for his chariots and horse-men. The land was divided into twelve districts, and over each was a governor who provided the food for the king's numerous court for a whole month.

Solomon was a wise king and an impartial judge. One cause which he decided early in his reign made him famous not only throughout Palestine, but
The Wise King. also in distant parts of the world. Even the Queen of Sheba, a country in Southern Arabia, heard of his fame and came to Jerusalem with a large company of courtiers to see with her own eyes the wise king of Israel. She was astonished at the magnificence of his court and the wisdom of his sayings.

Yet this great and wise king proved in the end foolish. He forgot to trust in God and made alliances with all the nations round about him in order to
Solomon's Decadence. keep his empire firm. To strengthen these alliances he married many wives from among the heathen nations — Moabites, Ammonites, Edomites, Phoenicians, and Hittites — and for them he built altars on high places to their heathen gods. On these high places abominable customs were practised,

and children were even passed through the fire and offered up as sacrifice to Moloch, the idol of Ammon. Solomon, by allowing these practices, helped to turn away the people of Israel from the pure worship of God as commanded by the Torah.

There was other cause for complaint. For his numerous palaces and buildings and for the upkeep of his large court Solomon had to tax the people. The peasants and farmers of Israel, living in plain fashion in their villages, could not help contrasting their simple life with the luxury of the capital and the other big cities. And all that luxury and wealth had come from their taxes. It is no wonder that many of the Israelites resented it.

Thus it came to pass that towards the end of his reign Solomon made many enemies. The bulk of the people groaned under the heavy taxation, but the **Ahijah and Jeroboam.** splendour of their king kept them from open revolt. The prophetic party, however, was more outspoken, and denounced the idol-worship which Solomon permitted. Ahijah the Prophet went so far as to promise a great part of the kingdom to a man named Jeroboam, whom Solomon had appointed chief tax-collector of the tribe of Ephraim. Once, Jeroboam was walking in a field outside Jerusalem when Ahijah the Prophet met him and, taking hold of a new garment which Jeroboam wore, tore it into twelve pieces. Ten of them he dramatically gave to Jeroboam, saying:

" Thus saith the Lord, the God of Israel. Behold I will rend the kingdom out of the hand of Solomon and will give ten tribes to thee. Yet to his son will I give one tribe, that David my servant may have a light always before Me in Jerusalem."

When Solomon heard of this event he sought to kill

Jeroboam, who fled to Egypt, to Shishak, the founder of the twenty-second dynasty of Pharaohs.

In this manner came to an end the reign of the third and last king of the whole of Israel. For many years during his long reign the Children of Israel **Solomon's Death.** lived in tranquil happiness, a notable and free people blessed by God whom they served with a perfect heart. But the folly of their wise king in his later years changed their joy into sorrow. He set an example of idol-worship which was soon followed, and a love of luxury and outward splendour which currupted the life of the people. But he did not live to see the result of the evils he introduced, for when he died Israel was still a great and united nation.

CHAPTER 10

POINTS TO REMEMBER

King Solomon:
Consolidation of the kingdom:
   a) internal

      Adonijah's second attempt to seize throne; rebels crushed; Adonijah and Joab put to death; Abiathar banished; Zadok appointed High Priest.

   b) external

      political alliances through marriage, with Moabites, Ammonites, Edomites, Phoenicians, Hittites and Egyptians.

Building of the Temple:

      begun in fourth year of reign

      took seven and-a-half years to build

      Hiram king of Tyre helped by providing skilled Phoenician craftsmen and stonemasons, as well as cedar and fir-trees cut from Lebanon

      Israelites and Canaanites mobilised for work

      built of hewn stone.

Plan of Temple: facing page 130.

Other Buildings:
   a) in Jerusalem

      palace for himself

      house for his Egyptian wife

      Court of Justice

      House of the Forest of Lebanon

   b) store-cities and armouries established throughout the country

   c) important cities fortified.

Life of People:
- a) agriculture main occupation
- b) cattle-rearing on hills and moors
- c) village life
- d) houses of timber or sun-baked bricks
- e) plain, home-made wooden furniture
- f) women wove and spun and helped their husbands in the fields and with their flocks
- g) children taught reading and writing.

Trade and Commerce:
- a) caravan trade passing through Palestine taxed by Solomon
- b) export of horses
- c) Solomon joined Hiram in sending merchant fleet to Spain, Africa, and possibly India
- d) towns filled with foreign craftsmen (from whom Israelites learnt trades), and with wealthier classes
- e) visit of Queen of Sheba to Solomon.

Seeds of Discontent:
- a) Prophetic party alienated by altars to foreign gods erected in Jerusalem
- b) luxury of court and capital, made possible by heavy taxes, resented by the peasantry
- c) Jeroboam promised the Ten Tribes by prophet Ahijah — fled to Egypt for safety.

CHAPTER 11

THE TWO KINGDOMS

When Solomon died, the elders of Israel recalled Jeroboam from Egypt and met under his leadership in Shechem, in the territory of Ephraim, to consider the succession to the throne. They could no longer bear the heavy taxes and the harsh burdens which Solomon had placed upon them, and therefore before making his son king they appealed that he should lighten their oppressive yoke. So Rehaboam, the son of Solomon, went to Shechem and was told the demands of the people.

The Revolt of the Ten Tribes.

" Your father made our yoke heavy," the elders said. " Do thou therefore lighten the heavy yoke which thy father put upon us, and we will serve thee."

Their request was both reasonable and justifiable. For the king of Israel was a constitutional monarch, a servant of his people, and not their master. Consequently the elder and experienced counsellors of Rehaboam advised him to redress the grievances of the people. But the son of Solomon was autocratic, wilful and arrogant, and answered the people roughly, according to the counsel of his youthful and foolish companions.

" My little finger," he said, " is thicker than my father's loins. My father burdened you with a heavy yoke, and I will add to your yoke. My father chastised you with whips, and I will chastise you with scorpions." Such a brusque rebuff was calculated to sting the people. Bitter

with resentment, they immediately raised the standard
of revolt against the insolent Rehaboam.

" We have no portion in David," they declared, " nor
inheritance in the son of Jesse. To thy tents, O Israel."
When Rehaboam sent Adoram, his chief tax collector,
to the rebellious tribes, they stoned him to death, and
Rehaboam at last realised that his folly had made him
forfeit a large part of his kingdom. The tribes of Judah
and Benjamin, however, remained faithful to the House
of David and crowned Rehaboam as their sovereign.

The elders of the remaining Ten Tribes met together
again and elected Jeroboam to reign over them. In
this manner the vast dominions of Solomon
Jeroboam King were split up and the kingdom of Israel
of Israel. was divided in two. The two tribes of
Judah and Benjamin, in the south of Palestine, became
the small kingdom of Judah, with the country of Edom
still tributary to it for a time. The territory of the
Ten Tribes, more extensive and better endowed by
nature, was known as the kingdom of Israel. It possessed
the fertile hills and plains of Palestine; through it ran
the caravan trade routes of the ancient world; to it
belonged the pasture-lands of Gilead and Bashan; Moab
paid it tribute. The kingdom of Israel in truth inherited
the empire of Solomon, and the kings of Israel might have
developed and enriched the life and culture of their
country. But Jeroboam was self-seeking and unscrupu-
lous, caring more for his personal ambitions than the
welfare and spiritual advancement of his people. Worldly
and irreligious, he corrupted the life of Israel and ruined
his own dynasty.

Since the days of David the religious centre of the
people of Israel was Jerusalem. In it stood the Temple

with the Ark of God, where the priests and the Levites ministered daily according to the commands of the

He Introduces
Calf-Worship. Torah. To Jerusalem, moreover, came every Israelite with his family three times a year, on the great festivals. But Jerusalem was the capital city of Judah, and Jeroboam was afraid to let the Israelites go there. For, he thought, " if this people go up to do sacrifice in the house of the Lord at Jerusalem, then shall the heart of this people turn again to their lord, even unto Rehaboam king of Judah, and they shall kill me."

For this reason Jeroboam made two golden calves and placed them in temples in the two end-cities of his kingdom, Dan in the north and Bethel in the south. Then he proclaimed to his people:

" It is too much for you to go up to Jerusalem: behold thy gods, O Israel, which brought thee out of the land of Egypt." The priests and the Levites, as well as the prophetic party living in Israel, were scandalised. They realised that Jeroboam's action struck at the very basis of the Ten Commandments, and it so degraded the idea of God that religious and moral progress were impossible. It could lead to only one end — the ultimate destruction of the kingdom of Israel.

Jeroboam, however, turned a deaf ear to the words of the Prophets. He dismissed the priests and the Levites for refusing to worship his idols, and consigned the office to other men. Consequently the priests and the Levites, who lived in thirty-five important cities in Israel, turned to Rehaboam of Judah as their king. Jeroboam called in the aid of Shishak, Pharaoh of Egypt, to subdue them. The Bible tells us that Shishak came and attacked Judah, entered Jerusalem and plundered the Temple of Solomon, taking away much of the wealth stored therein. An Egyptian record of this attack mentions also the places in Israel which Shishak captured, and they are all cities where the priests and the Levites dwelt.

Greatly disturbed by the invasion of Shishak, Rehaboam strengthened his fortress-cities on the hills of Judea, to make them safe from any further attack. **Rehaboam, King of Judah.** He fortified Bethlehem and Hebron, and the numerous strongholds in the Shephelah which were once the scene of battle between Israel and the Philistines. In all these cities Rehaboam also stored supplies of food and weapons, under the charge of trusted officers. The priests and Levites and many Israelites from the Northern Kingdom who would not worship the idols which Jeroboam had set up, flocked to the little kingdom of Judah and helped to strengthen it.

Rehaboam now turned to wage war on his rival Jeroboam. The people of Israel, once united by ancestry, religion, language and ideals, fought one another as enemies through the folly of their leaders. Jeroboam was troubled on other sides as well. The Syrians, who had paid tribute to Solomon, had revolted towards the end of his reign and disturbed the peace of Israel in the north. The Philistines also refused to submit to Israel. Thus Jeroboam had an uneasy reign. Once he was so hard pressed by enemies that he had to remove his capital from Shechem to Penuel, on the east of Jordan. Shechem, though situated in the centre of the land, was not a strong city, and Jeroboam finally established his capital in Tirzah, on the eastern slopes of the hills of Ephraim. There his son Nadab succeeded him, after a reign of twenty-two years.

Nadab ruled for only two years. While he was besieging the city of Gibbethon, which was held by the
The House of Jeroboam Destroyed. Philistines, Baasha, one of his generals,
conspired against him and usurped the
throne. So that he might have no rivals,
Baasha killed every member of the House of Jeroboam.
In other respects he followed the policy of Jeroboam.
He made Tirzah his capital, worshipped the golden calves
at Dan and Bethel, and constantly warred with Judah.
In order to blockade the king of Judah, he started to
fortify Ramah, four miles north of Jerusalem. At that
time, Asa, the son of Abijah, and grandson of Rehaboam,
was king of Judah. To rid himself of Baasha, Asa made
a league with Ben-hadad, the king of Syria who ruled
at Damascus, and bribed him to attack the kingdom of
Israel. Ben-hadad answered the call of Asa and ravaged
the cities of Naphtali on the north of Palestine. Owing
to this counter-attack, Baasha had to abandon the
fortification of Ramah. Asa ordered his men to carry
away the stones and timber left there, and, to guard his
frontier against further invasion, he seized the opportunity to strengthen the northern fortresses of Judah, Geba
and Mizpeh.

Otherwise Asa was a wise and successful monarch.
During the reigns of his father and grandfather the
Asa, King of Judah. idolatry which Solomon had introduced
into Jerusalem spread both in the capital
and in the other cities of Judah. Fortunately the Temple and its service centralised the true
worship of God and kept the people mindful of the Torah;
but in many parts of the kingdom, and even in Jerusalem
itself, there were temples to the idols of other nations.
Round these idolatrous temples companies of worshippers

settled and committed abominable crimes. You must remember that foreign merchants of all nations came to Jerusalem to do trade, and they were glad to find a place in it where their gods were worshipped. Many Judean traders and nobles imitated the heathen worship, and even the queen mother was guilty. Asa set himself the task of destroying these idols, and also deposed his mother from her high position at court.

He showed his martial ability when the country was invaded by Zerah, the Ethiopian, who had succeeded Shishak as Pharaoh of Egypt. Zerah came against Asa with a force of one million men and three hundred chariots, and advanced as far as Mareshah, an important city in the Shephelah. Asa was undismayed, and his smaller force of five hundred and eighty thousand men succeeded in putting the enemy to flight and driving them back to Gerar in the Negeb, on the road to Egypt. In their flight the Egyptians left behind much spoil of flocks and herds and camels, which the Judeans joyfully seized. This victory increased the fame of Asa, and many more Israelites from the Northern Kingdom came to join him. In the fifteenth year of his reign he made a great feast in Jerusalem, and the people solemnly renewed the covenant to serve only God and to fulfil His Laws. Asa ruled for forty-one years, and when he died the kingdom of Judah was firmly established and at peace.

In his footsteps followed his son Jehoshaphat. A great organiser and administrator, he made the country safe

Jehoshaphat. from war by placing strong garrisons in every fortified city of Judah. Courts of Law were set up in every city, and a supreme court in Jerusalem, with the High Priest at its head. He appointed also a commission of five noblemen, nine Levites, and two priests to go through the cities of Judah and teach the Law of Moses in the land. Around him he had wise and fearless Prophets as counsellors. His people were happy and contented in their villages and cities. Jehoshaphat was a brave and powerful king, and the Philistines, the Edomites and the Arabs paid him tribute. His son married a daughter of the king of Israel, and for the first time since the days of Solomon the two nations of Judah and Israel lived together in peace and friendship.

Yet this league of peace with the king of Israel brought well-nigh fatal consequences to Judah. In Israel the fifty-five years after the death of Solomon were years of confusion and anarchy. You remember that the House of Jeroboam was wiped out by Baasha, a general of the Israelite army. Baasha, after ruling for twenty-four years, was succeeded by his son Elah, but this king and all his family were destroyed within two years by Zimri, one of his cavalry officers. Zimri reigned for only seven days in Tirzah, when he was besieged by Omri, the energetic Israelite general who had been fighting the Philistines at Gibbethon. When Zimri saw that all was lost, he set fire to his palace and perished in the conflagration. Omri struggled for six years against another usurper, and finally established himself as king. A far-sighted man, he realised that the throne of Israel would not be safe until the king had a strong capital, and could grant security to the people.

Anarchy in Israel.

About eight miles north-west of Shechem, and in the midst of a well-watered and fertile countryside, there rises an isolated hill over three hundred feet high. Enclosed on three sides by the mountains of Ephraim, and open only to the west, no enemy could ever capture it with the simple weapons of those days, except from the west. Its position was impregnable, **Omri Founds Samaria.** and Omri chose it for his capital and called it Samaria after Shemer, the name of the man from whom he bought the site. From the beautiful city he built on the crest of the hill, Omri ruled Israel for six years. His son Ahab succeeded him and completed his father's work by making an alliance with the Phoenicians, who dwelt on the coast-land of northern Palestine. By this alliance Samaria was made secure on all sides, and quickly sprang into importance. The dynasty of Omri was firmly established and ruled for nearly fifty years in Israel. And even when it was destroyed, the next and every succeeding dynasty retained Samaria as the capital, so that it sometimes gave its name to the kingdom, and Israel was called Samaria.

Ahab allied himself to Phoenicia by marrying Jezebel, the daughter of Ethbaal, king of Tyre, who was also **Ahab Introduces Baal-Worship.** High Priest of the Phoenician sun-god Baal. Ethbaal himself had gained the throne of Tyre by murdering his brother, and Jezebel possessed her father's bold and depraved character. A strong-minded, callous-hearted woman who would stop at nothing to obtain what she wanted, she menaced the internal peace of Israel and caused a grave religious crisis. From Tyre she brought the worship of the Phoenician Baal and prevailed on Ahab to build a magnificient temple for her god in Samaria. In it she placed statues of Baal and other Syrian gods. She also brought with her four hundred and fifty priests from Tyre who ate at her table and enjoyed the royal favour. Through her example the worship of Baal quickly spread and corrupted the life of both the court and the people. It was far worse even than the golden calves at Dan and Bethel. In the calf-worship at least the people thought they were worshipping the God who had brought them out of Egypt. But the Phoenician Baal was an entirely new god, and its degenerate worship was so opposed to the service of the God of Israel that the two could not exist together. The challenge was direct and unmistakable.

CHAPTER 11

POINTS TO REMEMBER

Kings of Israel:

1. **Jeroboam**
   a) recalled from Egypt on death of Solomon
   b) made king by rebellious Ten Tribes
   c) introduced Calf-worship at Dan and Bethel
   d) warred with Judah, Syria, and Philistines
   e) made Tirzah his capital
   f) called in aid of Shishak, king of Egypt, to subdue the Levitical cities for him
   g) died after reign of 22 years.

2. **Nadab**
   a) son of Jeroboam
   b) reigned 2 years
   c) murdered by Baasha.

3. **Baasha**
   a) destroyed House of Jeroboam
   b) attacked Judah
   c) forced to withdraw on account of invasion by Ben-hadad king of Syria
   d) reigned 24 years.

4. **Elah**
   a) son of Baasha
   b) murdered after reign of 2 years by Zimri.

5. **Zimri**
   a) reigned only 7 days
   b) set fire to his palace on approach of Omri and perished in flames.

6. **Omri**
   a) chosen king of Israel in camp at Gibbethon
   b) struggled with Tibni for 6 years

149

c) founded Samaria
d) reigned 12 years.

7. Ahab
a) son of Omri
b) married Jezebel, daughter of Phoenician Priest-King Ethbaal
c) introduced Phoenician Baal worship into Israel.

Kings of Judah:
1. Rehoboam
a) son of Solomon
b) met Israelites at Shechem
c) refused to lighten their burdens
d) Ten Tribes rebelled against him
e) Judah and Benjamin were faithful to him
f) Priests, Levites, and Prophets went over to him when Jeroboam introduced Calf-worship
g) suffered invasion from Shishak, king of Egypt
h) fortified cities of Judah
i) warred with Jeroboam
j) reigned 17 years.

2. Abijah
his son, reigned 3 years.

3. Asa
a) son of Abijah
b) attacked by Baasha
c) called in aid of Ben-hadad
d) fortified northern fortresses of Judah
e) defeated army of Zerah the Ethiopian
f) destroyed idol-worship in Judah
g) renewed covenant to serve God faithfully
h) reigned 41 years; wise and successful king.

4. Jehoshaphat
a) son of Asa
b) re-organised and strengthened country
c) received tribute from Philistines, Edomites, and Arabs
d) made league of peace with Ahab.

KINGS OF JUDAH AND ISRAEL

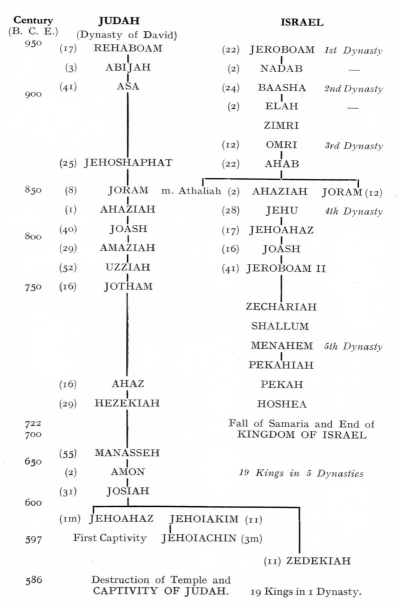

Century (B. C. E.)	JUDAH (Dynasty of David)		ISRAEL	
950	(17) REHABOAM		(22) JEROBOAM	*1st Dynasty*
	(3) ABIJAH		(2) NADAB	—
900	(41) ASA		(24) BAASHA	*2nd Dynasty*
			(2) ELAH	—
			ZIMRI	
			(12) OMRI	*3rd Dynasty*
	(25) JEHOSHAPHAT		(22) AHAB	
850	(8) JORAM m. Athaliah		(2) AHAZIAH JORAM (12)	
	(1) AHAZIAH		(28) JEHU	*4th Dynasty*
800	(40) JOASH		(17) JEHOAHAZ	
	(29) AMAZIAH		(16) JOASH	
	(52) UZZIAH		(41) JEROBOAM II	
750	(16) JOTHAM			
			ZECHARIAH	
			SHALLUM	
			MENAHEM	*5th Dynasty*
			PEKAHIAH	
	(16) AHAZ		PEKAH	
	(29) HEZEKIAH		HOSHEA	
722 700			Fall of Samaria and End of KINGDOM OF ISRAEL	
650	(55) MANASSEH			
	(2) AMON		*19 Kings in 5 Dynasties*	
600	(31) JOSIAH			
	(1m) JEHOAHAZ JEHOIAKIM (11)			
597	First Captivity JEHOIACHIN (3m)			
		(11) ZEDEKIAH		
586	Destruction of Temple and CAPTIVITY OF JUDAH.	19 Kings in 1 Dynasty.		

PART III

THE AGE OF THE PROPHETS

CHAPTER 12

ELIJAH

The beginning of the ninth century B. C. E. saw the rise of a new and powerful empire in the history of Palestine—Assyria. The Assyrian people were

The Assyrians. Semites who came originally from Babylonia and formed a colony on the banks of the river Tigris. While the great empires of Babylon, Egypt, and the Hittites fought for the possession of Palestine, Assyria was quietly developing its strength. When the great empires collapsed after the long struggle, Assyria saw its opportunity and determined to make itself master of the Mediterranean sea-board.

The chief cities of Assyria were: Nineveh, on the eastern bank of the Tigris; Calah, about twenty miles south of Nineveh; Resen, between Nineveh and Calah; and Ashur, the furthest south of all. In area the country of Assyria was at first no more than 100 miles long and 70 miles wide, but at the time of its greatest prosperity the empire stretched from the Median mountains on the east to Egypt on the west.

The soil of Assyria was very fertile, and the people engaged mainly in agriculture. Strong and well-built, they were a war-like race. Their warriors went to war in well-ordered ranks, with chariots and horses, and armed with gleaming arrows and drawn bows. Often the mere sight of them struck terror into their enemies. Moreover, they were great builders and made good use of the stone which abounded in their land. They loved painting, as well as sculpture, and in the British Museum you can see many examples of these arts. Their sculptures usually depict hunting scenes, or the tribute of defeated enemies. The Assyrians were a cruel people and their treatment of prisoners and other enemies was ghastly. One characteristic of theirs, when their empire grew, was to transport all the inhabitants of a captured district, so that they should never again know their native land.

In religion and culture the Assyrians borrowed much from the Babylonians. They worshipped the same gods, although their chief god was Ashur. Among their other gods were Nebo, who had a temple at Calah; Sin, the moon-god, and Shamas, the sun-god. The priests wielded great power, for they received lavish gifts from the superstitious worshippers, and were always consulted before any important work was undertaken. They used enchantments to drive away disease, and divination and astrology in order to have foreknowledge of the future.

The king was also high priest and chief judge, and had absolute power. Some of the kings were scholars, and it is due to the work of Ashur-bani-pal, one of the last and most renowned of the Assyrian kings, that we know so much about Assyrian life and history. This king collected a great library at Nineveh, consisting of thousands of clay tablets inscribed in Babylonian cuneiform writing. They deal with many subjects; history, litera-

ture, copies of political dispatches, letters and treaties, as
well as religious stories and charms.

Such was the people which began to appear in Syria
even before Ahab mounted the throne of Israel. In the
Ahab. year 876 B.C.E. Ashur-nazir-pal, the king of
Assyria, led an army to the Mediterranean
Sea. The Phoenician cities of Tyre, Sidon and Gebal,
among others, at once rushed to submit to him and pay
him tribute. The danger was near enough to Israel for
Ahab to determine to be at peace with all his neighbours.
We have seen that Ahab was allied to the royal house of
Tyre. He also made peace with Jehoshaphat king of
Judah. Later the alliance was sealed by the marriage
of Ahab's daughter Athaliah to Joram, the heir of Jehoshaphat. Ahab in many respects was a wise and statesmanlike king. He strengthened the defences of his kingdom and encouraged trade and commerce. His friendship with the commercial kingdom of Tyre was very
helpful in this connection. During his reign trade
flourished and the wealth of Israel increased abundantly.
The Israelite farmers sold their surplus corn and fruits
to Phoenician merchants. The nobles and traders grew
rich and, imitating the king, built themselves stone
houses. Ahab even built himself an ivory palace in
Samaria, which has only recently been discovered by
archaeologists.

As the nobles grew wealthy they sought to enlarge
their possessions. You remember that when the Children
of Israel entered Palestine under Joshua, each family
in every tribe of Israel received a portion of land which
was handed down from father to son and could never be
permanently alienated. If a farmer became poor through
a bad harvest, or through extravagance, he could sell

his inheritance, but not for ever. Every fiftieth year was observed as the Jubilee, when the land returned to its original owners and slaves became free men. In this way the Law of Moses sought to attach the people to the soil, and to create a contented peasantry.

But neither the king nor the wealthy men of Israel cared much for the Law of Moses. Under the evil influence of Jezebel, they abandoned themselves to the superstitious and corrupting worship of the Phoenician sun-god, Baal, which broke down the moral basis of the Torah. Ignoring social right and justice in the pursuit of their desires, they connived at every form of baseness. One instance recorded of this time shows how much the spiritual life of Israel had degenerated and at what low ebb was their moral sense.

Adjoining the palace of Ahab in the city of Jezreel lay the vineyard of a man named Naboth. Ahab wished to buy this vineyard from him, but Naboth replied, "God forbid that I should give the heritage of my fathers to thee."

Ahab returned to his palace, sorely displeased. Jezebel however, took the matter in hand for him. She wrote a letter to the elders of Jezreel commanding them to try Naboth on a charge of high treason, and to condemn him to death. The obsequious elders and faithless judges of Jezreel performed the diabolical command of the queen, and unjustly put Naboth to death. Then Jezebel turned to Ahab and said:

" Arise, take possession of the vineyard of Naboth the Jezreelite, who refused to give it to thee for money, for Naboth is not alive, but dead." When Ahab heard these words he went down to the vineyard of Naboth, accompanied by several of his officers. Among them was one named Jehu, of whom we shall hear more later.

This hideous crime did not go unchallenged. There were still in Israel many hundreds of God-fearing men who had not worshipped Baal. There was also in existence a trained Prophetical Order consisting of pious men who sternly denounced wrong, turpitude and injustice. Of this type was Elijah, a man of fiery energy who came from the land of Gilead to Samaria. Clothed in a hairy mantle which was bound with a girdle of leather round his loins, after the manner of the Prophets, he was afraid of no man, and fearlessly defied the Baal-worship of the court. When he heard that Ahab had gone down to take possessions of Naboth's vineyard in Jezreel, he went to confront the king.

They met at the entrance to the vineyard. Fearlessly, in the presence of Ahab and his courtiers, Elijah thundered:

"Thus saith the Lord, hast thou murdered, and wilt thou also take possession?"

Crestfallen, Ahab could only weakly answer,

"Hast thou found me, O mine enemy?"

Elijah's words produced their effect. Ahab was conscience-smitten, and, though a king, he humbled himself, and expressed his profound sorrow for the wrong he had committed.

Jezebel, however, was mistress of the kingdom. Self-willed, she asserted her dominance and trampled upon Ahab's good qualities. She hated **The Corruption of Israel.** the Prophets of Israel with a fierce hatred because they denounced the abominable Baal-worship which she had introduced in every city of Israel. In her fury she fiendishly persecuted and killed the Prophets, so that for fear of her they had to hide in caves and undergo great discomfort and privation. The moral laxity of Israel grew steadily worse. The example of Jezebel in stealing the land from its rightful owners, perverting justice and even murdering to gain her selfish ends, was followed by many. By oppressing the poor and crushing the needy, the rich extended their estates. Flagrant unrighteousness prevailed. Instead of the pure worship of God, the superstitious and grossly impure worship of the Phoenician Baal was the religion of the state. This was the root of all the evil. Elijah, the champion of true religion, could not be silent.

Before the astonished court of Ahab he appeared suddenly and prophesied:

The Challenge on Mount Carmel. "As the Lord God of Israel liveth, before whom I stand, there shall not be dew nor rain these years, but according to my word."

Then, as suddenly, he disappeared. For three years the drought afflicted the land. Harvests were spoiled, grass failed, and cattle languished. During the drought Elijah lived in the house of a widow in Zarephath, near the Phoenician city of Tyre. Ahab searched for the Prophet far and wide, but it never occurred to him to look for him in Phoenicia. At last, in the third year of the drought, Elijah boldly appeared before Ahab. When Ahab saw him he cried out:

"Is it thou, thou troubler of Israel?"

"I have not troubled Israel," Elijah sternly answered, "but thou and thy father's house, because you have forsaken the commands of the Lord and gone after Baal."

Elijah was determined to show and convince the people of Israel that there was only One God, and that Baal was a worthless idol. With this end in view he commanded Ahab to summon all Israel and the prophets of Baal to Mount Carmel. This mountain, jutting out to the

Mount Carmel, from the sea

Newtonian Illustrated-Press Service.

Ruins at Samaria

by courtesy of the Jewish National Fund.

Mediterranean Sea, was an ideal site for the test of the true God. Standing solitary above the plain, with grass and flowers covering its pleasant slopes and rocky platforms, it looked upon the sea and could be seen from every part of the land. On Mount Carmel Elijah addressed the assembled people and challenged the prophets of Baal.

" How long," he asked, " halt ye between two opinions? If the Lord be God, follow Him, and if Baal be god then follow him."

The Israelites stood in silence and made no answer. Elijah proposed a simple test. The prophets of Baal were four hundred and fifty in number, while he was only one man. " Let each party prepare a sacrifice," he said, " and put no fire under it. The God who will answer with fire, He will be God."

" The thing is good," shouted the Israelites.

The prophets of Baal prepared their sacrifice and, leaping frenziedly about, called upon their god from morning till evening, but received no answer. At noon Elijah mocked them, saying,

" Call loudly, for he is a god. Either he talketh, or is on a journey. Peradventure he sleepeth and must be awakened."

The prophets of Baal wildly gashed and cut themselves with swords and spears, but all to no avail.

Towards evening Elijah took twelve stones, according to the number of the Tribes of Israel, and built an altar to God. On it he laid the sacrifice anad drenched it with water. Then he uttered this simple prayer:

" O Lord, God of Abraham, Isaac and Israel, let it be known this day that Thou art God in Israel and I am Thy servant.... Answer me, O Lord, answer me, that this people may know that Thou, Lord, art God."

No sooner had he finished speaking than fire fell from the sky and consumed the sacrifice.

When the Israelites saw the miracle, they were overawed. Bowing their heads in reverence, they shouted:

"The Lord, He is God! The Lord, He is God!"

Urged on by Elijah, they seized the prophets of Baal and massacred them by the river Kishon. The test on Mount Carmel was followed by a thunder-storm which ended the long and terrible drought. Soon the heavens grew black with clouds, and the sorely-needed rain poured abundantly down upon the dry earth. Elijah was victorious. He felt that the worship of Baal had been decisively wiped out from Israel and that faith in the One God had been restored.

However, his triumph was short-lived. Jezebel was by no means defeated. She regarded the events on **Jezebel's Wrath.** Mount Carmel as a coincidence, and was moved to fury by the murder of her prophets. She was also afraid of the effects of Elijah's influence, and sent a messenger to him with these threatening words:

"The gods do so to me, and more also, if by this time to-morrow I make not thy life as the life of one of them." Worn out by his struggle, Elijah wearily fled to Beer-sheba, where he left his servant. Alone, he went further south to the desert of Sinai, and considered his work a failure. While resting in one of the caves, which abound there, he saw a vision. First he heard a shattering wind, then an earthquake and the noise of a great fire. Next he heard a still small voice.

"What doest thou here, Elijah?" it asked.

"I have been very zealous for the Lord God of Hosts," he answered. "For the Children of Israel have forsaken

Thy covenant, broken down Thine altars and slain Thy prophets.... I alone am left, and they seek to take away my life.''

But Elijah's work on earth was not quite over, and his experience at Sinai strengthened him and taught him to be patient. He was encouraged to know that he was not the only Israelite faithful to God. For among the farmers and shepherds of Israel there were many who had turned away from the immoral worship of Baal, scorned the luxurious life of the rich, and longed for the reformation of Israel. One of these farmers, Elisha of Abel-Meholah, left his home to follow Elijah, and became his disciple and attendant. There was also a party of Nazarites founded by Jonadab the son of Rechab, who would not build houses or cultivate land. Living simple lives in tents like shepherds, they drank no wine, and called themselves Rechabites, after the name of Jonadab's father. In this way did this little group of nomadic people protest against the corrupt life of the cities of Israel.

Opposition to Jezebel.

Elijah turned back to the land of Israel and to Syria, where great events were about to happen. The long peace between Israel and Syria during the days of Omri and Ahab was broken by the Syrian king Ben-hadad II. This monarch probably feared the growing power of Ahab, and decided to subdue him completely. Accompanied by a large army and thirty-two vassal kings, Ben-hadad appeared before the gates of Samaria. Ahab was prepared to submit to his overlord, but finding Ben-hadad's conditions harsh and humiliating, made ready for war. Encouraged by a prophet, the king of Israel made a surprise-attack and defeated the Syrian army. The following year the

Wars with Syria.

Syrian host, greatly strengthened, returned to the attack. This time they chose to battle in the plains, which were more suitable than the hills for their chariots and horses. Ahab on this occasion achieved a still greater victory, and Ben-hadad was made a prisoner of war. The Syrian king, who had a high opinion of the kings of Israel and considered them merciful, abjectly begged for his life before Ahab. In those days it was more usual to torture and kill a captured enemy than to send him away with honour. But Ahab was lenient. He made a treaty with Ben-hadad, and the two kings parted in peace.

Within a short time, however, they were both facing a grave danger. In the year 853 B. C. E., Shalmaneser III, king of Assyria, following in the footsteps of his father, made an attempt to conquer the Mediterranean sea-board. Ben-hadad, as the most powerful monarch in the Syrian confederacy, took the lead in opposing the advance of the Assyrian army. Under Ben-hadad were the kings of the other states in Syria and northern Palestine. From the Assyrian record of the battle we learn that Ahab's host of 2,000 chariots and 10,000 footmen was the second largest contigent in the force. The two armies of Syria and Assyria, each with about 80,000 men, faced each other at Karkar on the banks of the river Orontes in Syria. Both sides fought fiercely and suffered heavy losses. Shalmaneser, however, did not advance, and returned to his own land.

Battle Against Assyria.

Immediately, the allies fell out among themselves. Ben-hadad, elated no doubt at his partial success against the Assyrians, violated the treaty by refusing to restore to Ahab the city of Ramoth-Gilead according to his promise. To recover the

Ahab's Death.

city by force, Ahab, accompanied by Jehoshaphat of Judah, marched to battle against the Syrians in Gilead. Though mortally wounded by a chance arrow, the king of Israel heroically stayed in his chariot to encourage his men until the sun had set. At evening time the Israelites retreated from the battlefield and brought back the body of their dead king to be buried in Samaria.

Thus ended the reign of one of Israel's best-known kings. He himself possessed noble and kingly qualities, and in many ways lent lustre to the history of his people. But he weakly allowed his wife Jezebel to introduce into Israel the corrupting Baal-worship of Phoenicia, with all its horrors and depravity. Thus, while he strengthened his kingdom politically and economically, he had to contend with the opposition of the Prophets. At his death, Jezebel lost her power. Her elder son Ahaziah reigned less than two years when he was killed through an accident. His brother Joram succeeded him and reigned for twelve years. He refused to follow the Baal-worship of his mother, although he still maintained the golden calves of Jeroboam.

Yet the danger of the Baal-worship was real so long as the family of Jezebel existed. A daughter of Jezebel, Athaliah, had married Joram, son of Jehoshaphat, king of Judah. Jehoshaphat was very friendly with the kings of Israel. We have seen how he went with Ahab to battle against the Syrians to retrieve Ramoth-Gilead. Furthermore, he co-operated with Ahaziah of Israel in sending a merchant fleet to Tarshish, thus reviving the navy of Solomon. Unfortunately the ships were wrecked in a storm at the Red Sea port of Ezion-geber, so the expedition failed. The king of Judah joined the king of Israel

The Danger to Judah.

in other enterprises too, and the prophetic party feared that the evil of Baal-worship would extend also to Judah. It was for this reason that before his end Elijah commissioned Elisha to anoint Jehu, the young officer who had accompanied Ahab to Naboth's vineyard, to be king over Israel in place of Joram.

With this final charge, Elijah thought his struggle against the Baal-worship introduced by Jezebel was over. The most mysterious of all Israel's prophets, he came unheralded from the east of Jordan to challenge the growing power of the disastrous Baal-worship in Israel. On Mount Carmel he stood majestically, alone and full of faith, against the four hundred and fifty false prophets of Baal. His abrupt coming and going, his remarkable appearance, and his blazing passion for righteousness, marked him out as an ideal mouthpiece of God. His ardent labour was not in vain. Before crossing the Jordan to be heard of no more, he had trained a faithful successor who would carry on and complete his work, and not rest until the last trace of Baal-worship was uprooted out of Israel.

CHAPTER 12

POINTS TO REMEMBER

The Assyrians:
- a) Semites from Babylonia who founded colony on banks of River Tigris
- b) country — 100 miles long by 70 miles wide
- c) chief cities — Nineveh, Calah, Resen, Ashur
- d) chief gods — Ashur, Nebo, Sin, Shamas
- e) occupation — farming
- f) character — strong, warlike, cruel; loved painting and sculpture; favourite sport, hunting
- g) great libraries collected by scholar kings
- h) political events:
  - 1) Ashurnazirpal II marched to Mediterranean Sea, 876 **B. C. E.**
  - 2) Shalmaneser III met Syrian confederacy at Battle of Karkar 853 **B. C. E.**

Kings of Israel:
7. Ahab (ctd.):
- a) wise and statesmanlike king
  - 1) made peace with Jehoshaphat of Judah and gave his daughter Athaliah as wife to Joram son of Jehoshaphat
  - 2) strengthened defences of his kingdom
  - 3) encouraged trade and commerce
- b) prosperity of reign — built ivory palace in Samaria
- c) was ruled by Jezebel
  - 1) built temple to Baal in Samaria
  - 2) allowed Prophets to be persecuted
  - 3) had Naboth killed and took possession of his vineyard
- d) foreign wars:
  - 1) defeated Ben-hadad II of Syria and spared his life
  - 2) joined Ben-hadad II against Assyria at Battle of Karkar, 853
  - 3) was killed in battle against Ben-hadad at Ramoth-Gilead, 853, after reign of 22 years.

8. Ahaziah:
- a) son of Ahab
- b) reigned 2 years
- c) died as result of accident

9. Joram:
- a) brother of Ahaziah
- b) refused to follow Baal-worship of Jezebel
- c) maintained Calf-worship of Jeroboam

Kings of Judah:
4. Jehoshaphat (ct.):
- a) joined Ahab in Battle of Ramoth-Gilead
- b) co-operated with Ahaziah in sending merchant fleet to Tarshish.

Prophets:
Elijah:
- a) origin — came from Gilead
- b) description — clothed in hairy mantle bound with leather girdle round his loins
- c) acts
    1) denounced Ahab in Naboth's vineyard
    2) challenged power of Baal-worship on Mount Carmel
    3) was threatened with death by Jezebel
    4) vision at Sinai
    5) took Elisha as his disciple
    6) commanded Elisha to anoint Jehu king of Israel
    7) disappeared after crossing Jordan with Elisha
- d) his fight for social justice and for the purity of religion.

CHAPTER 13

ELISHA

The death of Ahab marked the beginning of the collapse of Omri's dynasty in Israel. To assert their independence, the Moabites, under their energetic king Mesha, rebelled against Israel. Joram, accompanied by Jehoshaphat of Judah and the tributary king of Edom, marched against Moab. After crossing the dreary and stony desert of Edom for seven days, they attacked Moab from the south-west. The Moabites fell upon the allied forces, but, severely repulsed, they retreated to their cities. The three kings pursued the fleeing army and laid waste the land of Moab. But the Moabites put up a stubborn resistance and it seems that the allied kings returned from the war without subjugating Moab, which incidentally regained its independence. Before the revolt, Moab, a rich pastoral people, used to pay an annual tribute to Israel of 100,000 sheep, and 100,000 rams, with their wool. The story of this rebellion is related in the early chapters of the Second Book of Kings. In the Louvre at Paris you can see a famous monument which gives an account of the war by Mesha, king of Moab, himself. This stone monument, which is known as the Moabite Stone, was found at Dibon, in the land of Moab, about four miles north of the river Arnon. Written in ancient Hebrew, it is most valuable for the light it sheds upon the life and culture of the tribes then living on the eastern borders of

The Rebellion of Moab.

Palestine. Opposite is a photograph of this monument, and here is a translation of a short extract from the inscription:

" I am Mesha, son of Chemosh king of Moab, the Daibonite. My father reigned over Moab for thirty years and I reigned after my father . . . Omri was king of Israel and he afflicted Moab for many days. And his son (Ahab) succeeded him and he also said, I will afflict Moab." The record goes on to state how Mesha reconquered the cities of Moab from Israel and set up this monument as a memorial of his victories.

The example of Moab must have fired the Edomites to throw off the yoke of Judah. With the aid of the

Jehoshaphat Dies.

Moabites and Ammonites, they invaded Judea by way of Engedi, the famous oasis on the western bank of the Dead Sea about thirty miles south of Jericho. Jehoshaphat went out to meet them in the wilderness of Judea, but there was no necessity to engage in battle with them. In this wild district, full of hills and water-courses, the enemy quarrelled among themselves and proved an easy prey to Jehoshaphat's army. The Judeans returned to their cities, joyful and laden with spoil. But within a few years Jehoshaphat died, leaving the kingdom to his son Joram, the brother-in-law of Joram of Israel. This Joram of Judah had an unhappy reign. On ascending the throne he put to death his six brothers and several nobles of Judah. In his days the Edomites again rebelled, this time more successfully, and established an independent kingdom. He also suffered from an invasion of Philistines and Arabs from the west, who ravaged Judah and carried off all his sons, except the youngest, as hostages. He ruled only eight years, and no one one regretted his death.

The Moabite Stone

Obelisk of Shalmaneser III, King of Assyria

(the second row from the top depicts Jehu's envoy kissing the dust of the earth before the king of Assyria)

World of the Bible.

His youngest son Ahaziah, who succeeded him, had been reigning for less than a year when he was swept away by the onrush of events in Israel.

Joram of Israel was king for twelve troubled years. After the Moabite rebellion he was faced with continuous raids by the Syrians. At last, however, **Joram of Israel.** Ben-hadad II of Syria was murdered by one of his counsellors, Hazael, who usurped the throne. Joram considered this an excellent opportunity to recover Ramoth-Gilead, where Ahab had lost his life. Together with Ahaziah of Judah he marched against and captured the city. Hazael fought desperately to regain it, and in the course of the battle Joram was wounded. He retired to the city of Jezreel, leaving the fortress in charge of his officers. Ahaziah followed Joram to Jezreel.

This moment Elisha, the successor of Elijah, chose to strike a death-blow at the House of Ahab. After the **Elisha and the** disappearance of Elijah, Elisha had lived **Guilds of the** with the guilds of the Prophets at Gilgal, **Prophets.** Bethel and Jericho. He had also visited many other cities in Israel, and had gone even to Damascus in Syria, where Hazael had consulted him during the illness of Ben-hadad. Wherever he went his fame as a Prophet, and his gentle and sympathetic nature, made him a welcome guest. In the city of Shunem, a wealthy and hospitable woman provided a small room, simply furnished, with a table, chairs, a bed and a candlestick, for the use of the Prophet and his man-servant Gehazi.

Elisha realised that so long as the dynasty of Ahab ruled there was no hope for the true religion of Israel. He knew that among the commanders at Ramoth-Gilead there was Jehu, the officer who had heard Elijah utter his fearless denunciation of Ahab in the vineyard of

Naboth. This man, you remember, had been marked out as the future king of Israel. To Ramoth-Gilead Elisha accordingly sent one of the sons of the Prophets, with orders to anoint Jehu king in the name of God. The scene at Ramoth-Gilead was highly dramatic. The young man, dressed in the hairy mantle which the Prophets wore, came to the Israelite headquarters in the fortress and gasped:

" I have a word for thee, O captain."

The captains were sitting at table, and Jehu asked, " For which of all of us?"

" For thee, O captain," was the answer.

The two men retired into a private chamber. There the young man poured a flask of oil on Jehu's head, thus anointing him to be king of Israel, and then fled. Jehu returned to the company and told them what had occurred. Immediately the captains took off their cloaks, laid them at Jehu's feet as a sign of submission, blew upon trumpets and shouted,

" Long live King Jehu!"

Jehu was astute, and a man of action. He forbade any one to leave the fortress and report the news in
Jehu Destroys the House of Ahab and the Baal-Worship. Jezreel. He himself, however, rode furiously to Jezreel, to meet the wounded king. When Joram saw the chariot of Jehu coming to the city, he rashly went out with Ahaziah to learn the reason for this sudden return of his captain from the battle-front. They met, ominously enough, in the ground which had once been the vineyard of Naboth.

" Is it peace, Jehu?" asked Joram.

" What peace can there be so long as the idol worship of thy mother Jezebel, and her witchcraft continue?" was his answer.

Joram realised his danger and turned to flee, shouting to his nephew,

"There is treachery, O Ahaziah!"

Jehu with his own hand drew his bow and killed Joram. Ahaziah, also, was murdered by Jehu's men. Meanwhile, Jehu hastened to Jezreel, where Jezebel the old queen still lived in her palace. Her, too, Jehu ordered to be slain. Then he sent to Samaria and brought about the death of all Ahab's family. Not content with this, he ordered the execution of all the brothers of Ahaziah, king of Judah. It was his intention to stamp out utterly the worship of the Phoenician Baal from Israel. To this end he proclaimed a great feast to Baal in the temple at Samaria. Every Israelite who worshipped Baal flocked to the feast, so that the concourse filled the temple from end to end. Jehu had placed eighty guards outside the temple. At a given signal during the service, the guards rushed into the building and killed every one of the worshippers. None escaped. They also pulled down the idolatrous altar and left the temple in ruins.

Thus Jehu exterminated the worship of Baal out of Israel. But the terrible slaughter with which he effected it shocked the conscience of the people and left a scar which was never effaced.

And yet, though he had destroyed the Baal-worship, Jehu, being insincere, did not return to the Law of Moses. The removal of possible rivals to the throne concerned him more than the reformation of the people. He had misgivings that, if he followed the Law of Moses, the people would again serve God in Jerusalem and consequently return to the House of David. So he retained the worship of the calves which Jeroboam had set up in Dan and Bethel.

Jehu was now firmly established upon the throne, and set about strengthening the position of Israel.   He could not count upon the support of either Phoenicia or Judah.   In Judah, Athaliah, the daughter of Ahab and Jezebel, had murdered all her grandsons and made herself the ruling queen.   Fortunately, however, one infant, Joash, was saved from the massacre by his aunt, the wife of Jehoiada the High Priest.   For six years the child was hidden in the Temple.   In the seventh year he was brought out and proclaimed king of Judah by the High Priest, in the presence of the people.   Athaliah rushed from her palace to the Temple, crying,

Athaliah of Judah Overthrown.

"Treachery!   Treachery!"

At the command of Jehoiada, she was hurried away from the sacred precincts and put to death.   The young king Joash ascended the throne and was guided for many years by his wise protector Jehoiada.   Under his guidance, the idolatrous Baal-worship of Athaliah was destroyed and the religious steadfastness of the country restored. The Temple was kept in good repair, and the people lived happily in their villages and towns.   The Davidic dynasty had been saved.

Meanwhile in Israel Jehu sought a new friend, Assyria, against his Syrian foe.   The king of Assyria, Shalmaneser III, made many expeditions into Syria, but without much success.   His sixteenth expedition was made in 841 B. C. E., the year in which Jehu usurped the throne of Israel.   This time Hazael of Syria suffered a severe defeat and was even besieged in his capital, Damascus.   Jehu thought it wise to send presents to Shalmaneser and be at peace with him.   Shalmaneser set up a monument of his victory, the

The Black Obelisk of Shalmaneser.

famous Black Obelisk, shown facing page 166. On it
Israelites can be seen bringing tribute to the Assyrian
king. The tribute of Jehu is said to have consisted of
"silver, gold, a golden cup, golden vases, golden buckets,
lead, a staff for the hand of the king, and sceptres."
Shalmaneser came only once more with his army to the
Mediterranean sea-coast. After that he was occupied
with a great rebellion in his empire until his death.
His son was too much concerned with wars in the empire
and its northern borders to venture far westwards.

The result was that the Syrians turned on Israel with
greater fury. The Syrian king captured the whole land
Hazael and of Gilead and Bashan, east of Jordan,
Ben-hadad III and cut off the tribes of Gad, Reuben, and
of Syria. part of Manasseh from Israel. In the days
of Jehu's son Jehoahaz the political condition of Israel
grew even worse. Hazael, and his son Ben-hadad III,
continued to harass Israel, whose army was finally
reduced to fifty horsemen and ten chariots, and ten
thousand footmen. Syrian armies plundered the land
and committed abominable atrocities. Troops of Syrian
robbers over-ran the farms of Northern Israel and Gilead,
burnt the homesteads, seized the corn and fruits, killed
the aged and the infants, and took captive the young
men and girls.

These were dark days for Israel, and a famine which
lasted for seven years increased the wretchedness of the
people. Yet Elisha the Prophet still tried to keep up
their courage, and counselled both king and people not
to submit to Syria. To the ordinary man this faith of
Elisha seemed foolish, especially when Ben-hadad III of
Syria invaded Israel and laid siege to Samaria. On
Elisha's advice the city held out heroically even when

the inhabitants were dying of hunger. Beside himself
with desperation, king Jehoahaz determined to take the
life of Elisha.   The Prophet, however, sat with the elders
of the people in his house, and confidently declared that
the Syrians would flee from the city, leaving their camp
with its rich stores as spoil for the Israelites.

And it was so.   One night the Syrians, encamping
outside Samaria, heard the tramp of horses and chariots
on the plains.   They were terror-struck.

" The king of Israel has hired the kings of the Hittites
and the kings of the Egyptians to come against us,"
they said to one another. Immediately they fled for their
lives, leaving their tents, and their horses and asses to
the mercy of the Israelites.

The relief of the besieged citizens knew no bounds when
they learnt of the miraculous flight of the Syrians.   This
event enhanced the reputation and honour

Elisha's Work.

of Elisha.   Even the Syrians respected
him and sought his advice.   Once, Naaman, the chief
captain of the Syrian army, who was a leper, came in
great state to Elisha to be cured of his disease.   Naaman
stood at the door of the Prophet's house, with his chariot
and horses, and surrounded by a large retinue.   He
thought the Prophet would come out to him, perform
some magic signs, and the leprosy would depart.   Instead,
Elisha sent his servant Gehazi to Naaman with this
simple message:

" Go and bathe seven times in the Jordan, and thy
flesh shall return to thee and be clean."   Naaman at
first was disappointed and angry, but his attendants
prevailed upon him to do the Prophet's bidding, and he
was healed.   So grateful was he that he returned to
Elisha and promised to worship no other god than the

God of Israel. Elisha refused to accept any gift from Naaman, thus showing him that he was different from the sorcerers of Syria, who took payment for the miracles they professed to perform.

Joash succeeded his father Jehoahaz as king of Israel, and during his reign of sixteen years defeated the Syrians three times in battle. In his days Adad-nirari III of Assyria struck low the power of Syria, so that they left Israel in peace.

Elisha died in the reign of Joash of Israel, after serving as a Prophet for over sixty years. He had lived through the reign of six kings of Israel and four kings of Judah. It is hard to estimate the importance of his work and influence. More is written about him in the Books of Kings than about any other Prophet of Israel or Judah. His life was an epoch in itself. When as a young man he followed Elijah, the state of Israel had been grave. The corrupting influence of Jezebel seemed all-powerful, and it looked as though Israel would sink to a mere province of Phoenicia and lose its identity. This crisis was met by the rebellion of Jehu. But the rise of Hazael of Syria threatened an equally great danger to the new dynasty of Jehu. Only the unfailing courage and firm faith of Elisha that Israel would not perish sustained his people. His courage and faith were rewarded; at his death he left Israel free from the menace of Syria, and dwelling in peace upon its own land.

CHAPTER 13

POINTS TO REMEMBER

Kings of Israel:

9. **Joram** (ctd.):
   a) reigned 12 years
   b) lost kingdom of Moab — the Moabite Stone
   c) suffered continuous raids from Syrians — was wounded in
      Battle of Ramoth-Gilead
   d) was murdered by Jehu.

10. **Jehu:**
    a) Founded fourth dynasty in Israel
    b) Rise to power
       1) was anointed king by prophet in camp at Ramoth-Gilead
       2) murdered Joram of Israel and brought about death of
          Ahaziah of Judah
       3) destroyed Ahab's family.
    c) wiped out all traces of Baal-worship from Israel
    d) maintained Calf-worship of Jeroboam
    e) sought protection of Assyria — paid tribute to Shalmaneser
       III (the Black Obelisk of Shalmaneser) 841 B. C. E.
    f) reigned 28 years.

11. **Jehoahaz:**
    a) son of Jehu
    b) reigned 17 years
    c) suffered from Syrian attacks
       1) Gilead and Bashan lost to Israel
       2) army reduced to 50 horsemen and 10 chariots
       3) Samaria besieged.

12. **Joash:**
    a) son of Jehoahaz
    b) reigned 16 years
    c) defeated Syrians 3 times in battle.

Kings of Judah:

4. Jehoshaphat (ctd):
   a) joined Joram of Israel in attack on Moab
   b) repulsed invasion of Edomites, Moabites and Ammonites in south of Palestine
   c) reigned 25 years.

5. Joram:
   a) son of Jehoshaphat, and brother-in-law of Joram of Israel
   b) reigned 8 years
   c) put to death his six brothers and several nobles of Judah
   d) lost kingdom of Edom
   e) suffered invasion of Philistines and Arabs, who carried off his sons (except youngest) as hostages.

6. Ahaziah:
   a) son of Joram
   b) reigned 1 year
   c) joined Joram of Israel in expedition against Ramoth-Gilead
   d) was killed by Jehu's men.

Athaliah, queen-mother, murdered all her grandsons, except one who was concealed in the Temple, and ruled the country by force for 7 years. She was put to death in the seventh year, when the true heir to the throne was brought out of hiding and anointed king.

7. Joash:
   a) son of Ahaziah
   b) saved by wife of Jehoiada the High Priest from Athaliah's massacre of Ahaziah's children
   c) was anointed king when 7 years old
   d) reigned 40 years
   e) was guided in first part of reign by High Priest Jehoiada
   f) kept Temple in good repair.

Prophets:
Elisha:
   a) farmer from Abel-Meholah
   b) became disciple and successor of Elijah

- c) lived with **guilds** of Prophets at Gilgal, Bethel and Jericho after disappearance of Elijah
- d) was provided with a room in the town of Shunem by a wealthy, pious woman there
- e) caused Jehu to be anointed king of Israel
- f) kept up courage of king and people in dark days of Syrian oppression
- g) prophesied that Syrian army besieging Samaria would flee without taking the city
- h) was consulted by Hazael and by Naaman, the Syrians
- i) was Prophet for over 60 years
- j) died in reign of Joash of Israel.

CHAPTER 14

AMOS

During the lifetime of the High Priest Jehoiada, the kingdom of Judah was happy and prosperous. But **Events in Judah.** when he died Joash fell into the hands of bad advisers who encouraged him to neglect the true service of God for the corrupt worship of the Canaanites. There were many in Judah who saw the danger of this idolatry, and they fearlessly condemned it. Zechariah the son of Jehoiada, in particular, cried out to the people:

" Why do ye transgress the commandments of the Lord?... Because ye have forsaken the Lord, He will forsake you."

These words infuriated Joash, and he ordered Zechariah to be stoned to death in the very courtyard of the Temple. The crime, and the gross ingratitude of the king, raised up many enemies against Joash, and he was murdered in his palace in the fortieth year of his reign. His son Amaziah, who succeeded him, put the murderers to death, but spared their children, according to the command of the Torah which says that children should not be put to death for the sins of their fathers.

Amaziah re-organised the army and attacked the Edomites in the Valley of Salt, sout-west of the Dead Sea. He was completely successful, and captured their fortress, afterwards called Joktheel. The relations between the two kingdoms of Judah and Israel were not as friendly as they had been in the days of Omri's dynasty. Amaziah may have planned to make Israel a part of his kingdom. If this was his design, he was sadly disappointed. Elated by his victory over the Edomites, he challenged Joash king of Israel to battle. Joash contemptuously laughed at the threat, but when provoked, he invaded Judah and severely defeated the Judean army at Beth-shemesh. Amaziah was forced to follow Joash as a prisoner in his triumphal procession to Jerusalem, and was so humiliated that for the rest of his reign he was almost tributary to the king of Israel.

Joash king of Israel was succeeded, after a reign of sixteen years, by his son Jeroboam II. This king ruled Israel for a period of forty-one years, **Jeroboam II and Uzziah.** and brought back to his country the glory and prosperity of Solomon's days. Against Syria, which had been weakened by the attacks of Assyria, Jeroboam waged war with confidence and success. He even captured Damascus and brought it once again under the dominion of Israel. Contemporary with him in Judah was king Uzziah. This son of Amaziah also enjoyed a long reign, and achieved for Judah what Jeroboam II did for Israel. He reconquered the territory in the south which had once been part of Solomon's empire. His greatest military enterprise was to regain possession of the important Edomite harbour of Elath by the Red Sea. This port has been called the " Gateway of Arabia," for from it branch the roads leading to Arabia, Egypt, and Syria. The wealth of Arabia passed through Elath, and by recovering it Uzziah made Judah master of this trade. To safeguard the merchant-caravans from the wild Bedouin tribes which inhabit the district, Uzziah built many fortresses in the hills of Edom. He

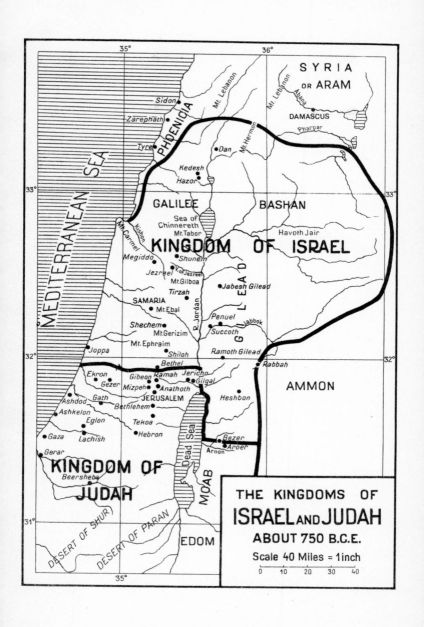

THE KINGDOMS OF
ISRAEL AND JUDAH
ABOUT 750 B.C.E.

Scale 40 Miles = 1 inch

0   10   20   30   40

also repaired and strengthened the fortifications of Jerusalem. His army was well organised and provided with shields, spears, helmets, coats of armour, bows, and slings. With his forces Uzziah advanced against the Philistines and broke down the high walls of their famous cities, Gath and Ashdod. On the other side of Jordan the Ammonites were subdued and paid him tribute.

Thus in the early part of the eigth century B. C. E. Israel and Judah, free from the fear of Syria and Egypt, **The Prosperity** were prosperous and powerful. We find no **of Israel and** record of war between Judah and Israel, **Judah.** and for nearly fifty years both nations must have felt happy and secure.

Uzziah of Judah loved the land and encouraged agriculture. He had many wells dug in the plains where shepherds tended innumerable flocks of sleep and other cattle. On the sunny hill-slopes peasants and vine-dressers cultivated vineyards and orchards. The country-side was dotted with little wooden dwellings, simple huts where the shepherds lived. Sometimes the roar of a lion or the growl of a bear told the shepherd that his flock was being attacked, and he would rush to save them.

In Israel life was lived on a more impressive scale than in Judah. The plains and valleys stretched over larger areas, and the country in general was more open. Villages and towns abounded, and magnificent buildings of stone, and of ivory too, beautified the spacious squares and pleasant streets of the cities. The wealthy nobles and traders of Israel possessed both summer and winter houses. In gorgeous and richly-furnished rooms they lay upon ivory couches and ate the most luxurious foods. Musicians played before them while they ate, and their meal was not complete without bowls of strong wine

secure impunity for their heartless oppression of the poor.

With such men in power, justice was often perverted. Bribery corrupted many a judge, and, since the poor had no bribes to offer, they had little chance of getting their rights in any lawsuit which they might bring before the judges who sat in the gate of the city. So their condition sank lower and lower, while the wealth of Samaria increased and its rich men and nobles lived on the fat of the land. It was a superficial civilisation, hollow, and with no real foundation.

Naturally, there were many earnest men in Israel who hated the life they saw around them. Neighbourly kindness and the charity and honesty which spring from true religion cannot have been absolutely wanting. But it was the bad side which roused a Prophet from Judea named Amos. This man was a herdsman in the hilly country round Tekoa. From the hills on which he fed his flock he could always see the desolation of the wilderness of Judea, stretching from the Central Plateau to the edge of the Dead Sea. The wild and untamed forces of nature impressed him, yet he realised that God controlled them. So, also, God controlled the life of man. Suddenly, how we cannot tell, Amos was inspired to be a Prophet. Bethel, the royal sanctuary of Jeroboam II, was only twenty miles to the north of Tekoa, and thither he went, with the word of God on his lips. His message was one which surprised and shocked his hearers. Amos had heard about the nations which surrounded Israel, and their deeds. He knew how savagely the Syrians had plundered Gilead; how barbarously the Philistines and Phoenicians had behaved in capturing prisoners of war and selling them as slaves to the wild Edomites; how

Amos, the Judean Shepherd.

the Ammonites, Edomites and Moabites had seized the moment of Syria's downfall to enlarge their own territory and practise unheard-of cruelties. All this Amos knew and condemned, and he threatened terrible retribution to the perpetrators. But his special message was for Israel who, because they knew God's Law, should have acted in a better manner than their neighbours.

" You only have I known of all the families of the earth, Therefore will I punish you for all your iniquities," declared Amos in the name of God.

His hearers were thunderstruck. They believed themselves to be the chosen people of God, and looked upon **His Denunciations.** the long prosperity of Jeroboam II's reign as a sign of His favour and protection. That they were doing wrong, and that God would punish them, was unbelievable. To them the Day of the Lord was the great Day when the surrounding nations would recognise them as the chosen people and serve them.

" Not so," thundered the shepherd from the Judean hills. " The Day of the Lord is darkness, and not light, thick darkness, and not brightness."

It will be for Israel a day of punishment, for following false gods, oppressing the poor, perverting justice, living a life of sinful extravangance, and disregarding every call to righteousness.

And the successive disasters that Amos threatened were dreadful indeed. In prophetic visions he saw calamity after calamity falling upon the people of Israel; earthquake, drought, and pestilence. Two years after he began to prophesy, an earthquake did occur in Palestine, so severe that the memory of it remained for generations afterwards. Blasting and mildew in the corn-

fields, locust plagues in the orchards and gardens, failure
of the rains before the harvest — all these visitations of
nature which troubled Palestine towards the end of
Jeroboam's reign, Amos regarded as a warning to the
people to turn from their ease and luxury to the true
service of God.

But the Israelites would not listen. They went on
in their carefree and indifferent way, paying no heed
to the words of the Prophet. They had confidence in
the House of Jeroboam and in their idols. Against
them Amos now directed his indignation. In Bethel
the Prophet uttered a dirge in the presence of the
incredulous Israelites:

> "Fallen, no more to rise, is the virgin daughter
> of Israel:
>
> She is cast down upon the ground, there is none
> to raise her."

For, said Amos, war was coming upon the land. An
enemy was approaching who would decimate Israel and
exile the remainder beyond Damscus.

> "The high places of Isaac shall be desolate;
>
> The sanctuaries of Israel shall be laid waste;
>
> And I shall rise against the House of Jeroboam
> with the sword," saith the Lord.

Consternation seized the people. Who could this
enemy be who would exile them beyond Damascus? Syria
was powerless. No other nation could rise
The Priest of against Israel. Amos must be a conspir-
Bethel Alarmed. ator. Amaziah, the priest of Bethel, sent
a message to Jeroboam with these words:

> "Amos hath conspired against thee in the midst
> of the House of Israel. The land is not able to bear
> all his words. For he saith that Jeroboam shall

die by the sword, and Israel shall surely be exiled from his land."

Not satisfied with this alone, Amaziah addressed Amos contemptuously:

" Seer, flee to the land of Judah and eat there bread, and there prophesy. And prophesy no more at Bethel, for it is a royal sanctuary and a king's chapel."

By these taunts he intended to insult Amos, intimating that he was like the many false prophets both in Israel and Judah, who prophesied for money. But Amos indignantly replied:

" I am no professional prophet, but a herdsman and a dresser of sycamore fruit. And the Lord took me from following the sheep and said unto me, Go prophesy unto My people Israel."

The enemy which Amos saw approaching was none other than the Assyrian. Although about the year 750 B. C. E., when Amos prophesied, there seemed little danger from that quarter, the Prophet was firmly convinced that Israel would be taken into exile by the Assyrians. It was the custom of this people, you remember, to transport the inhabitants of a conquered country to another district, where they would be swallowed up and lost as a nation. This fate Amos now saw was lying in wait for Israel, despite all their indifference and self confidence.

Yet the Prophets of Israel were no mere prophets of woe. They laid bare the weaknesses and imperfections **Amos' Message** of the people and chastised them with **of Consolation** burning words. But they also believed **and Hope.** in the purpose of Israel's existence. Amos is the first of the Prophets who has left a Book of his Prophecies. His words, he realised, were meant not only for his time, but for as long as the descendants of the Patriarchs existed on earth.   So we find that after all his passionate denunciátion of Israel's backsliding and the punishment which it must involve, the Book ends with a beautiful passage of consolation and hope:

" I shall not utterly destroy the House of Jacob," says Amos in the name of God,

" But behold, I shall sift the House of Israel among all the nations

As one sifts with a sieve,

And not a grain shall fall to the ground . . .

In that day I shall set up the tabernacle of David which has fallen,

And I shall close up its breaches,

And its ruins shall I raise up,

And I shall rebuild it as in the days of old . . ."

POINTS TO REMEMBER

Kings of Israel:

12. **Joash** (ctd.):

    a) defeated Amaziah of Judah at Battle of Beth-shemesh and entered Jerusalem in triumph.

13. **Jeroboam II:**

    a) son of Joash

    b) reigned 41 years

    c) restored dominions of Solomon to Israel — captured Damascus

    d) prosperity of long reign:

        1) peace with Judah

        2) villages and towns abounded

        3) houses of stone and ivory

        4) nobles possessed summer and winter houses

        5) rooms richly-furnished — ivory couches

        6) luxurious foods

        7) music

        8) wines in profusion

    e) calamities towards end of reign:

        1) earthquake

        2) drought

        3) pestilence

        4) blasting and mildew in the cornfields

        5) locust plagues in orchards and gardens

        6) failure of rains before the harvest

Kings of Judah:

7. **Joash** (ctd.):

    a) turned to idolatry on death of High Priest Jehoiada

    b) ordered death of Jehoiada's son Zechariah, who protested against this return to idolatry

    c) was murdered in fourtieth year of his reign.

8. Amaziah:

    a) son of Joash

    b) put his father's murderers to death

    c) re-organised army

    d) captured Edomite fortress of Joktheel

    e) challenged Joash of Israel to battle

    f) was defeated by Joash at Battle of Beth-shemesh

    g) was murdered after reigning 29 years.

9. Uzziah:

    a) son of Amaziah

    b) reigned 52 years

    c) reconquered territory in south which had been part of Solomon's dominions

    d) regained possession of Edomite port of Elath, " the gateway of Arabia "

    e) built many fortresses in hills of Edom

    f) repaired and strengthened fortifications of Jerusalem

    g) had well-organised army

    h) made Philistines and Ammonites tributary to Judah

    i) loved the land and encouraged agriculture.

Prophets:

Amos:

    a) a herdsman of Tekoa

    b) went to Bethel to prophesy

    c) threatened punishment to Syrians, Philistines, Phoenicians, Edomites, Ammonites, Moabites, for their cruelties

    d) his special message was to Israel

    e) he denounced wrong-doing in Israel

        1) injustice in the courts — bribery

        2) corruption in trade — false weights, bad foodstuffs

        3) oppression of the poor

        4) women encouraged their husbands to crush the poor

        5) idol-worship at Bethel, Gilgal.

    f) his threats of punishment

    g) prophesied that House of Jeroboam would be destroyed and Israel would go into captivity

    h) was charged by Amaziah, Priest of Bethel, with conspiring against Jeroboam

    i) his message of hope and consolation.

CHAPTER 15

ISAIAH

THE END OF THE NORTHERN KINGDOM

In the month of Iyyar in the year 745 B. C. E., an Assyrian general by the name of Pul usurped the throne

Assyria Again. of Assyria. This monarch, who is known to history as Tiglath-pileser III, began a new epoch in the annals of his empire. It was his aim to make Assyria the foremost country in the world of his time. Babylon to the south, Armenia to the north, and Egypt far away to the west, were the lands which he set out to pacify, weaken or conquer. Our interest lies in his struggle for the West, because the way to Egypt lay through Syria and Palestine. The rise of Tiglath-pileser therefore spelt troubled days for Israel and Judah. The careless ease and confidence of the preceding half-century were about to end, terribly and suddenly, even as the prophet Amos had already foretold.

Events in Israel hastened the catastrophe. Two years after the accession of Tiglath-pileser in Assyria, Jeroboam

Anarchy in Israel. II of Israel died. His son Zechariah was a weak king, and within six months was murdered publicly and openly, by a man named Shallum, who seized the throne. Scarcely a month passed before he in turn was slain by Menahem of Tirzah, a brutal man, who held the kingdom by force for about ten years.

Four kings in the space of one year! It was anarchy, and on one person at least in the kingdom of Israel, these royal assassinations by military usurpers made a lasting impression. Hosea the son of Beeri was a deeply religious man in the Northern Kingdom who had seen the prosperity and security of Jeroboam II's reign. But, like Amos, he had witnessed also the depravity and callousness which this material prosperity covered. The false worship and hypocrisy of king, prince, priest and prophet pained him deeply. He went about the country and saw Israelites worshipping idols and images upon the hills and mountain-tops, beneath oak-trees and poplars. He saw the idolatrous altars at Bethel and Gilgal, where false priests had betrayed their sacred calling. In Samaria and the fortress cities of Israel, king and nobles were shamefully neglecting their trust. The House of Jehu, he felt, was no better than the dynasty of Omri which it had destroyed. In the name of God, he cried out that the House of Jehu would be punished, and that the kingdom of the House of Israel would become extinct.

The Prophet Hosea.

When Zechariah was murdered by Shallum, Hosea saw his prophecy being fulfilled. King followed king, and the nobles of Israel swore allegiance to them, only to break their oath in a moment. In those days there were two parties in Israel. It was already apparent that Assyria meant to attack Palestine. One party therefore favoured an alliance with Assyria, against Egypt. The other thought it wiser to join with Egypt and oppose the Assyrian advance. It is possible that Shallum, the murderer of Zechariah, was instigated by Egypt. His murder by Menahem meant that the Assyrian party was again in power. Each party in turn sent bribes and gifts, coupled with all sorts of hollow promises, to Egypt and Assyria. It was this shifty policy, together with the gross idolatry of the people, which roused the anger of Hosea. He felt that God could never forgive such wrongdoing, and he foresaw the time when, as a punishment, Israel (or Ephraim as he called the Northern Kingdom) would be a captive in both Egypt and Assyria; when the idolatrous altars would be overthrown and covered with thorns and thistles; when the joy of the festival, New Moon and Sabbath, of every solemn occasion, would cease because of trouble; when the land also would be utterly desolate and, in place of vine and fig-tree, weeds would cover the face of the ground.

This was the terrible vision which Hosea saw. He felt that Israel deserved it because the people had not been true to their history. Instead of observing the Torah, they had mingled themselves with the surrounding nations and learnt to imitate their ways. Yet — and this is the great teaching of Hosea — God acts not only with justice but also with love. His own domestic tragedy gave the Prophet an insight into God's relations with His backsliding people. Though his wife proved faithless to him, Hosea still loved her and was moved to buy her back from slavery. In like manner, the Prophet taught, although the people of Israel had sinned and merited punishment, God still loved them and eagerly desired them to return to Him. Righteousness, justice, loving-kindness, mercy and faithfulness, ought to be the watchwords of the covenant between God and Israel. Let Israel only turn away from idolatry and from vain intrigues with both Egypt and Assyria.

But Israel was mixed up too much in idolatry and political intrigue to heed the words of the Prophet. The

Northern Kingdom was rushing to its ruin. In the year 738 B. C. E. Tiglath-pileser came against the lands of the west and, among others, exacted tribute from Syria and Israel. Menahem sent a gift of one thousand talents of silver, which he levied by taxing every man of substance in Israel fifty silver shekels. The danger, however, was by no means over. After Menahem's death his son Pekahiah was murdered by a member of the anti-Assyrian party, Pekah, who made a league with Rezin king of Syria to stir up war against Assyria. They wanted to force Judah to join them, but the situation there, also, had changed and Judah was not prepared to help.

In his later years, Uzziah king of Judah was smitten with leprosy, and his son Jotham acted as regent. **The Prophet Micah.** Although, like his father and grand-father, he set an example of devoted loyalty to the Torah, conditions in Judah were almost as bad as in Israel. The nobles and the wealthy men were the worst. They enlarged their possessions by buying up or taking by violence the land of the peasants, and they denied the poor man justice. At the same time false prophets encouraged these leaders and assured them that God was on their side. The words of the prophet Micah, from the town of Moreshah in Judah, paint a vivid picture of the unbridled venality and dishonesty in those days.

" Hear now this," he says to the heads of the House of Jacob,

" Ye abhor justice and pervert all righteousness,
Building Zion with blood, and Jerusalem with unrighteousness."

" Her leaders," he continues, " judge for bribes;
Her priests give instruction for profit;

> Her prophets prophesy for silver.
> Yet they rely upon the Lord, saying:
> Is not the Lord in our midst? Evil shall not come
> upon us."

Everybody, it seems to the Prophet, runs after money,
and pursuing it is faithless even to relative and friend.

> "The pious man has perished from the land,"
> the Prophet mourns,
> "There is no upright man....
> Believe not in a friend,
> Trust not in a counsellor....
> The enemies of a man are his own household."

He feels that the wealth and prosperity of Uzziah's reign
are responsible, by making the people love the power
and the comforts which money can buy. Therefore he
sees the time coming when God will destroy the city-
life of Israel, and cause the people to live again simply
as shepherds and nomads.

> "I shall cut off," Micah declares in the name of God,
> "Thy horses from the midst of thee,
> And I shall destroy thy chariots.
> I shall cut off the cities of thy land,
> And I shall pull down all thy fortresses."

To him the superstitious worship which passes for true
religion is meaningless. Burnt offerings and sacrifices
by themselves are worthless, and worse than nothing
when they are offered to graven images and idols, or
used with enchantments at the command of wizards
and soothsayers. Not in this manner, says the Prophet,
should one come before the Lord, and worship the God
on High.

> "What then," he asks dramatically, "does the
> Lord require of man?"

Without pause he himself gives the answer:

"To do justice,
To love lovingkindness,
And to walk humbly with God."

These word shave been described as the noblest definition of true religion in the world.

Yet even in the towns and cities there were some who had a nobler vision of life than merely to pile up money by fraud, deceit, and oppression of the poor. **Life in Jerusalem.** The pious had not quite perished out of the land, and there still existed some upright men. In the capital city, Jerusalem, there grew up at this time a young man who was destined to influence the people of Judah and the world more than any Prophet since Moses. This was Isaiah. He was born in Jerusalem during the reign of Uzziah, and his observant eye noted all that happened around him in the capital of Judah. The streets near the Temple were a frequent haunt of his, and there, on the Sabbath, New Moon and Festival he watched the Judeans thronging the Temple courts, leading their sacrifices of bulls and rams, lambs and goats. Then after they had offered their sacrifice he followed them trooping out of the Temple courts, in multitudes, and swarming round soothsayers and wizards in the streets, seeking by witchcraft to know the future. In the streets of Jerusalem he saw also heroes and warriors proudly strutting along; Judean girls, who, bedecked from head to foot in all kinds of finery, walked with outstretched necks and haughty looks as though they owned the land. These were the ladies of Judea. At the gates of the city, and by the Temple, he saw the courts where justice was dispensed. Again and again his heart burned with indignation when he saw the

judges accepting bribes. At these courts he learnt how
the peasants were dispossessed of their land and oppressed
with heavy taxation, until they sold their children and
themselves as slaves. The countryside was being emptied,
and the cities were being filled with slaves and beggars.
Yet the streets of Jerusalem re-echoed with the sound of
horses and chariots, while the clink of silver and gold
was music in the ears of the merchants and nobles.

All this Isaiah observed and was deeply stirred. Then,
in the year of King Uzziah's death, he had a vision of

Isaiah's Call. God sitting upon a high and exalted throne.
Fiery angels stood over Him and chanted
one to the other,

> " Holy, holy, holy, is the Lord of hosts,
> The whole earth is full of His glory."

Isaiah felt that he could not stand in the presence of
such a vision.

> " Woe is me, I am undone," he exclaimed,
> " For I am a man of unclean lips,
> And dwell among a people of unclean lips;
> Yet my eyes have seen the King, the Lord of
> hosts."

But he was reassured. His lips were touched with a
burning coal held by a seraph, and he heard a voice saying,

> " Whom shall I send, and who will go for us?"

Without hesitation came his reply:

> " Behold, here am I, send me!"

He was warned that the people of Israel would not
listen to his words, "even until cities were wasted without
inhabitant, and the whole land was utterly desolate." Yet
he was consoled as well, for his message would bear fruit
and a remnant of Israel, perhaps only a tenth part, would
follow his teaching and remain faithful to God.

Thus inspired, Isaiah began his long work as a Prophet. The first crisis occured early in the reign of Ahaz, who

The Syro-Ephraimitic War. succeeded Jotham as king of Judah. Rezin of Syria and Pekah of Israel thought this moment suitable to force Ahaz to join the league against Assyria. If he were unwilling, they planned to depose him and set up a king of their own in Jerusalem. Rezin did not advance at once against Jerusalem. He first captured from Judah the port of Elath by the Red Sea and allowed the Edomites to re-settle in it. He accomplished two things by this act. Firstly, he strangled the commerce of Judah which came through this port, and secondly he placed an enemy of Judah at the southern door of the country. Pekah also ravaged the land of Judah. Then the kings joined forces and marched against Jerusalem. Ahaz, a little over twenty years old at the time, was terrified at the approach of the two kings. The prophet Isaiah counselled him to have no fear of his assailants. They were of no account, and would soon be crushed by a mightier power, without any intervention of his.

Already the energetic Assyrian monarch Tiglath-pileser was completing his schemes for the destruction of Syria.

The First Captivity of Israel. His method of attack was masterful. He decided to cut off Syria's help from the south, before advancing against Damascus. With this end in view, in the year 734 he led an army against the Philistines in the south of Palestine and plundered the city of Gaza. Ahaz, spurning the advice of Isaiah, determined to call in the help of Assyria against his two foes who were besieging Jerusalem. To the camp of Tiglath-pileser at Gaza he sent an embassy with much silver and gold, and this message:

" I am thy servant and son. Come up and save me from the hand of the king of Syria and from the hand of the king of Israel, who have risen against me."

Instantly the Assyrian king turned northwards. Rezin and Pekah were dismayed and, giving up the siege of Jerusalem, fled to protect their own lands. Tiglath-pileser captured the fortresses of Israel on his way, and deported large numbers of their inhabitants to Assyria. Historic cities and districts such as Gilead, Galilee, and Naphtali were devastated in this manner and wrenched from Israel. So great was the calamity that it has been called the First Captivity of Israel.

But the Assyrian monarch had no time to stay long in Israel, and did not even attempt to besiege Samaria. He pressed on to Damascus, the capital of Syria, where Rezin was hemmed in without allies, like a caged bird. For over a year the city of Damascus withstood the siege. At length, in the year 732, it fell and Rezin was slain. The district was laid waste, and its inhabitants were carried into exile. Syria was humbled to the dust.

The effect in Judah, with Ahaz on the throne, was to be expected. The man who had spurned Isaiah's advice

Ahaz. attributed the success of Assyria to the help of her gods. Moreover, he was anxious to stand well with Tiglath-pileser. So he went personally to Damascus to offer tribute to the Assyrian monarch, and on his return introduced the worship of the Assyrian gods in Judah.

Isaiah was by no means defeated. The court would not accept his counsel, but he could go

Isaiah in Retirement. among the people of Jerusalem and teach them the message of God which inspired him. His voice might be unheard, yet he could write his prophecies in a book and keep them for the time to come, when men would see clearly that his attitude was the true and right one. So it was during the reign of Ahaz that Isaiah gathered round him a band of followers and revealed to them his beautiful visions of the days to come. The prophet Micah had the same conception as he of the end of days, when:

" The mountain of the House of the Lord shall be established on the top of the mountains,

And shall be exalted above the hills,

And all the nations shall flow unto it.

And many peoples shall go and say,

Come, let us go vp to the mount of the Lord, to the House of the God of Jacob,

That He may teach us of His ways and that we may walk in His paths.

For out of Zion shall Torah go forth, and the word of the Lord from Jerusalem.

And He shall judge among the nations and reprove many nations,

And they shall beat their swords into ploughshares and their spears into pruninghooks.

Nation shall not lift up sword against nation,

Neither shall they learn war any more."

Contrast this ideal picture with the actual conditions in Jerusalem in the days of Ahaz! Jerusalem was full of heathen altars and images to the Assyrian gods. The altar in the Temple of Solomon was displaced, and an Assyrian one erected for sacrifice. Ahaz caused his son to pass through the fire, which was a revolting custom practised by the worshippers of the god Moloch. And you have already seen from the words of the Prophets how little the leaders of the people respected justice and goodness. The example of Ahaz led to further evils, and this king did much to make the Torah forgotten in Judah.

In Israel the Torah had long ceased to be the guide of the state. The Northern Kingdom was now in no way different from the other small nations **End of the Nor-** on the western borders of the Assyrian **thern Kingdom.** Empire, and it suffered the same fate. About two years after the fall of Damascus, the Assyrian party in Israel made a successful conspiracy against Pekah, killed him, and put Hoshea on the throne of Samaria. Shortly afterwards Tiglath-pileser died and was succeeded by Shalmaneser V. The change of monarch in Assyria was the signal for revolt in the west. Hoshea made a secret intrigue with Egypt and, on receiving promise of help, rebelled against his overlord, the king of Assyria. Retribution was not long in coming. Shalmaneser hastened to Palestine and imprisoned Hoshea. Then he ravaged the land of Israel and finally besieged Samaria. The doomed city put up a stubborn defence, and for three years the Assyrian army was kept outside its gates. During the siege Shalmaneser died, and the throne of Assyria was seized by a usurper, Sargon II. This event happened early in the year 722 B. C. E. The same year Samaria fell and the kingdom of Israel came to an end. The Assyrian records tell us that 27,290 inhabitants were carried away into captivity, and from the Bible we know that they were transported to Halah, and to the cities of the Medes. We can imagine the feelings of the captives, the aristocracy of the country, as they were driven away from their home-land to the distant and unknown cities of their conquerors. Perhaps at that moment some of them may have felt that this sad fate would not have overtaken them, if only they had been faithful to their religion. As it was, they were uprooted from their land and torn away from all association with the Torah. In the cities of the Medes on the eastern borders of the Assyrian Empire they were lost among the other inhabitants, and their name was no more known among men. Their desolate land was filled with settlers from other parts of the Assyrian Empire. These new colonists, or at least a section of them, became known in history as the Samaritans. They occupied the cities of the Israelites and learnt to worship the God of Israel, as well as the idols of Assyria. It was a strange mixture. " They feared the Lord, and served their own gods, after the manner of the nations whom they carried away from thence." In time they considered themselves also heirs of Abraham and observed the laws in the Five Books of Moses. We shall hear more of them in the pages of our history.

CHAPTER 15

POINTS TO REMEMBER

Kings of Israel:

14. Zechariah:

    a) son of Jeroboam II

    b) reigned 6 months

    c) was murdered by Shallum.

15. Shallum:

    a) reigned 1 month

    b) was murdered by Menahem of Tirzah.

16. Menahem:

    a) founded fifth dynasty in Israel

    b) reigned 10 years

    c) sent gift of 1,000 talents of silver to Tiglath-pileser of Assyria — raised money by taxing the wealthy.

17. Pekahiah:

    a) son of Menahem

    b) reigned 2 years

    c) was murdered by Pekah.

18. Pekah:

    a) made league with Rezin king of Syria against Assyria

    b) tried to force Ahaz of Judah to join league—ravaged land of Judah

    c) besieged Jerusalem with Rezin

    d) suffered invasion from Tiglath-pileser — Gilead, Galilee. Naphtali devastated — First Captivity of Israel

    e) murdered by Hoshea.

19. **Hoshea:**
    a) reigned 9 years
    b) intrigued with Egypt to rebel against Assyria
    c) suffered invasion from Shalmaneser V of Assyria
    d) Samaria besieged 3 years
    e) Fall of Samaria — Captivity of Israel, 722 B. C. E.

END OF KINGDOM OF ISRAEL, after 209 years.

Kings of Judah:
9. **Uzziah:**
    a) smitten with leprosy towards end of reign.

10. **Jotham:**
    a) son of Uzziah
    b) reigned 16 years
    c) acted as regent in Uzziah's lifetime
    d) set example of devoted loyalty to Torah.

11. **Ahaz:**
    a) son of Jotham
    b) reigned 16 years
    c) called in help of Assyria against Rezin of Syria and Pekah of Israel
    d) went personally to Damascus to offer tribute to Assyria
    e) introduced worship of Assyrian gods in Judah
    f) caused his son to pass through the fire to the god Moloch

Prophets:
Hosea:
    a) lived in Northern Kingdom
    b) was deeply pained by
        1) idolatry and falsehood of king, prince, priest and prophet
        2) shifty policy of intrigue with Egypt and Assyria
        3) gross idolatry of people
    c) prophesied that House of Jehu would be punished and that kingdom of the House of Israel would cease to exist
    d) foresaw captivity of Israel and desolation of land
    e) taught that God acts with love and desired Israel to return to Him.

Micah:

    a) from town of Moreshah in Judah

    b) prophesied in days of Jotham, Ahaz, and Hezekiah

    c) declaimed against faithless judges, untrue priests and false prophets

    d) prophesied that city-life of Israel would be destroyed

    e) his definition of true religion — " to do justice, to love lovingkindness, and to walk humbly with God."

Isaiah:

    a) born in Jerusalem in days of Uzziah

    b) received call to prophesy in year of Uzziah's death

    c) counselled Ahaz to have no fear of Rezin of Syria and Pekah of Israel

    d) his advice was spurned by Ahaz

    e) lived in retirement — his visions of the end of days

    f) denounced evils of Ahaz's reign — idolatry, superstition, corruption, false prophets.

Kings of Assyria:
Tiglath-pileser III:

    a) usurped throne, 745 B. C. E.

    b) received tribute from Menahem of Israel, 738 B. C. E.

    c) answered call of Ahaz and attacked Syria and Israel

    d) captured Damascus, 732 B. C. E.

Shalmaneser V:

    a) reigned from 727 to 722 B. C. E.

    b) ravaged land of Israel

    c) besieged Samaria for 3 years.

Sargon II:

    a) usurped throne, 722 B. C. E.

    b) captured Samaria, 722 B. C. E.

    c) carried 27,290 Israelites into captivity.

CHAPTER 16

ISAIAH — THE SIEGE OF JERUSALEM

Meanwhile, in Judah, Ahaz had died and had been succeeded by his son Hezekiah. He was of an entirely different character from his father. Hezekiah was a pious and god-fearing king, and he inaugurated a religious reformation. One of his first acts was to cleanse the land of Judah of the idolatries of Ahaz, and to restore the pure service of the Temple. In his zeal to destroy every kind of idol, he broke in pieces even the brazen serpent which Moses had made in the Wilderness, because the Judeans were worshipping it. One of the great religious events in his reign was the observance of the Passover. It was held in the second instead of the first month, as the Temple was not completely cleansed and purified, and the priests and the people could not reach Jerusalem by the fourteenth of Nisan. Messengers were sent also to the Northern Kingdom to announce the Passover, and some Israelites from the tribes of Asher, Manasseh, and Zebulun did actually come to observe the Festival of Passover in Jerusalem. The Judeans, whose enthusiasm to follow their king seemed to know no bounds, went throughout the cities of Judah breaking down every Asherah, pillar and idolatrous altar they could find. The reformation was thorough, and for the first time since the days of Solomon the Temple was the only place of sacrifice in the whole of Judah.

Naturally the prophet Isaiah was delighted with this turn of affairs in Judah. The king held him in high honour and consulted him and his follow-

The Anti-Assyrian Party. ers on every important matter affecting the life of the state. Yet Isaiah was not completely satisfied. At court there was a party of nobles who still hankered after an alliance with Egypt and wanted to throw off the Assyrian yoke. These nobles cared little for religion and saw no higher purpose in the existence of the Jewish people. To them Judah was a country like all other countries and must be governed in accordance with the needs and circumstances of the time.

Against this party Isaiah used all his eloquence and power. He tried to show them that the strength of the

Isaiah's Policy. people lay not in horses and chariots, nor in gold and silver which could buy political alliances, but in a perfect trust in God and the observance of His laws. Unfortunately, Hezekiah allowed himself to be influenced by his nobles, and planned, with the help of Egypt, to rebel against Assyria. Philistia, Moab, and Edom were prepared to join in the revolt, but Sargon's army arrived promptly at Ashdod and easily put down the rising. At this time Isaiah removed the hairy mantle which he wore, and walked about the streets of Jerusalem half-clad and barefoot. For three years he went about in this manner, proclaiming that in the same way would Egypt and Ethiopia be led captive by Assyria. His object was to discourage the Judeans from relying on Egypt and from rebelling against Assyria:

" In returning and rest shall ye be saved;

In tranquility and confidence shall be your strength."

But Isaiah seemed powerless against the nobles who advised Hezekiah. The death of Sargon in the year 705

Merodach-Baladan. strengthened the hands of the anti-Assyrian party. Merodach-baladan, king of the Chaldeans near Babylon, planned a widespread revolt against Sargon's son, Sennacherib. He relied upon the help of the Babylonian cities and won over the Arabs of the great desert separating Babylon from Palestine. Through this desert, protected by the Arabs, an embassy went from Merodach-baladan to Hezekiah. Ostensibly, the reason for the mission was to congratulate Hezekiah on his miraculous recovery from an illness which had threatened to cut short his life. Hezekiah was honoured at the visit of these strangers from such a distant country as Babylon, and showed them his armoury and wealth, and the treasures of his kingdom. The ambassadors returned, pleased with their reception. Hezekiah would be a powerful ally against Assyria.

Isaiah, however, was not pleased. He considered it folly on Hezekiah's part to let them into the secrets of his kingdom. For, although they came from a far country and could not be considered foes, Isaiah foresaw the day when these very Babylonians would be masters of Judah.

Sennacherib, however, was watchful, and pounced upon Merodach-baladan before his conspiracy was ripe. Merodach-baladan was defeated decisively in battle, and fled. The strong cities of Babylonia were besieged and taken. The Chaldean rising had failed.

What was its effect upon Hezekiah? Instead of submitting to Assyria, he continued his intrigues with Egypt, despite the strong opposition of Isaiah. The Prophet has given us some unsurpassed descriptions of the caravans laden with treasures which Hezekiah sent down

Intrigues with Egypt. from the hills of Judea through the desert to the flat land of the Delta of Egypt.

" The burden of the beasts of the Negeb," declares the Prophet ironically.

" In a land of trouble and anguish,

Whence come the young and old lion,

The viper, and the flying fiery serpent,

They carry their riches upon the shoulders of young asses,

And their treasures upon the hunches of camels,

To a people who cannot help!"

All this trouble in order to get the valueless help of Egypt! For Egypt would not help in the day of need. She had been treacherous and faithless on earlier occasions.

" Ho! perverse children," says Isaiah in the name of God,

" Taking counsel but not from Me....

Who go down to Egypt and ask not My advice,

To strengthen themselves in the strength of Pharaoh,

And to take refuge in the shadow of Egypt.

The strength of Pharaoh shall be your shame,

And the refuge in the shadow of Egypt shall be your disgrace."

These outspoken words on the part of Isaiah aroused intense opposition against him from the anti-Assyrian

Jerusalem Fortified. party at court and among the people. They mocked and derided him, telling him to go out of their way and to stop talking about God, the Holy One of Israel, as Isaiah called Him. At the same time Hezekiah prepared for active rebellion

Siloam Inscription

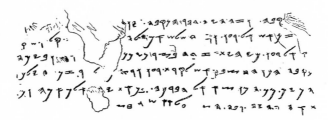

Text of inscription—note the ancient Hebrew characters

World of the Bible.

Translation of text—"The cutting. Now this is the matter of the cutting. While the hewers were yet raising the axe one towards the other and while there were yet three cubits to cut through ... they cried out one to the other, for there was a crack in the rock on the right. But on the day of the break-through the hewers struck each towards his neighbour, axe on axe, and the waters flowed from the source to the pool twelve hundred cubits, and a hundred cubits was the height of the rock above the heads of the hewers".

against Sennacherib. He subdued the Philistines, who were pro-Assyrian, and then strengthened the defences of Jerusalem. His first object was to cut off from the enemy the supplies of water outside the city. A new aqueduct was hewn through the eastern hill and a pool made inside the wall. This aqueduct and pool are known as the Siloam Tunnel and Pool. The story of how they were constructed is given on an inscription which was discovered in June 1880. A photograph of the Siloam Inscription, as it is called, together with a translation of its contents will be found facing page 206. The citizens also feverishly pulled down old houses and strengthened the wall of the city with their bricks and stone.

Sennacherib Invades Palestine. But the Prophet could not be silent, for he knew the calamity which threatened the land.

The Assyrians, he said, "shall come with speed, swiftly.

None shall be weary nor stumble among them;
None shall slumber nor sleep.

Neither shall the girdle of their loins be loosed,
Nor the latchet of their shoes be broken.

Their arrows are sharp and all their bows are drawn.

Their horses' hoofs are accounted as flint,
And their wheels as the whirlwind.

They roar like a lion, yea like young lions.

They roar and snatch the prey and carry it away,
And none can deliver it from them."

Soon the Prophet's fears were realised. A rising against the Assyrian governors in the Philistine cities, and the sending of the pro-Assyrian king of Ekron as a hostage to Hezekiah, marked the beginning of the rebellion. Early

in the year 700 B. C. E., Sennacherib's army marched
against Palestine. The Phoenician cities of Tyre and
Sidon submitted without a blow. Philistia's turn came
next. The fortified cities of Judah, forty-six in number
and containing over 200,000 inhabitants, surrendered to
the Assyrian monarch. Hezekiah, alarmed at the rapid
progress and success of the enemy, sent messengers to
Sennacherib's camp at Lachish with an offer of submission. The Assyrian exacted a heavy tribute from
the rebellious king, which Hezekiah paid by stripping the
Temple of its treasures. In the Assyrian Saloon at the
British Museum you can see enormous wall sculptures
transported from the palaces of Nineveh. One of these
walls depicts in bas-relief the assault and capture of
Lachish by Sennacherib, and also shows the king seated
on his throne while the spoils of the city passed before
him. Remarkable discoveries of considerable value have
been made in the past few months on the site of this
ancient city.

Still Sennacherib was not satisfied. From Lachish he
sent three of his chief officers, with a large force, to
capture Jerusalem. The Assyrian envoys
Jerusalem were met by three representatives of Heze-
Threatened. kiah, and they parleyed by the wall of the
city. The Assyrians spoke loudly in Hebrew, and stressed
the hopelessness of Hezekiah's revolt against Sennacherib,
in order to win over the inhabitants to their side. But
the men of Jerusalem were loyal to their king and made
no answer.

At this critical moment in the affairs of his kingdom,
Hezekiah turned to Isaiah and implored the help of God
against the enemy. The Prophet was calm. It was
his firm conviction that the Assyrian army would never

enter Jerusalem. His belief was strikingly confirmed when the Assyrian envoys returned to Sennacherib. They found that he had left Lachish to meet an Egyptian army which was advancing against him. The relief of the Judeans was indescribable. They made a festive day, killing oxen and slaughtering sheep, eating meat and drinking wine. To the Prophet this was all wrong. The citizens should have held a solemn day of repentance for their folly, looked to improve their ways, and trusted in God for help. The envoys of Sennacherib, however, soon returned and again threatened the city. They reminded Hezekiah that no city or kingdom had yet withstood the might of Assyria. How then could Jerusalem be delivered?

"Shall I not do to Jerusalem and her idols, as I have done to Samaria and her idols?" was the proud boast of the Assyrian.

But the Assyrians had made one mistake. The God who protected Jerusalem was not an idol such as the

The Holy City Saved.

gods of the cities which the Assyrians had conquered and laid waste. The God who protected Jerusalem, Isaiah taught, was the creator and ruler of the world, to whom even Assyria was only an instrument working out His purpose. Therefore Isaiah was confident that Jerusalem would not be captured by the Assyrians. Her time was not yet. This message the Prophet gave to Hezekiah, and the king was reassured. Though the enemy was at the gate, he had courage. The words of Isaiah rang in his ears:

"Therefore thus saith the Lord concerning the king of Assyria.

He shall not come into this city, neither shall he shoot an arrow there,

He shall not come with a shield against it,
Neither shall he cast a mound against it.
By the way that he came shall he return,
And into this city shall he not come, saith the Lord.
I shall protect this city to save it, for My own sake,
And for the sake of David My servant."

That same night the Assyrian army was destroyed by a sudden plague, and Sennacherib returned with all haste to his own land. He never again came against Palestine. The Assyrian records make no mention of the plague, and they suppress every reason for Sennacherib's sudden return to Nineveh. Isaiah's firm conviction was brilliantly justified. Jerusalem was still safe.

CHAPTER 16

POINTS TO REMEMBER
●

Kings of Judah:
12. Hezekiah:
- a) son of Ahaz
- b) reigned 29 years
- c) character — pious and god-fearing
- d) religious acts
    1) cleansed Judah of idolatries of Ahaz
    2) restored Temple service to God
    3) broke in pieces brazen serpent which Moses had made in Wilderness
    4) arranged observance of Passover, in second month
- e) foreign policy
    1) planned rebellion against Assyria, with help of Egypt
    2) first attempt put down by prompt action of Sargon
    3) entertained envoys of Merodach-baladan, who had come to congratulate him on his miraculous recovery from illness
    4) continued plan of rebellion against Assyria even after defeat of Merodach-baladan
    5) sent gifts to Egypt, for help
    6) subdued Philistines, who were pro-Assyrian
    7) fortified Jerusalem — built Siloam Tunnel
    8) submitted to Sennacherib when he invaded Palestine
    9) turned to Isaiah for help when Jerusalem was threatened.

Prophets:
Isaiah (ctd.):
- a) denounced Hezekiah's policy of league with Egypt
- b) expressed his displeasure at welcome which Hezekiah extended to envoys of Merodach-baladan — prophesied that Babylon would one day take Judah captive

c) fiercely opposed Hezekiah's intrigues with Egypt
d) was mocked and derided by anti-Assyrian party
e) assured Hezekiah that Jerusalem would not be captured by Sennacherib.

Kings of Assyria:
Sargon II (ctd.):

a) filled Northern Kingdom with colonists from other parts of Empire — Samaritans
b) besieged Ashdod, 712 B. C. E., to put down anti-Assyrian rising.

Sennacherib:

a) became king, 705 B. C. E.
b) defeated conspiracy of Merodach-baladan, king of Chaldeans
c) invaded Palestine, 700 B. C. E.
d) 46 fortified cities of Judah surrendered
e) received submission of Hezekiah
f) threatened Jerusalem
g) his army smitten by plague — returned in haste to own land.

CHAPTER 17

JEREMIAH

The few remaining years of Hezekiah's reign were a period of peace and prosperity. The mighty name of

Hezekiah's Last Years.

Assyria held in check the peoples of Moab and Edom who used to raid the eastern borders of Judah. The farmers of Judah could plough and sow their fields without fear that enemies would rob them of their harvest. In the cities and throughout the country, the fact that Jerusalem had been saved from attack made a tremendous impression. Isaiah was held in honour and his counsel taken at the court. We are told that, for the instruction of the people, Hezekiah appointed men to copy some proverbs of Solomon. Here is an example of one:

"Keep thy foot from going too often to the house of thy friend, lest he be full up with thee and dislike thee."

The king was also guided by the picture of the ideal monarch which the Prophet painted. A sovereign should reign righteously, and princes should rule for justice. Faithless judges were removed and upright men selected in their place. Jerusalem was once again a city of righteousness. There, at the festivals three times a year, the citizens flocked from all parts of the country to affirm their loyalty to God and king.

Unfortunately, when Hezekiah died his son and successor, Manasseh, was a boy only twelve years old. The princes whom Hezekiah had driven from court returned and seized power. While Manasseh was a minor they

Manasseh. ruled the country, and when he was older he allowed himself to be misguided by them. Manasseh ruled over Judah for fifty-five years, and during his long reign he undid all the good which Hezekiah his father had effected. The Prophets were scorned and rejected, and the worship of Baal and of the Assyrian gods was introduced once more. High places and altars to Baal were set up everywhere, and a graven image of Ishtar, or Ashtoreth, the Assyrian queen of heaven, was placed in the Temple itself. The Assyrians worshipped the sun, the moon, and the planets. In Jerusalem and in the other cities of Judah the winged disc of the sun-god Ashur, with its chariots and horses, made its appearance. In the two courts of the Temple similar images and others in adoration of the planets were erected. Judah was fast becoming like every other province of Assyria.

The danger which this threatened to the existence of the Jews, as we may now call the citizens of Judah, was obvious to Isaiah and his followers. They were cruelly persecuted, and many of them were killed. We are told that Manasseh shed much innocent blood in Jerusalem; the blood of little children who were burnt as sacrifices to the god Moloch in the valley of Ben Hinnom, south of Jerusalem; and the blood of men put to death because they protested against the abominable Assyrian customs which the court introduced into Judah.

It is said that Isaiah was murdered during the reign of

Egypt Conquered. Manasseh. But his enemies at the court of Manasseh could not kill his teachings. Men and women in Judah treasured his words and recalled them even in the darkest days of persecution, and when Assyria was so strong that many believed that her empire would last for ever. For, during the seventh century B. C. E., Assyria reached the zenith of her power. At its beginning she was mistress of the lands from the Persian Gulf to the borders of Egypt. The mere mention of the provinces and kingdoms which paid her tribute or over which her governors ruled would sound like a catalogue of the states of the ancient world. Babylonia, Elam, Media and all the peoples of Syria and Palestine were subject to her. Only Egypt was unconquered. For Sennacherib had failed to subdue that ancient land. In the year 681 B. C. E., Sennacherib was murdered in his palace at Nineveh by two of his sons who then fled to Armenia. A third son of his, Esarhaddon, mounted the throne and took up the struggle against Egypt. Assyrian armies poured through Palestine year after year in campaign after campaign. Many Jews had to join these armies, just as other subject nations were compelled to send contingents. At last, in the year 671 B. C. E., the Egyptian Pharaoh was completely defeated and Egypt was made a part of the Assyrian empire. The country was divided into districts, and an Assyrian governor was placed in charge of each of them. Two years later Esarhaddon died, and left to his son Ashur-bani-pal the greatest empire of the ancient world.

Assyria could aspire no higher. All lands were obedient to her. To prevent any possibility of revolt, Ashur-bani-pal removed whole masses of his subjects from one end of his empire to the other. To the cities of Samaria he brought many peoples from Media and other eastern lands. Seals and cylinders of this period, unearthed at Gezer in Southern

The Age of Ashur-bani-pal.

Palestine, show that Assyrian colonists penetrated even
into this district.   Subject kings provided the materials
for the prosperity of the empire and sent them, or even
brought them themselves, to Assyria. Manasseh, king
of Judah, was no exception. His name is mentioned,
on an Assyrian inscription, among a list of twenty-two
kings of the western lands who, with much toil and
difficulty, brought a tribute of cedar and cypress-trees
to Nineveh. For these lands were rich in timber
which could be used for building, and the Assyrian
monarchs were great builders. Ashur-bani-pal was not
only a powerful king but also a famous scholar who
prided himself upon his skill in the art of tablet-writing.
He collected two great libraries at Nineveh, and from
these we have learnt much about Assyrian life and
history. The reign of this renowned king saw indeed
the highest expression of Assyrian culture.

Yet the religion of Assyria, with its worship of the sun,
the moon and the planets, and with its superstitious belief
in demons and evil spirits, was a danger
to the worship of the true God. Already
ten of the Twelve Tribes of Israel had been swallowed up
and lost in the Assyrian empire. Only the little kingdom
of Judah remained to bear witness to the existence of
the One God. Yet even in Judah true religion was being
forgotten and the worship of the Assyrian idols was taking
its place. But the Prophets were not silent, and continued to spread the knowledge of God throughout the
land. They tried to bring back the people to the old
paths, and at the same time foretold that the power and
might of Assyria would not last.

Fall of Assyria.

Suddenly, as in a moment, the might of Assyria was
broken. Egypt was the first to throw off her yoke, but

that loss troubled Ashur-bani-pal only a little. The last years of his reign ended in sorrow and despair. From the steppes of the Caucassus wild hordes of nomadic tribes pressed southwards upon the cultivated lands of the empire. To plunder and ravage was their object, and they struck terror wherever they came. Through Syria and Palestine these Scythians poured, and were only bought off by a bribe at the gates of Egypt. Their coming marked the end of the Assyrian rule in the west, while Nabopolassar the Chaldean, and Cyaxares the Mede established their independence in the east.

At this time Josiah the grandson of Manasseh was on the throne of Judah. He is one the great figures of our history. His father Amon had ruled for less than two years before he was murdered.

King Josiah.

Josiah was a boy of eight when he began to reign. When he reached manhood Assyria was beginning to collapse. A seriously-minded man, he listened to the words of the prophets Nahum and Zephaniah, who were proclaiming the imminent fall of Assyria.

In the twelfth year of his reign he began to purge his country of the idolatries of his father and grand-father. Like Hezekiah, he swept Jerusalem and the cities of Judah clean of images, altars, and high places. Not content with this, he went into the territory which formerly belonged to Northern Israel, and broke down the golden calf of Bethel, besides heathen altars as far north as Naphtali. Assyrian influence in Palestine was so weak that there was nobody to stop him.

On his return to Jerusalem he decided to purify the Temple and to repair it thoroughly. Long years of neglect had made the glorious golden Temple of Solomon an unsightly ruin. Carpenters and builders were soon busy with wood and hewn stone rebuilding the House of God. While the dust-covered chambers were

The Finding of the Torah. being cleared and the foundations strengthened, Hilkiah the priest came upon an old book. It was the Law of Moses! So thorough had been the idol-worship of Manasseh that every copy of the Law had been ruthlessly destroyed. In those days books were rare and precious because they were written by hand, and sometimes only one copy might exist. If that were lost or destroyed, the book was lost for ever. This fate nearly overtook the Law of Moses.

The Law of Moses and therefore the commands of God to His people! Eagerly Hilkiah handed the book to the king's scribe, and the scribe read it in the presence of the king. Josiah listened with horror to the denunciations of wilful and presumptuous misdeeds which applied so literally to the conditions of his own time. When the scribe had done reading, the king arose with tears in his eyes and rent his garments.

" Great," he exclaimed, " must be the anger of the Lord against us because our fathers have not kept the command of the Lord, to do according to all that is written in this book." Hurriedly a deputation was sent to the Prophetess Huldah, who lived in Jerusalem, to find out the will of God. She replied that the doom pronounced in the Torah would be fulfilled, but that disaster would not come in the days of Josiah.

Immediately the king summoned the elders of Judah to the Temple, and there, standing upon a dais in the presence of the priests, prophets and elders of the people, he renewed the covenant that Judah should observe the commandments of the Torah. And the people solemnly

gave their assent. It was nearing the time of Passover,
and Josiah at once made preparations to observe the
festival in the manner prescribed by the Torah, much as
Hezekiah had done before him. Those priests who were
unclean because they had offered sacrifice on high places,
ate their unleavened bread in their own homes. The
others observed the Passover at the Temple in Jerusalem.
The Bible tells us that never since the days of Samuel
was such a Passover kept as in the eighteenth year of
King Josiah.

Meanwhile the enemies of Assyria were gathering to
strike a mortal blow against the empire. Ashur-bani-pal
Death of Josiah. died in the year 626 B. C. E. During the
next twelve years the Assyrian-trained
armies of Babylon and Media were joined by the barbaric
hordes of Scythians, and the three allied forces marched
against the cities of Assyria. Ashur fell in the year
614 B. C. E. and was sacked with savage ferocity. Two
years later Nineveh itself, the capital of Assyria, the
richest and most powerful city in the empire, was taken
and reduced to mounds of ruins. The Assyrian king fled
and established a shadow kingdom at Harran in Syria.
At this juncture, Egypt, fearing the fast-growing power
of Babylon, came to his help. Pharaoh Necho marched
with an army through Palestine. The Philistine city
of Gaza barred his way along the coast. It met with
short shrift. Josiah too decided to oppose the Egyptian
advance through his country. He waited for the Egyptian army beyond the heights of Carmel, in the Plain of
Megiddo. The battle was of short duration. Josiah was
mortally wounded and his army fled defeated to Jerusalem, where the king died.

A sound of mourning was heard in the cities of Judah

and in the streets of Jerusalem. Josiah, the good king,
who had served God faithfully, who had executed
justice and righteousness in his kingdom,
The Return to Idolatry. had come to an untimely end. In fact he
was the last king of any consequence. The
nobility chose his youngest son Jehoahaz to succeed him,
but Pharaoh Necho showed his power by deposing him
and taking him captive to Egypt. In his place he
appointed his brother Jehoiakim as king and made the
country pay a fine of one hundred silver talents and one
gold talent. These two calamities had a pronounced
effect upon both the common people and the ruling party.
They believed that their troubles had come upon them
because they had given up the worship of Ishtar, the
queen of heaven, and the other heavenly bodies. So in
the days of Jehoiakim the old idolatries came back to
the land. The Bible narrates how in the streets of
Jerusalem boys were again to be seen gathering wood,
old men lighting fires and women kneading dough in
order to make cakes for the queen of heaven. Images
and idols again reared their head by the side of altars
upon every high hill and under every green tree, so that
the gods of Judah were more numerous than the number
of her cities or her streets.

It may surprise us that amidst all this idolatry the
services in the Temple were still maintained. In the
Temple itself burnt-offerings and sacrifices were offered
daily upon the altar, with incense brought from Sheba
and other distant countries. In the courts of the Temple,
and in the squares and streets leading to it, princes,
priests, nobles and prophets met and talked and dispensed
justice to the people of the land. Yet it was all a mockery.
For most of the prophets were quacks and hirelings of the

party in power. They preached just what was popular.
The priests and the princes were not much better. The
rich men and the judges cared nothing about the plight
of the poor and defenceless. Violence and oppression
were common things in Jerusalem. The commands of
the Torah, which teach social justice and humanity, were
flouted. The Sabbath ceased to be a day of rest. Merchants brought in their wares from the countryside and
sold them in the market-places of the capital. Craftsmen
went about their work as on other days.

This was the state of Judah at the beginning of the
reign of Jehoiakim. The reforms of Josiah seem to have
left no effect. At least so it appeared to

Jeremiah.

Jeremiah, a priest from the town of
Anathoth in the territory of Benjamin, almost four miles
north of Jerusalem. The word of God came to him in
the thirteenth year of the reign of Josiah and he felt
compelled to publish it. For it seemed to him that a
divine hand touched his lips and granted him the gift of
eloquence. By that act Jeremiah was consecrated as a
Prophet to the nations. It was his mission to root up,
to pull down, to destroy and to overthrow, yet also to
rebuild and to plant. Courageously he supported King
Josiah in his reforms in his own town as well as in Jerusalem. He was glad at Josiah's success and praised the
king for the way in which he judged the cause of the poor
and the needy. The death of Josiah came as a shock to the
Prophet and the people's return to idolatry disappointed
him bitterly. He spoke against their treachery to the Torah
and consequently became unpopular. Even his own countrymen and the members of his own family turned against
him. The men of Anathoth said to him, "Prophesy not
in the name of the Lord, lest thou die at our hands."

In Jerusalem an even worse fate awaited him. At the beginning of Jehoiakim's reign he stood at the gate of the Temple and cried out to the worshippers that they should mend their ways. He rebuked them for doing every kind of wrong and trusting in the magic of the words " The Temple of the Lord," as if the Temple would never be destroyed, and would always save and protect them.

> " Act justly one towards another;
> Oppress not the stranger, the orphan, the widow ;
> Shed not innocent blood;

Go not after other gods to your own hurt," the Prophet declared vehemently. Otherwise, he threatened, God would destroy the Temple and cast out the Jews from their land even as He had done to the House of Ephraim.

The priests and prophets and the people in the Temple courts, resenting his words, gathered round him, shouting, " Thou shalt surely die!" He was hurried to the new gate of the Temple where the princes sat to judge lawsuits. The priests and the prophets charged him before them. Jeremiah replied to his accusers:

" The Lord sent me to prophesy unto this Temple and unto this city all the words which you have heard. Mend your ways and the disaster will not happen. I am in your hands, do to me what is good and right in your eyes. But know that if you put me to death you will be laying innocent blood upon yourselves." This speech pleased the princes and the people, for they said to the priests and the prophets: " This man does not deserve to die, for he has spoken to us in the name of the Lord our God."

The priests, however, were not defeated. Many a time

Jeremiah stood in the courts of the Temple and prophesied doom upon the city. Often he used a parable to illustrate his teaching. On one such occasion the chief governor of the Temple struck Jeremiah and put him in the stocks at one of the Temple gates for a day. This public disgrace hurt the sensitive Prophet deeply. He saw everybody mocking him, and in the bitterness of his anguish he cursed the day on which he was born.

His life was very hard and lonely. He felt that in such troublous times it would be wrong for him to marry and have a family. He took no part in joyous celebrations. People shrank from him and cursed him as a prophet of woe. Yet he had a generous heart and a noble disposition, and he prayed frequently that God would pardon the people and give them joy and peace again. One faithful follower, a man named Baruch, acted as his scribe and wrote down his prophecies at his dictation.

The fourth year of Jehoiakim marked a crisis in the Prophet's life. In that year the armies of Egypt and **Babylon Victorious.** Babylon met at Carchemish on the Euphrates, and the battle decided who was to be master of Western Asia in place of fallen Assyria. Pharaoh Necho was defeated, and retreated to his land. So Nebuchadnezzar the famous king of Babylon became the unquestioned master of the former Assyrian Empire. For twenty-three years Jeremiah had been prophesying that the Babylonians would come and take Judah into captivity. Now the Babylonian was overlord of Judah. The false prophets, however, saw in the defeat of Pharaoh Necho the beginning of a new era of peace and happiness. Egypt was powerless. Distant Babylon, they argued, would never reach Judah. Jeremiah, however, for his part still insisted that Babylon was certain to overwhelm them, and that their only chance lay in a timely submission. In order to bring this teaching vividly before the people, the Prophet made himself bonds and a wooden yoke, as a symbol of servitude to Babylon.

Naturally Jeremiah's teaching was unpopular, and he was flung into prison, where his prophecies were written **Jehoiakim.** down by Baruch. On an appointed day a year later a fast was proclaimed, when Baruch read the prophecies in the upper court at the new gate of the Temple. The princes called him to a chamber where he again read the words of Jeremiah. They were so impressed that they reported them to the king. It was a wintry day and Jehoiakim was sitting in a winter house heated by a brazier. The princes stood about him while he sat and listened to a courtier reading the prophecies. The king's impatience rose as he listened, and after he had heard four columns he could contain himself no longer. Snatching the scroll from the courtier's hand, he impiously tore it into pieces with a knife and cast them on the fire.

For a time it seemed that the false prophets were right and Jeremiah wrong. Nebuchadnezzar did not at once invade Judah, and the country was left undisturbed. Jehoiakim began to erect ostentatious buildings and to live a selfish life of luxury in his capital. For these purposes he engaged forced labour and oppressed the people. Fearlessly Jeremiah denounced his conduct and repeated his prophecies of doom. Soon Jehoiakim recklessly brought trouble upon himself and his kingdom. He intrigued with Egypt against Babylon. Nebuchadnezzar immediately incited the neighbouring tribes and peoples to invade and despoil Judah. Syrians, Moabites and

Ammonites eagerly seized the opportunity to enlarge their territory at its expense. Gone was the prosperity of the early years of Jehoiakim's reign. Trade was at a standstill in the cities. Farmers and peasants saw their crops ruined or stolen and their land despoiled. Shepherds, tent-dwellers, and land-workers fled to the fortified cities for refuge. In the cities the increase in the population and the loss of the produce brought starvation and famine. The fields were desolate. Orchards and vineyards on the hill-slopes, with no grapes on the vines and no figs on the fig-trees, presented a pitiful sight.

At last Nebuchadnezzar himself with his army of Chaldeans came against Judah. After a reign of eleven years, the miserable Jehoiakim died before **The First Captivity.** he reached Jerusalem. His son Jehoiachin opened the gates of Jerusalem to the Babylonian monarch and gave himself up as a prisoner. Nebuchadnezzar confiscated the treasures of the Temple and palace and cut off all the gold work in the Temple. He led Jehoiachin, the queen-mother, the court and the nobility to the number of one thousand, as well as seven thousand warriors and craftsmen and smiths, as captives to Babylon. It was the First Captivity of Judah.

Only the poorest in the land were left. Over them Nebuchadnezzar appointed Zedekiah, another son of Josiah, as king, and bound him by a most solemn oath to be faithful to Babylon. Jeremiah did not despair of the exiles. Indeed, he thought that there was more hope for them than for the people who remained in Judah under Zedekiah. In one of his striking parables he compared the exiles and those who remained to two baskets of figs. The good basket of figs corresponded to

the exiles, who would become the future builders of the
new state of Judah. To them the Prophet dispatched
a letter by the hand of messengers whom Zedekiah sent
to Babylon.

> " Build houses and dwell in them;
> Plant gardens and eat their fruit....
> Seek ye the peace of the city in which ye are,
> And pray for it unto the Lord.

For in its peace ye shall have peace," he declared.

There were many exiles in Babylon, however, who
cherished hopes of a speedy return to Judah. These
men wrote back to the priests in charge of the Temple
that Jeremiah ought to be punished for his advice.

In Jerusalem at this time the same hopes of the speedy
collapse of Babylon ran high. False prophets paraded

**Zedekiah's
Conspiracy.**

the Temple area crying aloud that the
sacred vessels which had been carried to
Babylon in the First Captivity would be
returned within two years. One of these false prophets
even went to Jeremiah, took off the wooden yoke from
his neck, and symbolically broke it in the presence of
the priests and the people. " Thus saith the Lord," he
added, "I have broken the yoke of the king of Babylon."

The excitement in Jerusalem was intense. Moreover,
messengers had come to the capital from Edom, Moab,
Ammon, Tyre and Sidon, to hatch in secret a gigantic
rebellion against Babylon. Egypt was urging Palestine
and Syria to throw off the shackles of Babylon. Zedekiah
of Judah, despite Jeremiah's strong warnings, joined the
conspiracy. He was called to Babylon to explain his
conduct. With one of the courtiers who accompanied
the king, Jeremiah sent a copy of his prophecies concerning Babylon, with orders that they should be read to

the Jews and then cast into the Euphrates. Zedekiah
returned from Babylon somewhat chastened, and for
four years nothing more was heard of the conspiracy.
But in Egypt there had succeeded to the throne a new
Pharaoh who strove to recover Palestine for his country.
He invaded Palestine and defeated the Babylonian
garrison. Zedekiah's hopes rose, and he threw in his
lot on the side of Egypt.

The king of Babylon thereupon set out to subdue the
rebellious state. The cities of Judah fell one by one
before his army until only three remained:
The Siege of Lachish, Azekah, and Jerusalem.
Jerusalem.
To the capital fled all the refugees from
town and country. In the ninth year of Zedekiah, in the
tenth month, Nebuchadnezzar's army encamped outside
the walls of Jerusalem. The siege had begun.

For one and-a-half years the Chaldean army was kept
without the city by the desperate defence of the brave
garrison. Famine and plague stalked through the streets,
yet the inhabitants would not open the gates. The
whole of this time the prophet Jeremiah urged the king
and the princes to submit to Babylon. He was called
a traitor and a deserter by the angry princes, but he
could not be silenced. Zedekiah had a secret interview
with him, and could extract no better counsel from him.
If Jerusalem was to be saved, then the city must yield
itself up peacefully to Nebuchadnezzar. This the ruling
party would not do, and Jeremiah was kept in prison.

At the end of one and-a-half years the enemy made
a breach in the outer wall and poured into the city.
Zedekiah and his warriors fled by night towards the
Plain of Jericho, hoping to cross the Jordan and set up
the kingdom in Eastern Palestine. But they were

forestalled. The Chaldean army pursued Zedekiah and overtook him in the Plain of Jericho. They brought him to Nebuchadnezzar at Riblah in Northern Palestine. His sons and the nobles of Judah were slaughtered; his eyes were blinded, and he was led in fetters to Babylon.

Meanwhile Nebuzaradan, Nebuchadnezzar's chief officer, took possession of Jerusalem and plundered it. The Temple and the palace, and every big house, was set on fire. To increase the conflagration the Chaldeans cast the choicest cedar-pillars upon the flames. The walls of Jerusalem were pulled down and the city was left a smouldering ruin. The High Priest and the principal men of the city were put to death. Only Jeremiah was set free and allowed to go wherever he wished. The other inhabitants of the city, to the number of 4,600, were led captive to Babylon.

But the Prophet who for forty years had prophesied woe and destruction felt his heart break as he watched the smoke rising from the city where once **Jeremiah's Lament.** had been the glory of God. His eyes filled with tears as he saw the lines of exiles trudging wearily in heavy chains along the unfriendly road to distant Babylon.

" How doth the city sit solitary that was full of people!" he lamented.

"The ways of Zion do mourn because none come to the solemn feasts.

All her gates are desolate....

Her adversaries are the chief, her enemies prosper....

Her children are gone into captivity before the enemy."

Was this the end of Judah's history? Judea was

desolate, and from her streets and cities had vanished the
sound of joy and the sound of gladness, the voice of the
bridegroom and the voice of the bride, and even the sound
of grinding millstones. The noblest and the most important of her inhabitants had been slain or taken into
captivity.   Only the poorest of the poor, who had nothing,
were left to take possession of the ruined vineyards and
fields.   The cities were for the most part uninhabitable.

Yet the Prophet who saw the fulfilment of all his
prophecies of doom never despaired.   He knew that the
people which carried with it the tradition
His Prophecy of the true God could not be destroyed.
of Hope. Therefore he was certain that fields and
vineyards would one day be again cultivated in Judah,
that there was yet hope for the land, and that the
Children of Israel would return to their own territory.
Therefore he could sing in the midst of his lamentation:

" There shall yet be heard in the desolate cities
of Judah and the streets of Jerusalem,
The sound of joy and the sound of gladness,
The voice of the bridegroom and the voice of
the bride,
The sound of those saying, Give thanks to the
Lord of hosts for He is good,
For His lovingkindness endureth for ever."

CHAPTER 17

POINTS TO REMEMBER

Kings of Judah:

12. **Hezekiah** (ctd.):

    remaining years period of peace and prosperity
    1) land free from attacks of border tribes
    2) Isaiah held in honour at Court
    3) faithless judges removed
    4) Jerusalem once again city of righteousness
    5) proverbs of Solomon copied by men of Hezekiah for instruction of people.

13. **Manasseh:**

    a) son of Hezekiah
    b) reigned 55 years
    c) was governed by princes whom Hezekiah had driven from Court
    d) state of land —
       1) prophets scorned and rejected
       2) worship of Assyrian gods re-introduced
       3) children burnt to death as sacrifice to god Moloch
       4) innocent men put to death
       5) paid tribute to Assyria.

14. **Amon:**

    a) son of Manasseh
    b) murdered after reign of 2 years.

15. **Josiah:**

    a) son of Amon
    b) reigned 31 years
    c) the last important king of Judah
    d) his reforms —

1) swept away images and idols in Judah
2) broke down golden calf of Bethel and heathen altars as far north as Naphtali
3) purified Temple and repaired it thoroughly — Book of the Law found
4) renewed covenant that Judah should observe commandments of the Torah
5) held Festival of Passover in 18th year of his reign;

c) foreign policy —
1) was independent of Assyria
2) opposed advance of Pharaoh Necho through Palestine
3) was killed at Battle of Megiddo, 609 B. C. E.

16. Jehoahaz:

a) son of Josiah
b) elected king by people on Josiah's death
c) reigned 3 months
d) deposed by Pharaoh Necho and led captive to Egypt.

17. Jehoiakim:

a) son of Josiah
b) appointed king by Pharaoh Necho
c) reigned 11 years
d) state of land —
1) return to idolatry
2) yet Temple services still maintained
3) false prophets
4) faithless priests and princes
5) violence, destruction and oppression common things in Jerusalem
6) Torah not kept — Sabbath not observed as day of rest;

e) home policy —
1) burnt prophecies of Jeremiah
2) lived life of luxury in capital
3) built ostentatious buildings
4) engaged forced labour and oppressed the people;

f) foreign affairs —
1) intrigued with Egypt against Babylon
2) land invaded by Syrians, Moabites and Ammonites at instigation of Nebuchadnezzar
3) invasion by Nebuchadnezzar.

18. Jehoiachin:
   - a) son of Jehoiakim
   - b) reigned 3 months
   - c) surrendered to Nebuchadnezzar — First Captivity of Judah; treasures of Temple and palace confiscated by Nebuchadnezzar; Jehoiachin, queen-mother, nobility, warriors and craftsmen taken as captives to Babylon.

19. Zedekiah:
   - a) son of Josiah, uncle of Jehoiachin
   - b) appointed king by Nebuchadnezzar
   - c) last king of Judah
   - d) reigned 11 years
   - e) conspired against Babylon
   - f) joined Egypt in rising against Babylon
   - g) besieged in Jerusalem by Nebuchadnezzar for $1\frac{1}{2}$ years
   - h) escaped from doomed city, but captured in Plain of Jericho
   - i) Jerusalem taken — the Temple burnt — 586 B. C. E.

END OF THE KINGDOM OF JUDAH, after 345 years.

Prophets:

Isaiah (ctd.):
   - a) met his death in reign of Manasseh
   - b) his teachings and writings treasured by his followers.

Nahum and **Zephaniah** prophesied downfall of Assyria.

Jeremiah:
   - a) priest from town of Anathoth in territory of Benjamin
   - b) received call to prophesy in 13th year of Josiah
   - c) his mission — " to root up, to pull down, to destroy and to overthrow, yet also to rebuild and to plant."
   - d) supported reforms of Josiah
   - e) lamented untimely death of Josiah
   - f) bitterly disappointed by return to idolatry in days of Jehoiakim
   - g) unpopular and driven from home town
   - h) arrested in Jerusalem for saying that Temple would be destroyed
   - i) put in stocks and publicly disgraced
   - j) lived lonely life — he sometimes doubted himself

k) yet prayed for his people
l) had one faithful follower — Baruch
m) his parables
    1) the linen girdle
    2) the potter
    3) the earthern bottle
    4) the baskets of figs
    5) the wooden yokes
n) was flung into prison time and again
o) denounced misdeeds of Jehoiakim
p) spoke against the false prophets
q) dictated his prophecies to Baruch, who read them to the people one Fast Day — Jehoiakim burnt the prophecies
r) sent encouraging words to the first exiles
s) his lamentation on the destruction of Jerusalem
t) his prophecy of hope.

Important dates:
1) Nineveh, capital of Assyria, destroyed by Medes, Scythians and Babylonians, 612 B. C. E.
2) Nebuchadnezzar defeated Pharaoh Necho at Battle of Carchemish and thereby became master of Western Asia. 605 B. C. E.
3) Temple burnt by Babylonians, 10th Ab 586 B. C. E.

PART IV

THE EXILE AND THE RETURN

CHAPTER 18

EZEKIEL

Over the poverty-stricken peasants who were left in the land of Judah, Nebuchadnezzar appointed a Jewish governor, Gedaliah. This man took up his residence in Mizpah, north of Jerusalem and, helped by the prophet Jeremiah, attempted to reshape the life of the small community. The news of the king of Babylon's clemency spread, and there gathered round Gedaliah members of the royal family, many soldiers, and a number of Jews who had fled for safety to the neighbouring countries of Moab, Ammon, and Edom. To all these people Gedaliah appealed for loyalty.

Gedaliah.

" Fear not to serve the Chaldeans," he declared. " Dwell in the land and serve the king of Babylon, and it shall be well with you."

On his advice the refugees gathered the harvest of grapes, summer fruits and oil from the fields (for it was now mid-summer) and established themselves in the desolate cities.

Yet all was not well. Ishmael, a member of the royal family, plotted with the king of Ammon to kill Gedaliah. Within less than two months after the destruction of

Jerusalem, the unsuspecting governor was treacherously slain by Ishmael at a banquet in Mizpah. For a moment all was confusion in the town. Some officers, however, who were faithful to Gedaliah, saved the situation, and Ishmael and his men were put to flight.

The remnant of the people were terrified lest the king of Babylon should punish them for the death of the governor. Their sufferings during the rebellion against Babylon had made them hate even the mention of the word war, or the sound of the trumpet. They remembered also how they had hungered for bread in the sieges. So, guided by the officers and their elders, they decided to escape into Egypt and thus be free from the fear of Babylon. Jeremiah warned them that the king of Babylon would conquer Egypt also, and advised them to stay in the land of Judah. But the officers would not listen to him, and taking with them the men, women, and children whom Nebuzaradan had left, as well as the king's daughters, the aged Prophet, and Baruch, they went down to Egypt.

The Descent to Egypt.

In Egypt colonies of Jews had existed from early times. Some may have accompanied the caravans which travelled between Palestine and Egypt during the prosperous days of the monarchy in Israel. Later many Jews fled from the sword of Assyria or joined the armies of Egypt and then settled in various parts of that country. Recently a number of old papyri documents were discovered at Elephantine, near the first cataract of the Nile. These papyri deal with the life of a colony of Jews who had established themselves there probably about the time of Josiah, king of Judah.

The Jews in Egypt.

So the Jews who fled to Egypt after the murder of Gedaliah soon felt secure. As before, they thought that the calamities which had overtaken them in Palestine were a punishment for not worshipping Ishtar, the queen of heaven, and once again they began to offer sacrifice to this idol. Great was the grief of Jeremiah when he realised that his people had learnt nothing from their sad fate. His last words were a vehement protest against their idolatry and an appeal that they should serve God in truth and faithfulness.

In Babylon, however, whither the bulk of the wealthier classes had been led captive, a different spirit prevailed. You must remember that the First Captivity took place in the year 597 B. C. E., eleven years before the destruction of the **The Jews in Babylon.** Temple. Among the exiles of that year were king Jehoiachin, the royal family, and the priest Ezekiel. The exiles did not find life too difficult in the plain of Babylon. Many of them received their freedom and some even reached high office in the state. The stories of Daniel and his three companions are well known. Most of the exiles settled in or near the city of Babylon, by the big canals which irrigated the land of the river Euphrates. They engaged in trade and agriculture. Several Jewish names have been found on Babylonian contract tablets of this period. These tablets give us a fairly complete picture of the life in that city of merchants and nobles, Babylon. On them we read, among other things, of land and slaves being bought and sold, boys apprenticed to masters, and property divided or left by will.

The city of Babylon itself had been rebuilt by Nebuchadnezzar. It was encircled by high walls of burnt brick, and contained many large open spaces covered with gardens, cornfields and orchards. Through the city flowed the Euphrates, with its numerous canals and water channels. Two great works of Nebuchadnezzar beautified the city and made it one of the wonders of the world. For his queen he built the famous Hanging Gardens. He also erected magnificent palaces and temples. In honour of the god Marduk he paved with slabs of limestone the great Processional Way along which the god was taken annually in solemn procession in the great festival of the New Year.

On a summer's day, five years after the First Captivity, Ezekiel the Priest was standing by the Great Canal, called the river Chebar, when it seemed **The Visions of Ezekiel.** to him that the heavens opened and a fiery vision appeared before his eyes. At once he fell upon his face in worship, when he heard a voice bidding him stand upright.

" Son of man," the voice said, " I send thee unto the Children of Israel.... They and their fathers have trespassed against Me until this very day.... Fear them not, but speak My words unto them, whether they hear or whether they will forbear to listen."

In this dramatic manner was Ezekiel consecrated as a Prophet of God. The Prophet tells us in his own words how he fulfilled his mission to his people. He went to the Jewish settlement at Tel-Abib by the Great Canal, near the city of Nippur, and for seven days sat in silence among the exiles.

The Jews among whom the sat seemed to have no idea of what was happening in Palestine. By means of emblems and symbols, Ezekiel lived the siege and the captivity before their eyes in order to make them realise how real these things were. Even then they asked him in wonderment, " What doest thou?" At once the Prophet answered,

" I am a sign for you. As I have done, so shall it be done to them. Into exile, into captivity, shall they go."

In prophetic visions Ezekiel saw the reason why disaster was coming over the inhabitants of Judah and Jerusalem. The elders and leaders of that unhappy land performed the most abominable practices in secret in the underground chambers of the Temple. There they felt themselves safe for they said,

" The Lord sees us not;
The Lord hath forsaken the land."

Therefore, the Prophet declared, God would uproot the Jews out of their land and give it into the hands of strangers.

Many of the exiles, however, laughed at the words of Ezekiel. You must remember that just at this time false prophets in Judah and in Babylon raised high the hopes of the people that Babylon was about to fall.

" The vision which he sees," they said of Ezekiel, " is for many days to come, and for times which are far off does he prophesy."

But the words of Ezekiel were fulfilled only too soon. The tenth day of the tenth month in the ninth year of the First Captivity the Prophet marked down as a day of sorrow. For on it the king of Babylon began the fateful siege of Jerusalem. One and-a-half years later, after terrible sufferings of which you have already heard, the Jews of Judea saw their city captured and their Temple burnt, and they themselves joined their fellow-exiles in captivity.

This tragic event marked a turning point in Ezekiel's life. No more did he prophesy against the Jews of Judea.

The Enemies of Judah. His prophetic eye saw the desolate lands of Judea seized by spiteful enemies, exultant at Judah's downfall. In dramatic fashion he tells us how the Ammonites clapped their hands and stamped their feet in joy when Judea was destroyed. The Moabites and the Edomites said, " Aha, the House of Judah is no different from all other nations." The Philistines and the Phoenicians were doubly glad because they thought the trade and commerce of Judah would now go to them. These neighbourly enemies of Judah were quick to pounce upon the desolate land. The Edomites did not scruple to hand over to the Babylonians refugees who fled to them for safety. Then they seized the territory of Judah and occupied it right up to Hebron.

So it was against these nations that Ezekiel poured out his prophetic wrath. To the exiles he was more kind.

Ezekiel's Prophecy of Hope. He saw in them the remnant of Israel through whom the knowledge of God and His ways would spread throughout the world. Therefore did he try to win them with words of comfort and a vision of the better days to come.

" I shall gather you from among the peoples," he declared in the name of God,

> " And I shall assemble you from the countries
>   where you are scattered,
>   And I shall give you the land of Israel....
>   I shall put a new spirit within you,
>   In order that you may walk in My statutes,
>   And keep and do My judgments.
>   Ye shall be My people,
>   And I shall be your God."

It was under the influence of the Prophet that the exiles met together in their communities in Babylonia and established what we may call syna-

His Influence. gogues. The word is Greek and means an assembly. The elders of the community used to come to the Prophet's house and seek the word of God from him. Whilst speaking to them he would naturally relate to them the history of their people and perhaps read to them portions of the Law. We know that some of the exiles offered prayers to God three times a day, with their faces turned westwards towards the Holy City, Jerusalem. We know also that they fixed four fast days to be observed in memory of the destruction of Jerusalem: the tenth day of the tenth month, the seventeenth day of the fourth month, the tenth day of the fifth month, and the third day of the seventh month. Each of these days was the anniversary of a sad event in connection with the destruction. The first marked the day when Nebuchadnezzar began the siege of Jerusalem; the second when the walls of the city were broken by the enemy; the third, most dreadful of all, when the Temple was burnt, and the last when Gedaliah was murdered.

By these assemblies, these prayers, and these fast days, the exiles remembered the land of their fathers and kept alive the spirit which bound them together as a people. But as the years passed and the conquests of Nebuchadnezzar were extended, so that by the end of his reign he was master of the whole of Western Asia and Egypt, the hopes of the Jews sank. They feared they would never again see Palestine, and that as a nation they were dead.

" Our bones are dry,
Our hope is lost.
We are cut off," they sighed.

Not so, declared the Prophet. He told them a wonderful vision which he had seen of a valley full of dry lifeless bones. At the word of God these dry bones had been inspired with life and stood upright as living men. In like manner would God deal with the House of Israel:

"I shall put My spirit in you and ye shall live;
And I shall place you upon your land.

And ye shall know that I the Lord have spoken, and performed it, saith the Lord."

So firm was this belief of Ezekiel that he wrote down in minutest detail the particulars of the new Temple which **His Teaching.** the exiles were to build in Jerusalem on their return. He also told them that in Palestine there would no more be two kingdoms, but one. The two Houses of Israel would be united under a king descended from David. Yet he warned them that they could not rely upon the righteousness of others to bring them happiness. Ezekiel taught that every single individual is master of his own destiny. A man must not rely upon the good deeds of his father. He must do good deeds himself. And to Ezekiel doing good deeds meant not only avoiding wrong things. It meant also giving one's bread to the hungry, clothing the naked, executing justice between man and man, walking in God's statutes, and keeping His judgments. The Prophet's great teaching is summed up in the following sentence:

"I delight not in the death of the wicked, saith the Lord,

But that he return from his evil way and live."

Teachings such as these sustained the spirit of the Jews in Babylon and made them look forward with eager longing to a release from their captivity and bondage. At the moment, however, the fall of Babylon seemed very far off indeed. Nebuchadnezzar was at the height of his power. As he stood upon the flat roof of his palace in Babylon and looked upon the beautiful city which he had adorned, he might well say:

" Is not this great Babylon, which I have built for a king's house by the might of my power and for the honour of my majesty!"

He died in the year 562 B. C. E. His son Evil-Mero-dach released King Jehoiachin from prison and treated him with kindness. Three kings of Babylon followed one another in quick succession until Nabonidus was placed on the throne in 556 B. C. E. He was a learned man full of love for his country and its long history. But he did not occupy himself with state affairs, and his son Belshazzar was the real ruler of the country.

The material lot of the Jews grew worse. Then, with dramatic suddenness, upon the stage of history a new figure burst — Cyrus the Persian. An unknown and insignificant Persian satrap, he became in a few years a conqueror of renown. The Median and the Lydian monarchies fell before him. With his army he crossed the Tigris and held Babylonia at his mercy. Only the strong walls of the capital barred his progress, for he could not take them by storm. Instead, he diverted the waters of the Euphrates and entered the city through the dry bed of the river. Babylon, taken by surprise, submitted without a blow.

Collapse of Babylon.

The career of Cyrus is traced in the latter chapters of the Book of Isaiah. He is there called the Anointed of God, entrusted with the mission of restoring Israel to their land. The imminent fall of Babylon, and the powerlessness of her idols to assist her in the day of her calamity, are vividly described. On the other hand, the majesty and power of the God of Israel, who guides the destiny of nations, form the central theme of these chapters. Hopes of a speedy and miraculous return to Palestine must have raised the spirit of the Jews to the point of ecstasy.

"A Voice cries, prepare ye in the wilderness the way of the Lord,

Make straight in the desert a higway for our God.

Every valley shall be exalted, and every mountain and hill shall be made low;

The crooked shall be made straight, and the rough places plain."

Within a year from the fall of Babylon, these expectations began to be realised. From his palace in Ecbatana, in 538 B. C. E., Cyrus issued an edict:

"Thus saith Cyrus king of Persia, all the kingdoms of the earth hath the Lord God of heaven given me, and He hath charged me to build Him a Temple in Jerusalem, which is in Judah. Whoever there is among you of all His people, his God be with him, and let him go up."

Ashurbanipal Feasting

(the king is reclining in a bower and drinking. The lower half of his body is enveloped in a coverlet; behind him stand two chamberlains keeping off the flies; by his side is a table; opposite him reclines the queen, also drinking)

World of the Bible.

Inscription commemorating the victory of Cyrus, King of Persia, over Babylon, "without battle and without fighting".

World of the Bible.

CHAPTER 18

POINTS TO REMEMBER

Judah:
   Gedaliah:
      a) made governor by Nebuchadnezzar
      b) took up residence in Mizpah
      c) murdered by Ishmael;
   Ammonites, Moabites, Edomites, Philistines and **Phoenicians,** glad at Judah's downfall, seized desolate land for themselves.

Egypt:
   Remnant of people escaped to Egypt against advice of Jeremiah after murder of Gedaliah; re-introduced worship of Ishtar
   Jeremiah taken unwillingly to Egypt
      protested vehemently against return of Jews to idolatry.

Babylon:
   Bulk of captives carried there
      a) nobler exiles of First Captivity already there
      b) life not hard
      c) many received their freedom and advanced to high positions
      d) lived near the capital
      e) engaged in trade and agriculture;
   Ezekiel.
      a) exiled in First Captivity
      b) began to prophesy 593 B. C. E.
      c) symbolically lived siege and captivity before eyes of exiles to make them realise what was happening in Palestine
      d) prophesied that God would uproot the Jews out of their land and give it into the hands of strangers
      e) people paid no heed to his prophecies

f) poured out his prophetic wrath against the nations on borders of Judah

g) was kinder to the exiles after destruction of Jerusalem

h) declared that they would be restored to Palestine

i) synagogues established through his influence

j) kept alive the spirit of the exiles (the vision of the dry bones)

k) wrote down minute particulars of the new Temple

l) taught that every individual is master of his destiny, and that God desires man to return from his evil ways and live;

Kings of Babylon:

a) **Nebuchadnezzar** — rebuilt city of Babylon

b) succeeded by **Evil-Merodach,** who released Jehoiachin from prison, 561 B. C. E.

c) **Nabonidus** and son **Belshazzar** were the last Babylonian rulers

d) **Cyrus the Persian** — his dramatic career traced in latter chapters of Isaiah

captured Babylon by surprise

issued edict for return of Jews, 538 B. C. E.

CHAPTER 19

ZERUBBABEL

42,360 people, not including 7,337 slaves and 2,000 singers, were stirred by the decree of Cyrus to return to the land of their fathers and to rebuild the Temple of God in Jerusalem.

Return of Exiles.

They were supplied with silver, gold, goods, and cattle, as well as with ample provisions for the long journey, by those Jews who remained in Babylonia. Cyrus, moreover, restored the treasures of silver and gold which Nebuchadnezzar had carried away from Jerusalem. He was very helpful to the Jews because he respected their religious feelings. He adopted the same attitude toward all the subject nations of his empire. In the case of the Jewish nation, however, there was also a political consideration. Like every earlier emperor and monarch from the north, he set his eyes upon Egypt and determined to conquer it. A friendly Palestine would naturally be a valuable asset in his campaign.

So, blessed with the good wishes of their fellow-Jews and their new ruler, the exiles took leave of Babylon. A joyous song was on their lips as they traversed the broad desert separating them from their homeland.

" When the Lord brought back the captivity of Zion," they sang,

" We were as those who dream.

Then was our mouth filled with laughter and our tongue with song.

Then was it said among the nations,
The Lord hath done great things for this people."
The company included many elders of Judah and Benjamin, priests, and Levites. At their head was Zerubbabel, grandson of King Jehoiachin, and Joshua the High Priest. The returned exiles took possession of Jerusalem and the land immediately around it, as far north as Mizpeh and Jericho, and as far south as the ancient cities of Keilah, Bethzur and Tekoa. They found the land in a pitiable state. For fifty years it had lain almost desolate and uncared-for. The Temple was a ruin, while the burnt walls of the once beautiful city of Jerusalem mutely told their story of destruction and desolation. The time of the newcomers was at first entirely taken up in building houses and reconstructing the farms which were allocated to them by their leaders. Zerubbabel and Joshua were faced with all the problems of organising a new life in the land, and establishing a well ordered community. But they were not unmindful of the main purpose which had inspired their return, namely to rebuild the Temple. So in the seventh month they called a great assembly of the people in Jerusalem, erected the stone altar in the Temple courtyard, and on it offered sacrifice of thanksgiving to God. That same month they kepth with gladness the Festival of Joy, the Feast of Tabernacles.

Immediately after the Festival they arranged for cedar-wood to be brought by the Phoenicians from the

The Foundation-Stone of the Temple Laid. Lebanon to the harbour of Jaffa, and they engaged masons and carpenters to rebuild the Temple. It is interesting to note that the workmen they paid in money, but with the Phoenicians they exchanged wheat, wine, and oil, for cedar-wood. The workmen worked with zeal, and in the year 537 B. C. E., the builders laid the foundation-stone of the second Temple amidst the loud rejoicings of the people. But many of the priests, Levites, and elders who had seen the First Temple, wept during the ceremony. For they remembered the glories of the First Temple, and contrasted them with the small beginnings of the Second Temple.

Yet there was hope that the work would go forward and succeed, even beyond the expectation of the leaders. **The Samaritans.** The inhabitants of Samaria saw the work of the Jews and came forward with an offer to take part in it.

" Let us build with you," they said, " for like you we seek your God and we sacrifice to Him since the days of Esarhaddon king of Assyria who brought us up here." Zerubbabel and Joshua took counsel with the elders and decided to refuse this request. The Samaritans, you remember, were not Israelites but settlers who had adopted the worship of the God of the land of Israel, after the Ten Tribes had been led into captivity. The Jews were anxious to keep their race pure, and could not risk the dangers which would arise from the Samaritans joining them as one people. It would be a repetition of what had happened when the Children of Israel had first entered Palestine under Joshua. They had mixed with the inhabitants of the land, forgotten God, and forsaken the Torah. Zerubbabel and Joshua were determined to avoid such a course.

When the Samaritans were told that their help could not be accepted, they were furiously angry. They sought every means in their power to hinder the work. They interfered with the builders and troubled them.

They also sought to influence government circles against the Jews. Unfortunately Cyrus died, and his successor Cambyses was too much occupied with the war against Egypt to pay any attention to the Jews. Consequently the minor officials in Palestine, influenced by the Samaritans, put a stop to the work.

Conditions in Palestine also helped to discourage the Jews. High taxes, drought and failure of the crops during these years brought poverty upon **Haggai.** the struggling community. The people looked in vain for the fulfilment of the glorious prophecies of a triumphant return, to be found in the last part of the Book of Isaiah. They began to believe that their difficulties and troubles were a divine punishment because they had begun the rebuilding too soon. Such an attitude roused the ire of the prophet Haggai, who prophesied in the second year of Darius, king of Persia. Darius ascended the throne in 521 B. C. E., and is among the most famous of the kings of Persia. On the great rock at Behistun in Persia there is an inscription of this Darius wherein he describes the greatness of his power. At the beginning of his reign Egypt and Babylon rose against him, and the empire seemed to totter. But he firmly withstood his enemies, and in a short time he could boast that twenty-three countries owned his sway, among them Persia, Elam, Babylonia, Assyria, Arabia, Egypt and the sea-lands (which included Palestine).

" Is it time to dwell in panelled houses," Haggai asked indignantly,

" While this Temple is desolate!"...

" Go up to the mountain,

Bring wood,

Build the Temple.

Then shall I be pleased with it and I shall be honoured," he declared.

" Take courage Zerubbabel,

Take courage Joshua,

Take courage all ye people of the land and work," he exhorted the leaders,

for " greater shall be the glory of this latter Temple than of the former."

Urged on by the prophet Haggai, Zerubbabel and Joshua resumed the work in the Temple. At the same time another Prophet arose, Zechariah, **Zechariah.** who also encouraged the leaders. Zechariah was confident that the city of Jerusalem, now half deserted, would be inhabited like a town without walls, because of the multitude of the people and the cattle in it. The cities of Judah would yet spread through prosperity, and God's presence would be felt in the Holy City.

" Old men and women," he declared, " shall yet sit in the broad squares of Jerusalem, every man with his staff in his hand for age. The broad squares of the city shall be full of boys and girls playing in them."

This prophecy seemed marvellous in the ears of the remnant of the people. Yet conditions did improve from the day that Zerubbabel and Joshua began again the work on the Temple. Zechariah continued his prophecies of comfort and hope:

" There shall be seed of peace;

The vine shall yield her fruit;

The ground shall gain its increase;

The heavens shall give their dew....

And it shall be that as ye were a curse among the nations, O House of Judah and House of Israel, so will I save you and ye shall be a blessing. Fear not, but let your hands be strong."

As the days passed and the Temple grew nearer completion, the prophet Zechariah felt it his duty to remind the Jews of the teachings of the former Prophets.

"These are the things that ye shall do," he said to the people.

"Speak truth to one another;
Execute the judgment of truth and peace in your gates.
Think not the hurt of your brother in your heart.
Love no false oath."

He foresaw that the time would arrive when

"Many peoples and mighty nations shall come to seek the Lord of hosts in Jerusalem and to pray before the Lord."

He had a message also for Zerubbabel and Joshua. There would be no antagonism between the Prince and the High Priest, as too often there had been in former times. Joshua was told by the Prophet:

"If thou wilt walk in My ways
And wilt keep My charge,
Thou also shalt judge My Temple
And shalt keep My courts."

It was the duty of the Priest to know the Torah and to teach it. As for the Prince, he was to lead and guide the community, and he must ever remember that real rule over men is

"Not by might, nor by power,
But by My spirit, saith the Lord of hosts."

Inspired by the prophets Haggai and Zechariah, Zerubbabel and Joshua went confidently about their work.

The Western Wall—all that is left of the Temple

by courtesy of the Jewish National Fund.

Tatnai, governor of Palestine, however, was suspicious and asked them,

"Who gave you permission to build this Temple?" They replied:

"We are the servants of the God of heaven and earth, and are rebuilding the Temple which was **The Completion** built aforetime by a great king of Israel. **of the Temple.** Our fathers sinned and were exiled.... Cyrus gave us permission to return and rebuild this Temple. The foundations were laid, but the work has not been finished."

Tatnai was not satisfied and reported the matter to Darius. Search was made in the records of Persia, and the declaration of Cyrus was found. Darius thereupon gave Zerubbabel permission to complete the work and forbade Tatnai to interfere with its progress.

The Jews now set to work with a will and prospered. On the third day of Adar in the year 516 B. C. E., seventy years after it had been destroyed, the Temple was finished. The following month, the exiles were able to observe the Passover in the Temple for the first time since the Return.

CHAPTER 19

POINTS TO REMEMBER

The Returned Exiles:
   a) nos. — 42,360, besides 7,337 servants
   b) took possession of Jerusalem and land immediately around it, as far north as Mizpeh and Jericho, and as far south as the ancient cities of Keilah, Bethzur and Tekoa
   c) led by Zerubbabel, grandson of king Jehoiachin, and Joshua the High Priest
   d) stone altar rebuilt in seventh month — Feast of Tabernacles observed with joy.

The Temple:
   a) arrangements begun for rebuilding — foundation-stone laid in 537 B. C. E.
   b) Samaritans asked to be allowed to help — sought to hinder work when request refused
   c) Jews discouraged also by high taxes, drought and failure of the crops
   d) work stopped for 16 years
   e) leaders returned to the work through inspiring message of the Prophets
   f) opposition of Tatnai, governor of Palestine, overcome by command of Darius
   g) Temple completed 3rd Adar, 516 B. C. E., 70 years after the destruction of First Temple.

The Prophets:
Haggai:
   a) prophesied in 520 B. C. E. (2nd year of Darius)
   b) encouraged Zerubbabel and Joshua to recommence work on Temple
   c) his prophecy — " Greater shall be the glory of this latter Temple than of the former."

Zerubbabel:

    a) prophesied from 520 B. C. E.

    b) also encouraged leaders to restart the work

    c) glowing prophecies of future prosperity

    d) reminded Jews of lessons of former Prophets

    e) taught that there should be no antagonism between Prince and Priest

    f) his great teaching — man rules

> " Not by might, nor by power,
>
> But by My spirit, saith the Lord of hosts."

CHAPTER 20

EZRA AND NEHEMIAH

The years slipped by without record. Only in Persia did an event occur the effect of which was felt in every land of the empire. It was in the reign of Xerxes, who succeeded Darius, that a certain courtier named Haman, hating a Jew Mordecai in the capital city of Susa, planned to destroy the whole Jewish race.

The Story of Purim.

" There is a certain nation," Haman said to Xerxes, " scattered abroad and dispersed among the nations in all the provinces of thy kingdom; and their laws are diverse from all people; neither keep they the king's laws. If it please the king, let it be written that they may be destroyed."

Xerxes took his signet ring from his hand, and gave it to Haman as a sign that he could do with this people as he pleased. The thirteenth day of Adar 475 B. C. E. was fixed as the day of the destruction of the Jews. Couriers were sent to every part of the king's dominions bidding the people do the royal command.

The story of this plot and how it was foiled is told in the Book of Esther. Since that time Jews all over the world keep the thirteenth day of Adar as the Fast of Esther, and the fourteenth day as the Feast of Purim. It is called Purim, which means lots, because Haman originally cast lots to determine the day on which to destroy the Jews.

Ten years later Xerxes died and was succeeded by the wise Artaxerxes. This monarch was favourably disposed towards the Jews, and in 457 B. C. E., the seventh year of his reign, he gave Ezra permission to go up to Jerusalem with as many Israelites, priests and Levites as wished to accompany him. He provided Ezra with silver and gold and provisions, charged him to appoint magistrates and judges in Judah, and released priests and Levites from paying taxes. Ezra was a zealous Jew who devoted his life to expounding and performing the Law of God and to teaching in Israel statute and judgment. He was the first of a class of men called Scribes, who occupied themselves with making copies of the Torah and explaining its words to the people. Ezra was also a priest who could trace his descent from Aaron the first priest.

Ezra.

Ezra gathered a company of 1,500 men, besides women, by the canal which ran to Ahava, and encamped there for three days. Before they began their long journey he proclaimed a fast and offered prayer to God. On the twelfth day of the first month the caravan started for Palestine, with no escort of soldiers or horsemen to protect them from Bedouin robbers on the way. No mischief occurred on the journey through the desert, and they reached Jerusalem safely in the fifth month.

Almost as soon he arrived Ezra saw the need for his coming. The appalling state into which Judah had sunk since the days of Zerubbabel is vividly described by the prophet Malachi.

The first and greatest evil was that which Zerubbabel had tried so hard to avoid, intermarriage. Israelites, priests, and Levites had taken husbands and wives from among the mixed peoples of Palestine: Canaanites,

Ammonites, Moabites and Egyptians. The lax princes and rulers were among the first offenders. The degen-

Malachi. erate priests and Levites were especially deserving of blame. They treated the Temple service lightly, and when they received no gifts or dues from the people they stopped to minister there and went back to the countryside. They favoured the rich and were partial in their interpretation of the Torah.

" Who among you," Malachi asks scornfully, "would close the gates or kindle fire on the altar for nought?

Ye have turned aside from the way;

Ye have caused many to stumble in the Torah."

This attitude on the part of the priests and Levites brought them into contempt among the people, who began to despair.

" Everyone who does evil is good in the sight of the Lord, and in them doth He delight," they asserted. Some even dared to ask: " Where is the God of judgment?" Yet it was the duty of the priests to honour God's name.

" A priest's lips should keep knowledge," declared Malachi, " and they should seek Torah at his mouth,

For he is the messenger of the Lord of Hosts."

Of the ideal priest, Malachi could truly say in the name of God:

" My covenant was with him life and peace....

The Law of Truth was in his mouth,

And unrighteousness was not found on his lips.

In peace and equity he walked with Me,

And many did he turn away from iniquity."

Ezra Stamps out Intermarriage. Such a man was Ezra. When he heard of the way in which the Jews had intermarried with the heathen nations he was overcome with grief and indignation, and spent the day in fasting and prayer. A great multitude of men, women and children gathered round him, weeping. One of their number adressed Ezra:

"We have trespassed against our God.... Now, let us make a covenant with our God to put away all the heathen wives and such as are born of them.... Arise, for the matter belongeth to thee, and we are with thee. Be of good courage and do it."

Ezra, assured of the support of the leaders, issued a proclamation throughout Judah for all the returned exiles to assemble in Jerusalem. Whoever would not come, the proclamation added, would forfeit his property and be excommunicated. The assembly met on the twentieth day of the ninth month in the broad square facing the Temple. The matter could not be settled in a moment. The people as one man agreed to repair the wrong that had been done, and set up a Commission to deal with it. The Commission sat from the first day of the tenth month until the first day of the first month in the following year.

Ezra had been successful in his first reform. But his action had stirred up powerful enemies among the **Nehemiah.** neighbouring peoples, whose feelings had been outraged. Jerusalem was a city with only ruined walls, and therefore at their mercy. The small Jewish community in Judah was in danger of destruction. Fortunately it had a powerful friend at the court of the Persian king. In the month of Kislev in the twentieth year of Artaxerxes, there came to Susa some men from Jerusalem. They reported to Nehemiah, the king's Jewish cup-bearer, that the community was in great affliction and reproach, and defenceless against its enemies, because the wall of Jerusalem was broken down and its gate burnt with fire. Nehemiah was grieved for

18

their sake, and obtained permission from Artaxerxes to go up to Jerusalem and rebuild its wall. The king gave him letters of safe conduct, provided him with a body-guard, supplied him with timber from the royal forest for the Temple and for the wall of Jerusalem, and ap-pointed him governor of Judah for a period of twelve years. On reaching Jerusalem Nehemiah stayed there for three days. Then, at night, with a few men, and only one beast on which he rode, he made a tour round the broken walls of the city. The next day he addressed the priests, the nobles, the rulers, and the rest of the people.

" Come," he said, " let us rebuild the wall of Jerusalem, that we be no more a reproach."

The people readily agreed. At the same time they took the opportunity to tell Nehemiah of their troubles. There had been a famine and the farmers were ruined. Some had sold their children as slaves for corn that they might live. Others had mortgaged their fields, vineyards and houses for corn. Others still had borrowed money on their fields and vineyards in order to pay the royal taxes. Nehemiah remonstrated with the nobles and rulers.

" We (in the Captivity) have redeemed our brethren the Jews who were sold to the heathen," he said. " Will you sell your brethren, or let them be sold to us?" They were silent and found nothing to answer. Then said Nehemiah:

" Restore their fields, vineyards, olive orchards and their houses; also the hundredth part of money, corn, wine and oil which ye exact of them."

" We will restore, and we shall not tax them," they replied. Nehemiah himself set them a praiseworthy example. During the twelve years of his governorship he waived the dues of his office. Previous governors had taken from the people annual bread and wine and forty silver shekels, while their servants burdened the people with other taxes.

The work upon the wall began at once. It was the turn of the enemies of Judah to be grieved. The leading spirits among these enemies were Sanballat **The Wall of Jerusalem.** the Samaritan, Tobiah the Ammonite and Geshem the Arabian. At first they mocked the Jews at their work.

" What are these feeble Jews doing?" Sanballat asked scornfully. " Can they fortify themselves? Can they put life into stones taken from burnt heaps of rubbish?"

" The wall which they build," rejoined Tobiah, " why, if a fox jumped over it he would knock it down."

Yet the days passed and the wall round the city grew steadily higher. The Arabians, Ammonites and Ashdodites tried more warlike methods. The Jews, however, under Nehemiah's resolute leadership, were not afraid. The builders went about their work on the wall armed with swords. A trumpeter stood by the side of Nehemiah ready to blow an alarm to the scattered builders on the wall. By night guards kept watch, armed with spears, shields, bows and habergeons. By day they all worked feverishly.

Sanballat, Tobiah and Geshem now adopted still another way of attack. They sent Nehemiah an open letter containing these words:

" It is reported among the nations that thou and the Jews think to rebel, therefore thou buildest the wall. Also that thou hast set up prophets to preach concerning thee in Jerusalem, saying, There is a king in Judah. Now it shall be reported to the king. Therefore come, and let us take counsel together."

Nehemiah was not to be deceived by such tactics. He replied with dignity to Sanballat's messenger: "The things that thou sayest have never happened." What made matters more difficult for Nehemiah was that many of the nobles of Judah held friendly correspondence with Tobiah, who had married a daughter of one of them. Sanballat also hired false prophets to compromise Nehemiah, but to no avail.

At last, after fifty-two days, on the twenty-fifth day of Ellul, the wall was finished. Nehemiah arranged a magnificient ceremony to mark its dedication.

The Dedication. The people were formed into two companies, Ezra at the head of one, and Nehemiah bringing up the rear of the other. The two companies made a circuit of the wall with its nine gates and met at the Temple court. The priests blew on trumpets, Levites sang, and men, women and children shouted for joy. The noise of the rejoicing was heard for many miles, and must have chilled the heart of the Samaritans and other enemies of Judah.

Jerusalem was once again a walled city, but it was not yet inhabited. The people lived in the countryside where they cultivated their farms. Only the princes dwelt in the city. Nehemiah decided to populate the city by casting lots.

Jerusalem Inhabited.

One family out of every ten was required to settle in Jerusalem.

Ezra realised that the time had come to spread a knowledge of the Torah among the Jews. On the first day of the seventh month the people assembled in the broad square before the Water Gate and asked Ezra the Scribe to bring out the book of the Law of Moses. Ezra mounted a wooden platform and, with leading men on either side of him, opened the book

The Great Assembly. in the sight of all the people. He blessed the Lord, the great God, and all the people answered Amen, amen. Then he read from the Torah from morning light till midday, and the ears of the people were attentive to his words. The Levites explained the Torah to the people, and as they understood they wept. But Nehemiah, Ezra and the Levites comforted the people, saying:

" This day is holy to the Lord your God.

Mourn not, nor weep,

Go, eat the fat and drink the sweet;

Send portions to them for whom nothing is prepared....

Be not troubled, for the joy of the Lord is your strength."

So the people went their way to make holiday.

On the second day the elders, the priests and the Levites gathered round Ezra to learn the words of the Torah. They read the law concerning Succoth, and at once the people went up to the hill-country to get branches of olives, pines, myrtles, and palms for the Festival. Every Jew made a hut either on his roof or in his court- yard, in the Temple courts, and in the broad squares before the Water Gate and the Ephraim Gate. Great was the rejoicing in the city throughout the Festival, and on every day, from the first to the last, Ezra read the Torah to the people.

Immediately after the Festival, on the twenty-fourth day of the month, the Jews entered into a solemn covenant to observe the Law of God given through Moses.

They assembled with fasting and with sackcloth. They separated themselves from the heathen and made confession of their sins and the sins of their fathers. For one part of the day they read the Torah, and for another part they made confession and worshipped. The Levites stood upon the Temple stairs and prayed. In their prayer they related God's kindness throughout the history of the Jewish people. In conclusion they exclaimed:

> " Behold, we are servants this day,
> And the land which thou didst give to our fathers
> — We are slaves upon it.
> And its produce goes to the kings whom Thou hast put over us.
> They rule over our bodies and over our cattle,
> According to their pleasure.
> And we are in great distress.
> Yet, we make a true covenant and write it,
> And our princes, Levites and priests do seal it."

Besides accepting the Torah in general, the community promised:

1) not to intermarry with the heathen,
2) not to buy merchandise on the Sabbath or Holyday,
3) not to exact any debts during the seventh year,
4) to pay a third of a shekel annually for the Temple service,
5) to bring the wood-offering for the altar by families (lots were drawn for this purpose),
6) to bring the first fruits of the land, of fruit, of cattle and of dough, to the Temple,
7) to separate the heave and tithe offerings.

Ezra's work was done. The Talmud says of him that he was a second Moses. The Torah was forgotten from

Israel and he came up from Babylon to teach it again. The solemn assembly on the twenty-fourth of Tishri, when the whole community bound itself to observe the Torah, was a triumph for his teaching.

Biblical history might well end here. The descendants of the Patriarchs had undergone a multitude of experiences in their role of the Chosen People. It was their duty to live the Torah and to teach the ways of God to man. Many a time throughout their history they had failed. The example of their Patriarchs, the guidance of their Judges, their Priests and their Kings, and the exhortation of their Prophets often seemed to be of no avail. Of the Twelve Tribes which left Egypt to receive the Torah at Sinai, Ten were lost in Captivity. Two only survived, under the name of one, Judah. Restored to their homeland, the lesson of the past burned itself deeply into their consciousness. Under the guidance of Ezra they learnt to love the Torah and to treasure the records of their long history.

Nehemiah's Return.

But the Bible does not end here. It tells of one more scene, which sheds much light upon the meaning of the whole drama. After twelve years Nehemiah returned to the court of Artaxerxes at Susa. A little while later he came again to Judah and to his horror saw the Torah again ignored. The Temple was forsaken. The Levites had not received their tithe offerings from the people and had left Jerusalem to live upon the produce of the countryside. The Sabbath was not kept. Farmers worked their wine-presses, loaded their asses with wine, grapes and figs and brought them into Jerusalem on the Sabbath day. Phoenician merchants established themselves in the city and sold fish and other goods on the

Sabbath to the inhabitants of Judah and Jerusalem. Moreover, the Jews had taken back their heathen wives, and their children could no longer speak Hebrew. A grandson of Eliashib the High Priest was a son-in-law of Sanballat! Tobiah the Ammonite was given the disused tithe chamber in the Temple by Eliashib!

Nehemiah put down these abuses with a strong hand. He expelled Tobiah and the grandson of Eliashib from Jerusalem. The Levites he brought back to the Holy City, and appointed faithful custodians to take charge of the tithe offerings of corn, wine and oil which the Jews were persuaded to bring again to the Temple. The Phoenician merchants were expelled from the capital and forbidden to bring wares into the city on the Sabbath day. To ensure this prohibition Nehemiah had the gates of Jerusalem closed from before the Sabbath until its end, and appointed Levites to guard the gates. The heathen wives were sent away, and the offenders took an oath not to intermarry any more.

With these last acts of Nehemiah the history of the Biblical period closes. We leave the Jews upon their own land enjoying the tolerant rule of the Persian kings.

Conclusion. The common people earn their living from the soil and are content to follow the guidance of their leaders. Among the leaders are the priests, the Levites, the Scribes, and the nobles. Upon them is the duty of maintaining the teaching of the Torah to the people so that in the fulness of time throughout the world, from the sunrising to the sunsetting, the name of God may be honoured among men.

POINTS TO REMEMBER

Persia: Story of Purim.
Palestine:

- a) Evils denounced by prophet Malachi —
    1) intermarriage of all classes with peoples of Palestine
    2) lax princes and degenerate priests deserving of blame
    3) priests forsook Temple service, favoured rich and were partial in interpretation of Torah
- b) hopelessness of people
- c) picture of ideal priest painted by Malachi.

Ezra:

- a) called by Talmud a second Moses
- b) priest who could trace his descent from Aaron
- c) first of the Scribes
- d) received permission from Artaxerxes to lead a second return from Babylon to Palestine, 457 B. C. E.
- e) joined by company of about 1,500 men, besides women
- f) reached Jerusalem after journey of 4 months
- g) dismayed at conditions in Judah
- h) took steps to stamp out intermarriage — called assembly at Jerusalem and had Commission appointed
- i) his action stirred up emnity of neighbouring peoples, who threatened the existence of the defenceless city.

Nehemiah:

- a) cup-bearer of Artaxerxes
- b) heard news of Jerusalem's danger
- c) obtained permission from Artaxerxes to go up to Jerusalem and rebuild its wall, 444 B. C. E.
- d) appointed governor of Judea for 12 years

    e) on arrival, persuaded nobles and rulers to restore property
       of farmers which they had sold during time of famine

    f) set example by waiving dues of office

    g) the rebuilding of the wall —
      1) at first work mocked by Sanballat, Tobiah and Geshem
      2) warlike methods adopted by them
      3) cunning tried
      4) in spite of all, wall finished in 52 days — dedication
        ceremony

    h) Jerusalem populated by casting of lots — 3,000 chosen

    i) abuses crept back after expiry of term of governorship —
      1) Temple forsaken
      2) Sabbath profaned
      3) heathen wives taken back

    j) put down abuses with strong hand on return to Judea.

Renewal of the Covenant:

    a) Torah read publicly by Ezra on first day of seventh month,
       after rebuilding of wall

    b) Fast kept on 24th day of same month and covenant sealed
       to observe the Torah.

Explanation of Weights, Measures and Money Referred to in Text

Cubit — אַמָּה .... 18 inches

Shekel — שֶׁקֶל 2–6d

Talent — כִּכָּר .... equivalent in weight
                                         to 3,000 shekels

                                   a) in silver £375
                                    b) in gold £6,750

INDEX TO BIBLICAL PASSAGES QUOTED

269

GENERAL INDEX

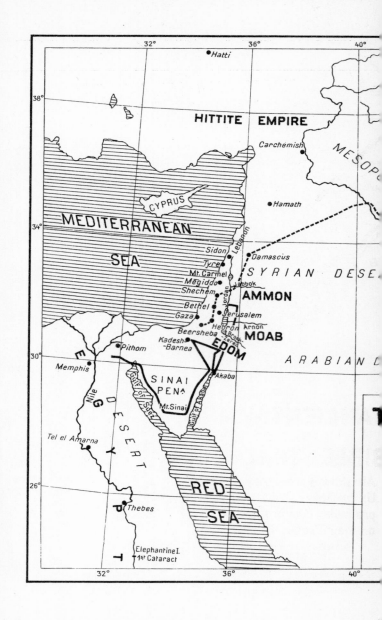

ANCIENT WORLD
IN
IBLE TIMES

Abraham's probable route from
Ur to Beer – sheba
probable route of the Israelites
on their Exodus from Egypt.

Scale 200 Miles = 1 inch

0   50   100   150   200